LAW OF
Termination
OF SERVICES
FOR GOVERNMENT SERVANTS

LAW OF Termination OF SERVICES

FOR GOVERNMENT SERVANTS

Containing:

- Up-to-date law on Termination of Services
- Latest Court Judgments
- Scope of Judicial interference in matters relating to security of services of temporary employees
- Model Forms for issuing various types of Memoranda, Orders etc. and much more

V. S. BHANOT

M.A. (Pol. Science and History); LL.B.

Author of

Law of Confidential Reports for Government Servants

Universal

Law Publishing Co. Pvt. Ltd.

2006 Edition

ISBN : 81-7534-530-6

Published by
UNIVERSAL LAW PUBLISHING CO. PVT. LTD.
C-FF-1A, Dilkhush Industrial Estate,
(Opp. Hans Cinema, Azadpur) G.T. Karnal Road,
Delhi-110 033
Tel : 011-27438103, 27215334, 42381334
Fax : 011-27458529
E-mail *(For sales inquiries)* : sales@unilawbooks.com
E-mail *(For editorial inquiries)* : edit@unilawbooks.com
Website : www.unilawbooks.com

Recommended citation: *Law of Termination of Services for Govt. Servants*, V.S. Bhanot (New Delhi: Universal Law Publishing Co. Pvt. Ltd., 2006)

Computer Typeset at Aesthetic & *Printed* at Taj Press, New Delhi.

PREFACE

The very utterance of word "termination" sends down a shock wave down the spine in a family where the services of the only bread-earner are suddenly dispensed with. There are, indeed, cases where visitation of this punishment is fully justified when the person is given to corrupt practices. But the instances are also not rare where an innocent person is thrown out of the services for his only "fault" of being "incorruptible".

It is often alleged and also not without reasons that masters often get rid of their recalcitrant servants by applying the shortcuts – *i.e.* by passing orders of termination simpliciter without following the elaborate procedure of holding regular inquiry under Article 311(2) of the Constitution as might be required. By passing termination orders simpliciter, they hide the real causes of dispensing with their services. Such orders are couched in a language which ensures that no stigma is attached to the character of the employee whose services have been terminated. In fact, they play hide and seek with the careers of such employees and such employees have then no legal remedy against such orders passed by the masters. It is gratifying that courts are coming up to the rescue of such unfortunate employees by lifting the veil from the innocuous looking orders of simple termination and seeing what is hidden behind them.

It is well settled for about a half of a century now since the decision of the Supreme Court in *Parshotam Lal Dhingra's* case, AIR 1958 SC 36 which has been described by the Supreme Court itself as "the Magna Carta of the Indian Civil Servants that employment of a temporary Government Servant can be terminated under the terms of his contract or under the rules of service applicable to him by a simple order of discharge without disclosing any reason and without casting any aspersion against him. But if it is shown that the order of termination casts or purports to cast some aspersion or stigma on them, such termination would amount to dismissal under Article 311 of the Constitution. Thus, even in the matter of temporary appointments, the State is not a free master to hire and then to fire an employee in any manner it likes in its absolute pleasure, because the position in law is that if the fired employee; even though employed temporarily, can show that such firing has left some scar on him, the firing would be declared unlawful. However, one may criticise this state of law as it is interpreted today. The fact remains that if an employer finds his temporary employee to be absolutely unsuitable or undesirable or inefficient and terminates his employment expressly and avowedly on such ground, the employer gets himself caught in the coils of law. But if the employer is cautious or clever enough to conceal the truth and takes care not to call a spade and terminates the temporary employment by just an order of termination simpliciter, his order is inscrutable and immune from all judicial scrutiny. The employers have rightly been advised to remember the good old precept....'Satyam Bruyat, Priyam Bruyat, Na Bruyat Satyam Apriyam' ... *i.e.* tell the truth, but only the pleasant truth and never the unpleasant truth, even though one might wonder as to whether the law intends to put a premium on concealment of truth.

The services of temporary employees are of a precarious nature which can be terminated on various valid and legitimate grounds *e.g.* on abolition of posts, unsuitability of the employee for the post, concealment of vital information at the time of his appointment or loss of confidence of the employer in the employee etc. etc. Despite many benevolent pieces of legislations passed by Government such as Industrial Disputes Act, 1947, Industrial Employment (Standing Orders) Act, 1946, Contract Labour (Regulation and Abolition) Act, 1970, the status of a temporary employee remains nothing better than that of a "bonded labour" who is subject to 'hire and fire' policy of his employers especially in Industrial Establishments. It is true that too much security for the employee is as bad as too much insecurity for them. A balance has therefore to be struck that is to say the spirit of work and initiative of a worker should not be killed but at the same time, he should not become too complacent and public interest and efficiency should suffer thereby.

I have been greatly encouraged in writing this book by Shri Manish Arora of Universal Law Publishing Co. Pvt. Ltd. But for his instinctive love for preservation of knowledge for the posterity, this book would not have seen the light of the day.

I will be failing in my duty if I do not refer to the continued help and support afforded to me by my wife Nirmal and other members of the family particularly my grand daughter Deepali aged about 6 years who always gave me a smile whenever I felt tired of writing the manuscript. My thanks are also due to Shri Yash Pal who did a commendable job in typing out the manuscript repeatedly with a smiling face.

Suggestions for improvement of this book are most welcome which will be duly acknowledged.

New Delhi
April, 2006

V.S. BHANOT

CONTENTS

CHAPTER 6

ROLE OF THE COURTS IN SAFEGUARDING THE INTERESTS OF THE TEMPORARY EMPLOYEES AGAINST MISUSE OF PROVISIONS OF CCS (TS) RULES BY THEIR EMPLOYERS IN TERMINATION CASES

CHAPTER 7

GIST OF THE LEADING JUDGEMENTS RELATING TO TERMINATION OF SERVICES OF TEMPORARY EMPLOYEES

CHAPTER 8
TERMINATION OF SERVICES OF A PROBATIONER

CHAPTER 9
TERMINATION OF SERVICES OF AD HOC EMPLOYEES

CHAPTER 10
TERMINATION OF SERVICES OF EMPLOYEES APPOINTED ON CONTRACT

CHAPTER 11
TERMINATION/REGULARISATION OF SERVICES OF CASUAL WORKERS

CHAPTER 13

RETRENCHMENT AND TERMINATION OF EMPLOYEES

TABLE OF CASES

A

C

D

E

F

G

H

I

J

L

M

N

O

P

R

S

T

U

V

W

Y

Z

Chapter 1
INTRODUCTION

SYNOPSIS

1.1 Categories of temporary employees

1.2 Rulings of the courts on the amelioration of the lot of *ad hoc*/ casual employees in the matter of security of their service

1.3 Salient propositions of law relating to termination of services of employees under terms of their contract or under Service Rules applicable to them

1.1 Categories of temporary employees

In the hierarchy of security of service in public employment, "permanent" service occupies the top position followed by temporary service, *ad hoc* service, full time casual employment with 'temporary status', full time casual employment without 'temporary status', part time casual employment, seasonal employment on daily rated or piece basis etc. Besides, we have also staff employed on contingencies, contract labour, apprentices, probationers, persons employed in Public Sector Undertakings, workers employed in industrial establishments, teachers working in educational institutions etc. etc. whose tenure of service is precarious because their services can be terminated with or without notice depending upon the terms of their contract or under the relevant service rules applicable to them. There have been innumerable cases where the services of such employees have been terminated at the whims and fancies of their masters and thrown on the road after they had put in long years of service. The lot of the servants employed in private employment is still worse.

1.2 Rulings of the courts on the amelioration of the lot of *ad hoc* / casual employees in the matter of security of their service

It is heartening to note that judiciary has come to the rescue of such unfortunate victims of official apathy by delivering classic pronouncements exhorting the Government to regularize such *ad hoc* employees in regular posts as far as possible. The Hon'ble Supreme Court while dealing with the case of a casual worker employed in the Railway Administration observed as under—

> "We would be guilty of turning a blind eye to a situation apart from being highly unethical, wholly contrary to constitutional philosophy of socio-economic justice if we fail to point out that Rule 2501 of Railway Establishment Manual which permits a man serving for 10, 20, 30 years at a stretch without break being treated as daily rated servant, is thoroughly opposed to the notions of socio-economic justice and it is high time that the Railway administration brings this part of the provision of the Manual, antiquarian and antediluvian, in conformity with the Directive Principles of State Policy as enunciated in Part IV of the Constitution".
>
> [*L. Robert D'Souza* v. *Executive Engineer*, 1982 (1) SLR 864.]

The Government has also been responsive to such exhortation made by the courts and have been issuing instructions from time to time to regularize the services of casual employees within the prescribed guidelines. These have been discussed in the book in detail at appropriate places.

1.3 Salient propositions of law relating to termination of services of employees under terms of their contract or under Service Rules applicable to them

(i) Central Civil Services (Temporary Service) Rules, 1965, were promulgated under Article 309 of the Constitution and came into effect w.e.f. 1-5-1965. These Rules regulate the conditions of service of temporary Central Government Employees. Rule 5 thereof is the most dreaded Rule according to which the services of a temporary Government servant can be terminated at any time forthwith or by a notice in writing without assigning any reason. Various State Governments have also framed similar rules on the pattern of C.C.S. (TS) Rules, 1965 which are applicable to the employees of their respective States. It may, however, be added that the State is not a free master to "hire and fire" a temporary employee in any manner it likes in its absolute pleasure. The position of the law is that if the "hired" employee even though temporarily employed can show that such a "firing" has left some scar on him, the "firing" would be declared unlawful unless the Constitutional requirements of Article 311 are fulfilled.

(ii) A person once employed however does not get a license to continue in service indefinitely irrespective of the fact whether there is any need for his services or not indeed, Government has the legitimate right to terminate the services of its employees on various valid grounds, namely:—

(a) when the post on which such an employee is employed is abolished by Government on *bona fide* grounds; or

(b) when the employee is found unsuitable for the post on which he is employed; or

(c) when it is revealed that he had obtained his employment by withholding vital information at the time of his recruitment; or

(d) when it is found that he was somehow wrongly appointed by the Appointing Authority to this post to which he was not eligible; or

(e) when his termination is effected on certain administrative grounds; or

(f) when there is justification for terminating his services while retaining his juniors in service; or

(g) when he is absent from duty unauthorisedly or has overstayed his leave; or

(h) when the employer has him lost confidence in his sincerity of his employee; or

(i) when there are charges of misconduct against him and he has been held guilty after holding the inquiry as contemplated in Article 311 (2) of the Constitution; or

(j) when the employee is declared physically unfit for being continued in service.

(iii) The burden of proof to convince the court that his termination 'simplicitor' is actually an order of 'punishment', lies on the employee.

(iv) The courts have also the powers to call for the records of the case to 'lift the veil' from innocuous order of termination to see what is actually hidden behind it.

(v) There is always some reason or cause for terminating the services of an employee. It is not necessary to state that reason in the order of termination communicated to him. But where there is a specific charge levelled by the employer of discrimination or some hostile motive on the authority terminating his services, it is incumbent on the authority making the impugned order to explain to the court the reasons for such impugned action.

(vi) The courts do not give relief to the persons who are appointed only as a stop-gap arrangement to meet emergent situations since they have no vested right to hold the posts.

(vii) If the material against the Government servant on which the competent authority has acted constitutes the "motive" but not the "foundation" then the order of his termination cannot be held as 'illegal". The function of the court in such cases is to discover the real nature of the order by attempting to ascertain what was the motivating consideration in the mind of the authority which had prompted passing of the impugned order.

(viii) Before a probationer is confirmed, the authority concerned is under an obligation to consider whether his work is satisfactory or whether he is suitable for the post. In the absence of any specific terms and conditions of his appointment, the authority may come to the conclusion that on account of inadequacy for the job or for any other such reason not involving moral turpitude, the probationer is unsuitable for the job and hence must be discharged. No punishment is involved in this. The authority could in some cases be of the view that the conduct of the probationer is such which may warrant dismissal or removal on an inquiry. But in those cases the authority may not hold an inquiry as such and may simply discharge the probationer with a view to giving him a chance to make good in other walks of life without a stigma. If, on the other hand, the probationer is faced with an enquiry on charges of misconduct of inefficiency or corruption, and if his services are terminated without following the provisions of Article 311(2), he can claim protection under the law.

(ix) Where the service regulations provide that an express order of confirmation is required to be passed even after completion of prescribed maximum period of probation, such an employee continues to remain a probationer till the order is issued.

(x) It is now well settled that an *ad hoc* appointment by its very nature is a stop gap arrangement made for a variety of reasons when the regular incumbent is not available or when the process of regular selection involves time and the exigencies of service are such that the post cannot be allowed to remain unmanned meanwhile.

(xi) Where an employee is appointed to a post on contract, he acquires a status and his duties and obligations are no longer determined by consent of both the parties but the statute or statutory rules which may be framed and altered unilaterally by the Government.

(xii) Rules and Regulations framed by statutory bodies have statutory force and the authorities functioning thereunder are statutory authorities and the employees of such Bodies also enjoy statutory status. They are entitled to protection of Articles 14 and 16 of the Constitution but not to the protection of Article 311 (2) of the Constitution.

(xiii) The services of even a permanent employee of a Corporation can be terminated by an order simplicitor on the ground of his unsuitability for the post.

(xiv) There is no security of service of contract labour and the system is archaic, primitive and is of baneful nature. It is nothing but an improved version of 'bonded labour'.

(xv) The services of teachers working in educational institutions receiving grant-in-aid from Government cannot be terminated at the whims and fancies of their management.

(xvi) If the services of a teacher are terminated by the school management after complying with the instructions contained in grant-in-aid code relating to prior consultation with the Director of Education etc., the concerned teacher has no remedy against his order of termination.

(xvii) In cases of termination of services of employees of private educational institutes, the normal rule for relief is not of reinstatement in service but claims for damages only.

(xviii) The management of an unaided minority educational institution cannot be permitted to exploit the employees under the garb of provisions of Article 30(1) of the Constitution.

(xix) "Retrenchment" of a worker amounts to termination of service but every termination is not retrenchment.

(xx) Termination of services of an employee on his having become 'surplus' due to recession in industry amounts to Retrenchment.

Note.—All the abovementioned propositions of law have been discussed at great length in the Book with case law and may be referred to in the relevant chapters.

Chapter 2

CENTRAL CIVIL SERVICES (TEMPORARY SERVICE) RULES, 1965

Central Civil Services (Temporary Service) Rules, 1965 are statutory rules framed under Article 309 of the Constitution of India in supersession of CCS (TS) Rules, 1949. These Rules regulate the conditions of services of temporary Government *servants. These Rules came into effect from 1-5-1965.*

SYNOPSIS

2.28 The services of a temporary employee can be terminated on the ground of his physical unfitness without notice

2.29 Case law on the subject of termination of services of services of employees on medical grounds

2.30 Terminal benefits available to a temporary employee whose services have been terminated under Rule 5(1) of CCS (TS) Rules

2.1 Text of C.C.S. (T.S.) Rules, 1965

1. Short title, commencement and application.—(1) These rules may be called the Central Civil Services (Temporary Service) Rules, 1965.

(2) They shall come into force with effect from 1st May, 1965.

(3) Subject to the provisions of sub-rule (4), these rules shall apply to all persons—

(i) who hold a civil post including all civilians paid from the Defence Services Estimates under the Government of India and who are under the rule-making control of the President, but who do not hold a lien or a suspended lien on any post under the Government of India or any State Government;

(ii) who are employed temporarily in work-charged establishments and who have opted for pensionary benefits.

(4) Nothing in these rules shall apply to—

(a) Railway servants;

(b) Government servants not in whole-time employment;

(c) Government servants engaged on contract;

(d) Government servants paid out of contingencies;

(e) persons employed in extra-temporary establishments or in work-charged establishments (other than the persons employed temporarily and who have opted for pensionary benefits);

(f) non-departmental telegraphists and telegraphmen employed in the Posts and Telegraphs Department; and

(g) such other categories of employees as may be specified by the Central Government by notification published in the Official Gazette.

2. Definitions.—In these rules, unless the context otherwise requires,—

(a) "appointing authority" means, in relation to a specified post, the authority declared as such under the Central Civil Services (Classification, Control and Appeal) Rules, 1965;

(b) [*Deleted*]

(c) [*Deleted*]

(d) "temporary service" means the service of a temporary Government servant in a temporary post or officiating service in a permanent post, under the Government of India; and

(e) "defence service" means services under the Government of India in the Ministry of Defence and in the Defence Accounts Departments under the control of the Ministry of Finance (Department of Expenditure) (Defence Division) paid out of the Defence Services Estimates and not permanently subject to the Air Force Act, 1950 (45 of 1950) or the Army Act, 1950 (45 of 1950) or the Navy Act, 1957 (62 of 1957).

3. [*Deleted*]

4. [*Deleted*]

5. Termination of Temporary Service.—(1) (a) The services of a temporary Government shall be liable to termination at any time by a notice in writing given either by the Government servant to the appointing authority or by the appointing authority to the Government servant;

(b) the period of such notice shall be one month:

Provided that the service of any such Government servant may be terminated forthwith and on such termination, the Government servant shall be entitled to claim a sum equivalent to the amount of his pay plus allowances for the period of the notice at the same rates at which he was drawing them immediately before the termination of his services or, as the case may be, for the period by which such notice falls short of one month.

Note.—The following procedure shall be adopted by the appointing authority while serving notice on such Government servant under clause (a)—

(i) The notice shall be delivered or tendered to the Government servant in person.

(ii) Where personal service is not practicable the notice shall be served on such Government servant by registered post acknowledgement due at the address of the Government servant available with the appointing authority.

(iii) If the notice sent by registered post is returned unserved, it shall be published in the Official Gazette and upon such publication, it shall be deemed to have been personally served on such Government servant on the date it was published in the Official Gazette.

(2)(a) Where a notice is given by the appointing authority terminating the services of a temporary Government servant, or where the service of any such Government servant is terminated either on the expiry of the period of such notice or forthwith by payment of pay plus allowance, the Central Government or any other authority specified by the Central Government in this behalf or a Head of Department, if the said authority is subordinate to him, may, of its own motion or otherwise, re-open the case and after making such enquiry as it deems fit,—

(i) confirm the action taken by the appointing authority;

(ii) withdraw the notice;

(iii) reinstate the Government servant in service; or

(iv) make such other order in the case as it may consider proper:

Provided that except in special circumstances, which should be recorded in writing, no case shall be re-opened under this sub-rule after the expiry of three months—

(i) from the date of notice, in a case where notice is given;

(ii) from the date of termination of service, in a case where no notice is given.

(b) Where a Government servant is reinstated in service under sub-rule (2), the order of reinstatement shall specify—

(i) the amount or proportion of pay and allowances, if any, to be paid to the Government servant for the period of his absence between the date of termination of his services and the date of his reinstatement; and

(ii) whether the said period shall be treated as period spent on duty for any specified purpose or purposes.

6. Termination of temporary service on account of physical unfitness.—Notwithstanding anything contained in Rule 5, the services of a temporary Government servant may be terminated at any time without notice on his being declared physically unfit for continuance in service by an authority who would have been competent to declare him as permanently incapacitated for service had his appointment been permanent.

7. [*Deleted*]

8. [*Deleted*]

9. [*Deleted*]

10. Terminal gratuity payable to temporary Government servants.—(1) Subject to the provisions of sub-rule (1B), a temporary Government servant who retires on superannuation or is discharged from service or is declared invalid for further service shall be eligible for gratuity on the same scale as admissible to a permanent Government servant under the Central Civil Service (Pension) Rules, 1972.

(1A) In the case of temporary Government servant who is compulsorily retired from service as a disciplinary measure, the provisions of sub-rule (1) shall apply subject to the modification that the rate of gratuity payable in his case shall not be less than two-thirds of, but in no case exceeding, the rate specified in sub-rule (1).

(1B) In the case of a temporary Government servant who retires from service on attaining the age of superannuation or on his being declared to be permanently incapacitated for further Government service by the appropriate medical authority, after he has rendered temporary service of not less than ten years or who has sought voluntary retirement by giving three months' notice in writing on completion of 20 years, provisions of sub-rule (1) shall not apply and in accordance with the provisions of Central Civil Services (Pension) Rules, 1972—

(i) such a Government shall be eligible for the grant of superannuation, invalid or retiring pension, as the case may be, and retirement gratuity; and

(ii) in the event of his death after retirement, the members of his family shall be eligible for the grant of family pension.

(2) In the event of death of a temporary Government servant while in service, his family shall be eligible for family pension and death gratuity at the same scale and under the same provisions as are applicable to permanent Central Civilian Government servants under the Central Civil Services (Pension) Rules, 1972.

(3) No gratuity shall be admissible under this rule to a Government servant,—

(i) who resigns his post or who is removed or dismissed from service as a disciplinary measure;

(ii) who is re-employed after retirement on superannuation or retiring pension:

Provided that a temporary Government servant who resigned from service to take up, with prior permission, an appointment under a Corporation or Company wholly or substantially owned or controlled by the Government or in or under a Body controlled or financed by Government shall be paid terminal gratuity at the rate prescribed under sub-rule (1) in respect of the service rendered by him under the Government:

Provided further that a temporary Government servant who has been absorbed in a Central Autonomous Body, with the permission of the parent department, shall have an option to count the service rendered under the Government for the purpose of pension under the autonomous body if it has a pension scheme, instead of drawing the terminal gratuity under the first proviso.

Explanation.—For the purpose of this sub-rule—

(i) "Central Autonomous Body" means a body which is financed wholly or substantially from cess or Central Government grants and includes a Central Statutory Body or a Central University but does not include a public undertaking falling under the purview of the Bureau of Public Enterprises;

(ii) "Financed substantially" means that more than 50% of the expenditure is met by cess or Central Government grants

(4) [*Deleted*]

(5) [*Deleted*]

(6) For the purpose of this rule,—

(a) gratuity shall be calculated on the basis of pay which the Government employee was drawing immediately before his superannuation/discharge/invalidation/absorption in an autonomous body or on the date of his death and Dearness Allowance on that pay;

(b) "Pay" shall mean pay as defined in Fundamental Rule 9(21)(a)(i);

(c) period of extraordinary leave, if any, availed of by the Government servant concerned shall be taken into account for computing the completed service on the same basis as it is taken into account for the purpose of calculation of pension and retirement gratuity/death gratuity under Rule 21 of the Central Civil Services (Pension) Rules, 1972, as amended from time to time; and

(d) an increment earned during the currency of earned leave not exceeding 120 days or during the first 120 days of earned leave exceeding 120 days expiring on the date of retirement though not actually drawn, shall form part of the pay for purposes of calculating terminal/death gratuity.

(7) The provisions of Rule 10 shall apply to Government Servants appointed on or before 31-12-2003.

11. [*Deleted*]

2.2 Central Civil Services (Temporary Services Amendment) Rules, 2003

Government of India (Deptt. of Personnel & Training amended Rule 10 of CCS (TS) Rules, 1965 *vide* Notification No. 12011/1/2003-Estts.(C) dated 4-12-2003 . The amendments have been carried out in the text of Rule 10 reproduced above. The explanatory Memorandum annexed thereto is reproduced below:

"Under the Central Civil Services (Temporary Services) Rules, 1965, Terminal gratuity is payable to a temporary Government employee who retires on superannuation or discharged from service or declared invalid for further service on the basis of length of service and the pay which was last drawn by him. On the recommendations of the Fifth

Pay Commission, the distinction between permanent and temporary Government employees who have rendered less than ten years of service has been removed. Since, the removal of distinction between permanent and temporary Government employees in the matter of payment of terminal gratuity is in the nature of liberalization, the interest of no one will be adversely affected by giving retrospective effect to the rule."

2.3 Meaning of the term "Holder of a Civil Post" used in Rule 1 (3) of CCS (TS) Rules, 1965

Rule 1(3) of CCS (TS) Rules, 1965 provides that these rules are applicable to persons who hold a civil post. This term has not been defined in these Rules nor indeed in the Constitution of India in relation to Article 311 thereof. It has also not been defined in the Civil Services (Classification, Control and Appeal) Rules. In fact, the expression 'holding a civil post' or 'civil post' has not been defined in any statute or rule. It may, however, to be stated that a civil post means a post not connected with defence. A person holding a post under a State is a person serving or employed under the State. A post under the State is an office or a position to which duties in connection with the affairs of the State are attached, an office or a position to which a person is appointed and which may exist apart from and independently of the holder of the post.

A "civil post" means a post other than a post connected with defence. The term "civil post" used in Article 311(1) of the Constitution also connotes the same meaning. The holder of a "civil post" means a person serving under the Government of a State in a "Civil" capacity.

[*R. Christopher* v. *Executive Engineer, Irrigation Workshop Eatanagar, Bareilly*, AIR 1966 All 97 (98)]

A civil post is under the administrative control of the State. The State may create or abolish such a post and may regulate the conditions of services of the person appointed to that post.

[*State of Assam* v. *Kanak Chandru Dutta*, AIR 1967 SC 884]

2.4 Applicability of CCS (TS) Rules, 1965 to Probationers

The question as to whether or not CCS (TS) Rules, 1965, are applicable to Probationers was considered by Ministry of Home

Affairs in their O.M. No. 4/10/66-Estts(c) dated 26-8-1967 and it was clarified that Rule 5 of CCS (TS) Rules, 1965, can be invoked in the case of persons appointed on probation, where in the appointment letter a specific condition regarding termination of service without any notice during or at the end of the period of probation (including extended period, if any) has not been provided. The position is that, the CCS (TS) Rules do not specifically exclude probationers or persons on probation as such. However, if a specific condition regarding termination of service without any notice during or at the end of the period of probation (including extended period, if any) has been specifically made in the letter of appointment, it would be desirable to terminate the services of the probationer/person on probation in terms of the letter of appointment and not under Rule 5(1) of the CCS (TS) Rules, 1965.

The question also came up for consideration before Bombay High Court in *Ishwar Lal J. Naik* v. *S.C.Arya, Principal,* Government *Arts & Science College, Daman*, 1984 (1) SLJ 1 (Bom), which in its judgment dated 8-8-1983 observed as under:

> "Sub-rule (4) of Rule 1 of the Temporary Service Rules specifies categories of Government servants to whom these Rules do not apply. A Government servant on probation has not been included in this sub-rule and has therefore not been excluded from the purview of the Temporary Service Rules."

2.5 CCS(TS) Rules, 1965 are not applicable to Permanent/ confirmed employees in relation to termination of their services

One S.N. Sharma was appointed as a teacher on a temporary basis on 8-6-1960 and it was stipulated in his letter of appointment that his services were terminable on 24 hours' notice. Subsequently, he was confirmed in the said post on 1-11-1966. His services were, however, terminated on 29-7-1970 under Rule 5(1) of CCS (TS) Rules against which he filed an appeal in Himachal Pradesh High Court pleading that he had acquired a lien on the post under F.R. 12-A and that in terms of the provisions contained in CCS (TS) Rules, he was no longer a temporary employee and that his services could not be terminated by taking recourse to Rule 5 *ibid.* The Court in its judgment dated 21-8-1990 quoted with approval the judgment in the case of *Beni Mudhale Pal Choudhri* v. *State of Assam,* (1968) SLR 616, which reads as under:

> "It is common knowledge that confirmation gives certain rights to the Government servant who is confirmed, the rights being that he cannot be removed from service except on disciplinary grounds or on medical unfitness. Here, in this case there is no question of any disciplinary grounds, nor of any question of medical unfitness. Such being the case and there being no power under the Rules to set side the confirmation of a Government servant, we must hold that the Government has no power to terminate the services. It would be most dangerous to assume that such a power exists in the Government; for, there will then be absolutely no certainty to the service of Government servant. Any such stand on behalf of the Government will certainly be contrary to all recognised principles of Government employment. It is because confirmation gives a permanent footing in the service that employees are anxious to get themselves confirmed and in the Central Government service."

The order of termination dated 29-7-1970 was quashed being clearly without jurisdiction.

[*Sachida Nand Sharma* v. *State of Himachal Pradesh,* 1981 (1) SLJ 9]

2.6 The services of a temporary employee cannot be terminated under CCS (TS) Rules if these Rules are not applicable to him

One Rai Singh was appointed as an Inspector in Border Security Force on 1-10-1968 in a temporary capacity. A court of Inquiry was ordered to investigate a complaint against him that he failed to carry out lawful orders of his superior officers and after the conclusion of the inquiry, his services were terminated under Rule 5 of CCS (TS) Rules without assigning any reason. He assailed the order on the ground that the said Rules were not applicable to him. This case came up for consideration before Delhi High Court, which in its judgment dated 20-11-1978 observed as under:

> "The petitioner is governed by Border Security Force Act, 1968 and the Rules of 1969 framed thereunder. There is no provision in the scheme of the rules of 1969 for any

termination simiplicitor as is envisaged in Rule 5 of CCS (TS) Rules. On account of this clear inconsistency, the employees of BSF would therefore be outside the scope of the said Rules of Temporary Service and as such Rule 5 has no application for them. The termination of service of the petitioner in purported exercise of the power under rule 5 is, therefore, in excess of authority and hence liable to be quashed on that ground.

It was further held that the impugned order is also vitiated because, even though it *ex facie* purports to be an innocent order of termination without any apparent stigma, the noting in official records, the circumstances antecedent to the passing of the order leave no doubt that order was punitive in character. The services of the petitioner were dispensed with on account of allegations that he had failed to carry out lawful orders and misbehaved with his superior officers and was found in a state of intoxication. These charges were subject matter of the court of enquiry ordered by Commandant and the DIG. It is well settled that when a seemingly innocent order of termination is assailed as being punitive in character on the ground that it was founded on charges of misconduct, judicial scrutiny need not be confined merely to the terminology used in the order and it would be open to the court as indeed it is obligatory on it, to go behind the order and to determine from circumstances antecedent to the order to see for itself if the charge of misconduct was the foundation of the order or mere motivation. Such an order could have been made only after giving the petitioner reasonable opportunity of being heard which was admittedly denied."

[*Rai Singh* v. *U.O.I.*, (1979) SLJ 101]

2.7 Rule 5(1) of CCS (TS) Rules, 1965 which vests unlimited powers in the appointing authority to terminate the services of a temporary employee is not ultravires of Articles 14 and 16 of the Constitution

The constitutional validity of this Rule came up for consideration in the Supreme Court in *Champaklal Chiman Lal Shah* v. *The Union of India*, AIR 1964 SC 1854, which in its judgment observed as under:

"Rule 5 gives power to the Government to terminate the services of the temporary Government servant by giving him one month's notice or payment of one month's pay in lieu of such notice. This rule is being attacked on the ground that it is hit by Article 16, which provides for equality of opportunity......... It is well recognised that the Government may have to employ temporary servants to satisfy the needs of a particular contingency and such employment would be perfectly legitimate. There can also be no doubt, if such a class of temporary servants could be recruited then there would be nothing discriminatory or violative of equal opportunity if the conditions of service of such servants are different in some respects from those of permanent employees... In particular the very fact that the services of a Government servant is purely temporary makes him a class apart from those in permanent service and such Government servants cannot necessarily claim all the advantages which a permanent servant, has in the matter of security of service. We are therefore of opinion that considering the nature of the employment of a temporary Government servant, a provision like that in Rule 5 in respect of termination of service is a reasonable provision which cannot be said to deny equality of opportunity provided in Article 16. The attack therefore on Rule 5 on the ground that it is hit by Article 16 of the Constitution must fail.".

This Rule also came in for consideration before Delhi High Court in *Jarnail Singh* v. *Supdt. of Police*, 1983 (2) SLJ 101, in which it was observed as under:

"It is not correct to say that Rule 5(1) of the Central Civil Services (Temporary Service) Rules, 1965 is *ultra vires* Articles 14 and 16 of the Constitution on the ground that it vests arbitrary powers in appointing authority to dispense with the services of the temporary employee. This type of argument is an argument of despair. The temporary servants form a class by themselves and there is a laudable object which is served by Rule 5 and that is that the services of a temporary employee may be dispensed with without taking any disciplinary action or casting any stigma against him. No guidelines are required for the exercise of such a simple rule. There is reasonable nexus between the Rule and the object and the rule cannot be considered either arbitrary or otherwise unconstitutional."

2.8 Observations of the Supreme Court on the constitutional validity of Rule 5 (1) of C.C.S. (TS) Rules, 1965

"Power was given by Rule 5(1) to terminate the services of existing employees by giving one month's notice or pay in lieu thereof. It is held that there is always a presumption of constitutionality of the rule. The court ought not to interpret the statutory provisions (unless compelled by their language) in such a manner as would involve their unconstitutionality, since the legislature of the rule-making authority is presumed to enact a law which does not contravene or violate the constitutional provisions. If the provision of a law or rule is such that if construed in such a way that it would make it consistent with the constitution and another interpretation would render the provisions or the rule unconstitutional, then the Court would lean in favour of the former construction – Rule 5 is capable of two interpretations. One view being that rule *per se* is arbitrary offending Article 14. The other view capable of being construed would be that the Government may form an objective opinion, on the basis of the material, that the post which the officer or the employee is occupying is no longer in need *i.e.* to abolish the post and in consequence the service of employee whether permanent or temporary can be terminated. In the light of this interpretation, Rule 5 is valid and does not offend Article 14."

[*M.L. Kumra* v. *New India Assurance Co. Ltd.*, 1992 (1) SLR 421 (SC)]

2.9 Distinction between a simple letter of resignation submitted by a temporary employee and a notice served by him on the appointing authority under Rule 5(1) of CCS (TS) Rules

"When a temporary Government servant submits a letter of resignation, a distinction should be drawn between a letter of resignation purporting to be a notice of termination of service and one which is not. A notice of termination of service given by a temporary Government servant under Rule 5(1) of the CCS (TS) Rules, 1965, is something different from a mere letter of resignation submitted by him without any reference, direct or indirect to the said rule. While the former is an exercise of the right conferred by statutory rules to enabling a temporary Government servant to cease performance of his duties automatically on the expiry of the prescribed period of notice, the latter requires acceptance by the competent authority in order to become effective. Therefore, if a temporary Government servant submits a letter of resignation in which he does not refer to Rule 5(1) of these rules or does not even say that it be treated as a notice of termination of service, the provisions of Rule 5(1) *ibid* will not be attracted. In such a case, he can relinquish his post only when the resignation is accepted and he is relieved of his duties. It will, therefore, be possible in such circumstances to retain the temporary officer even beyond one month if it takes time to make alternative arrangements. This will not be repugnant to the provisions of these rules in any way because when a temporary Government servant submits a letter of resignation without invoking the provisions of the said rules, these will not come into the picture, notwithstanding the fact that, being a temporary Government servant, he is governed by these rules."

[G.I., M.H.A., O.M. No. 4/1/65-Estt. (C) dated the 25th May, 1966]

2.10 No formal relieving of a temporary employee is necessary on the expiry of the notice period served on him under Rule 5(1) of CCS (TS) Rules

"It has been decided that once a notice is issued to a temporary employee under Rule 5(1) of CCS (TS) Rules, 1965, he ceases to be in Government service on the expiry of one month from the date on which the notice was served on him. The question of formally relieving him on the due date does not arise. It should be ensured that no such employee is allowed to be kept on duty from the date on which he ceases to be in Government service."

[D.G., P & T, N.D. No. 29/3/69–SPB II, dated the 23rd July, 1970]

2.11 Break in service to be condoned if Government servant is appointed to another post within the notice period

"Where a Central Government servant whose services have been terminated on payment of pay and allowances in lieu of a period of notice is able to secure another appointment under the Central Government within that period, the break in service may be condoned by the appointing authority and service in the new appointment treated as continuous with that in the previous appointment for all purposes including fixation of pay, seniority, leave and gratuity or other retirement benefits; provided that he shall refund to Government the pay and allowances of the former post for the unexpired portion of the notice after his re-employment as well as any gratuity or other termination benefits in respect of his previous service."

[G.I., M.H.A. O.M. No. 9/1/54-RPS dated the 9th October, 1956]

2.12 Reasons for termination of services should not be mentioned in the termination order

When action is taken under Rule 5 to terminate the services of a temporary employee, reasons for termination should not be mentioned.

[M.H.A. O.M. No. 39/14/56-Estts. (A) dated, 22nd June, 1956]

2.13 Order of termination of services under Rule 5(1) of CCS (TS) Rules, cannot be passed from a retrospective date

One Ms Machchia, an *ad hoc* stenographer was sanctioned maternity leave which was later on cancelled on 30-6-1983 on the ground that she was not entitled to it. In lieu, thereof, earned leave for 25 days from 1-6-1983 to 25-6-1983 which was due to her was sanctioned. Subsequently, the said order letter dated 30-6-1983 was also cancelled and her services were terminated under Rule 5 of TS Rules on 17-8-1983 with effect from 25-6-1983. She challenged the order of her termination before CAT (Ahmedabad Bench) which in its judgment dated 20-6-1989 observed as under:

"Learned advocate for the petitioner has pointed out that in *Ram Pal Singh* v. *U.P. State Electricity Board*, 1983 (2) SLR 677, the Allahabad High Court has ruled that an order having retrospective operation is not legal and valid. Even otherwise it is amply clear and obvious that normal rules of jurisprudence do not allow retrospective operation of administrative orders as clearly these would be unjust so far as the parties affected therein are concerned. We are not impressed by the arguments of the learned Government advocate that either in terms of appointment order or in terms of the rule referred to, there is any valid right or power allowed to them to terminate the services of the employee from a date prior to the date of the order."

[*Smeetaben P. Kachachia* v. *U.O.I.*, 1989 (4) SLJ CAT 820]

2.14 Services of a temporary employee can be terminated during his suspension and/or during pendency of departmental proceedings against him

In the case of a temporary Government servant if the term of his temporary post held by him at the time of suspension is likely to expire or if he otherwise becomes liable to be retrenched from service before the disciplinary proceedings are likely to be completed, it may be considered on merits whether –

(a) he should be discharged from service on the expiry of the term of the post held by him; or

(b) his services should be terminated under Rule 5 of the Central Civil Services (Temporary Service) Rules, 1965; or

(c) the disciplinary proceedings should be continued to its logical conclusion.

If it is decided to continue the disciplinary proceedings, the tenure of the temporary post should be extended for an appropriate period under order of the authority competent to sanction and such extension. If delay is anticipated in obtaining the sanction of the Competent Authority, the authority competent to dismiss or remove the Government Servant concerned from service may issue orders extended the post without reference to the Competent Authority. The vacancy caused by such extension should not, however, be filled.

(Rule 36 of Posts and Telegraphs Manual, Volume III)

2.15 Prescribed Standard proforma should be used for issuing orders of termination of services of temporary employees under Rule 5(1) of CCS (TS) Rules

Standard proforma have been prescribed for issuing orders of termination of temporary Government servants under Rule 5 of the CCS (TS) Rules, 1965, which are reproduced below. Forms I and II are meant for use in cases where the Appointing Authority is other than the President of India. Forms III and IV are to be used in cases where the Appointing Authority is the President of India. Forms V and VI are to be used by the President of India or the Appointing Authority for termination of services of the employees during the currency of the notice of termination of services already served on them.

FORM I

NOTICE OF TERMINATION OF SERVICE ISSUED UNDER RULE 5 (1) OF THE CENTRAL CIVIL SERVICES (TEMPORARY SERVICE) RULES, 1965

In pursuance of sub-rule (1) of Rule 5 of the Central Civil Services (Temporary Service) Rules, 1965, I……………. (Name & Designation) hereby give notice to Shri /Smt./ Kumari…………..that his/her services shall stand terminated with effect from the date of expiry of a period of one month from the date on which this notice is served on, or, as the case may be, tendered to him/her.

Station

Date: Signature of the Appointing Authority

ACKNOWLEDGEMENT

I hereby acknowledge the receipt on this day of the notice of termination from service.

Station Signature of the individual

Date: Designation

FORM II

ORDER OF TERMINATION OF SERVICE ISSUED UNDER THE PROVISO TO SUB-RULE (1) OF RULE 5 OF THE CENTRAL CIVIL SERVICES (TEMPORARY SERVICE) RULES, 1965

In pursuance of the Proviso to sub-rule (1) of Rule 5 of the Central Civil Services (Temporary Service) Rules, 1965, I……………. (Name & Designation) hereby terminate forthwith the services of Shri /Smt./Kumari…………..and direct that he / she shall be entitled to claim a sum equivalent to the amount of his/her pay plus allowances for the period of notice at the same rates at which he/she was drawing them immediately before the termination of his/her service or, as the case may be for the period by which such notice falls short of one month.

Station

Date: Signature of the Appointing Authority

FORM III

NOTICE OF TERMINATION OF SERVICE ISSUED UNDER RULE 5 (1) OF THE CENTRAL CIVIL SERVICES (TEMPORARY SERVICE) RULES, 1965, WHERE THE APPOINTING AUTHORITY IS THE PRESIDENT

In pursuance of sub-rule (1) of Rule 5 of the Central Civil Services (Temporary Service) Rules, 1965, the President hereby gives notice to Shri /Smt./Kumari.............. that his/her services stand terminated with effect from the date of expiry of a period of one month from the date on which this notice is served on, or, as the case may be, tendered to him/her.

By order and in the name of the President

Station Signature of the Authority empowered to

Date: authenticate documents in the name of the President

ACKNOWLEDGEMENT

I hereby acknowledge the receipt on this day of the notice of termination from service.

Station Signature of the individual

Date: Designation

FORM IV

ORDER OF TERMINATION OF SERVICE ISSUED UNDER THE PROVISO TO SUB-RULE (1) OF RULE 5 OF THE CENTRAL CIVIL SERVICES (TEMPORARY SERVICE) RULES, 1965, WHERE THE APPOINTING AUTHORITY IS THE PRESIDENT

In pursuance of the Proviso to sub-rule (1) of Rule 5 of the Central Civil Services (Temporary Service) Rules, 1965, the

President hereby terminates forthwith the services of Shri /Smt./ Kumari..............and directs that he /she shall be entitled to claim a sum equivalent to the amount of his/her pay plus allowances for the period of notice at the same rates at which he/ she was drawing them immediately before the termination of his/her service or, as the case may be for the period by which such notice falls short of one month.

By order and in the name of the President

Station Signature of the Authority empowered to
Date: authenticate documents in the name of the President

FORM V

ORDER OF TERMINATION OF SERVICE ISSUED UNDER THE PROVISO TO SUB-RULE (1) OF RULE 5 OF THE CENTRAL CIVIL SERVICES (TEMPORARY SERVICE) RULES, 1965, DURING THE CURRENCY OF THE NOTICE OF TERMINATION OF SERVICES ALREADY SERVED ON HIM, WHERE THE APPOINTING AUTHORITY IS THE PRESIDENT

In modification of Notice No. ...., dated ....of termination of service of Shri/Smt./Kumari............. and in pursuance of the Proviso to sub-rule (1) of Rule 5 of the Central Civil Services (Temporary Service) Rules, 1965, the President hereby terminates forthwith the services of Shri/Smt./ Kumari............. and directs that he/she shall be paid a sum equivalent to the amount of pay and allowances for the period by which the said notice falls short of one month calculated at the same rates at which he/she was drawing them immediately before the date of this order.

By order and in the name of the President.

Station Signature of the Authority empowered to
Date: authenticate documents in the name of the President

FORM VI

ORDER OF TERMINATION OF SERVICE ISSUED UNDER THE PROVISO TO SUB-RULE (1) OF RULE 5 OF THE CENTRAL CIVIL SERVICES (TEMPORARY SERVICE) RULES, 1965, DURING THE CURRENCY OF THE NOTICE OF TERMINATION OF SERVICES ALREADY SERVED ON HIM

In modification of Notice No. .... dated ....of termination of service of Shri/Smt./Kumari.................. and in pursuance of the Proviso to sub-rule (1) of Rule 5 of the Central Civil Services (Temporary Service) Rules, 1965, I............... (Name & Designation) hereby terminate forthwith the services of Shri /Smt./Kumari..............and direct that he /she shall be paid a sum equivalent to the amount of pay and allowances for the period by which the said notice falls short of one month calculated at the same rates at which he/she was drawing them immediately before the date of this order.

Station Signature of the Appointing Authority

Date:

[G.I.,M.H.A., O.M. No. 4/1/65-Estt. (C) dated the 30th March, 1967; 4/12/67-Estts. (C) dated the 8th January, 1968 and G.I., C.S. Deptt. of Pers. F. 4/1/73-Estts. (C) dated the 1st September, 1973 and dated the 11th January, 1974]

2.16 Manner in which the notice of termination of services should be served on the employees by the appointing authority

The procedure which should be adopted by the Appointing Authority in serving the notices issued under Rule 5(1) of CCS (TS) Rules on the employee is explained in the "Note" below Rule 5(1) ibid reproduced earlier in the text of CCS (TS) Rules and may be referred to:

"Ordinarily when a Government servant is actually in service, there would not be any difficulty in serving the notice on him personally or tendering the same in the presence of some other officer, if he has refused to accept the same. In cases where it is apprehended that service is likely to be evaded by the employee e.g. when the officer is on long leave etc., services should be terminated forthwith by issuing an order mentioning therein the offer to pay him a month's salary in lieu of notice period as provided in the Rules."

[G.I., M.H.A., O.M. No. 4/1/65-Estts. (C) dated the 30th March, 1967]

2.17 Is it necessary to make payment of Pay and allowances to an employee in lieu of the notice period simultaneously with the serving of the notice of termination of his services on him under Rule 5 of CCS (TS) Rules?

Proviso to Rule 5 of CCS (TS) Rules, 1965, as it originally stood prior to its amendment on 23-6-1972 provided for payment of pay and allowances etc. in lieu of the notice period to the employee simultaneously with the serving of the notice of termination of his services on him under Rule 5 (1) of CCS (TS) Rules, 1965. However, with the amendment of the said provision on 23-6-1972, the position has changed. It is now no longer obligatory to pay to the Government servant pay and allowances etc. for the notice period simultaneously with the notice of termination of his services. He is now entitled to claim the said amount from the Government .

This Rule came up for consideration before Punjab & Haryana High Court in the case of *Des Raj, Ex-Peon* v. *U.O.I.*, 1984 (1) SLJ 623. The Court had, before it, both the original as well as the amended version Rule 5 which read as under:

"5. *Termination of Temporary Service (Original Rule)*.—(1)(a) The services of a temporary Government servant shall be liable to termination at any time by a notice in writing given either by the Government servant to the appointing authority or by the appointing authority to the Government servant;

(b) the period of such notice shall be one month:

Provided that the services of any such Government servant may be terminated forthwith by payment to him of a sum equivalent to the amount of his pay plus allowances for the period of the notice at the same rate at which he was drawing them immediately before the termination of his services or, as the case may be, for the period by which such notice falls short of one month."

2.18 Amended Rule 5

"(a) The services of a temporary Government servant who is not quasi permanent service shall be liable to be terminated at any time by a notice in writing given either by the Government servant to the appointing authority or by the appointing authority to the Government servant;

(b) The period of such notice shall be one month. Provided that the services of any such Government servant may be terminated forth with and on such termination the Government servant shall be entitled to claim a sum equivalent to the amount of his pay plus allowances for the period of notice at the same rate, at which he was drawing them immediately before the termination of his service or as the case may be, for the period for which such notice falls short of one month."

After going through both the versions of Rule 5, the Court in its judgment dated 30-1-1984 observed as under:

> "By amendment of Rule 5, a new rule has come into being from the date the Central Civil Services (Temporary Service) Rules, 1965 came into force with the result that it would be deemed as if Rule 5 as amended, was in the rules since the year 1965. In other words, the earlier Rule 5 stood completely effaced and in its place the amended rule came into existence. The validity of the order has to be judged in the light of the rule as it has been now incorporated in the rules with retrospective effect."

2.19 Government of India decision relating to amendment to Proviso to Rule 5(1) of CCS(TS) Rules, 1965

> "The Amendment to Proviso to Sub-rule (1) of Rule 5 of the CCS (TS) Rules, 1965, introduced by Department of Personnel, Notification No. 4/2/72-Estts. (C) dated the 23rd June, 1972 came up for discussion in the meeting of the National Council set up under the Joint Consultative Machinery in its meeting held on the 28th and 29th July, 1972. During the discussion, the Staff side *inter alia* pointed out that the amendment might lead to delay in making payment of pay and allowances in lieu of notice to temporary Government servants discharged summarily. In order to allay this apprehension, it was agreed by the Official Side that

Rules of 1965, provides that upon the termination of services of a temporary Government servant forthwith, he would be entitled to claim his pay and allowances in lieu of notice. Executive instructions would be issued to the effect that the Ministries/Departments should make payment of pay and allowances to such Government servants immediately on their discharge.

2. The agreement reached in the National Council is brought to the notice of the Ministry of Finance, etc. for issuing suitable instructions to the appointing authorities under them."

[G.I.C.S. Deptt. of Pers. No. 4/2/72-Estts(C) dated the 4th November, 1972]

2.20 Rulings of the Courts on the subject of making simultaneous payment to the employees with the order of termination

It was held by the Apex Court in *Raj Kumar* v. *U.O.I.*, AIR 1975 SC 1116 that it is not obligatory to pay to the Government servant the salary for the notice period simultaneously and that Government servant is only entitled to claim the same.

Termination of services of a temporary employee without tendering payment of one month's salary in lieu of notice simultaneously is illegal.

[*Textile Committee* v. *K.A. Malani*, 1983 (1) SLR 416]

Under Rule 5(1) of T.S. Rules, while terminating the services of a temporary employee, simultaneous payment of notice salary is not mandatory.

[*U.O.I.* v. *Arun Kumar Roy*, 1986 (1) SLR 476 (SC)]

Where the rules of Corporation require that termination of services of a temporary employee should be either by notice or payment of one month's salary in lieu of the notice period, pay must be tendered. The fact that "No dues" certificate was wanting, is no excuse.

[*Kusum Gupta* v. *Haryana State Small Scale Industries Corporation*, 1986 (3) SLR 14 SC]

Where the services of a temporary employee are terminable by one month's notice, the one month notice or tender of one month pay in lieu of notice is a condition precedent to his discharge. An order of termination with a concluding sentence that the employee "will be given one month's salary in lieu of notice" is illegal and has to be quashed.

[*Dina Nath Srivastava* v. *Haryana Agricultural University*, (1983) 1 SLR 280]

Regulation No. 12 of National Cooperative Development Corporation Service Regulations does not require payment of one month salary in lieu of the notice period simultaneously with the termination order.

[*Bachi Ram* v. *U.O.I.*, ATR 1986 (2) SC 248]

2.21 There is no reciprocal provision for insisting on the employee for payment of one month's pay in lieu of the notice period in cases where his request for relieving him forthwith is accepted by the competent authority

"Rule 5 enables Government to dispense with the services of a temporary employee forthwith on payment of one month's pay and allowances in lieu of notice but does not provide for the forfeiture to Government of a similar amount when the employee does not give the requisite notice. The practice of obtaining an undertaking from temporary employees regarding forfeiture of pay and allowances should be discontinued where this has not already been done."

[G.I.,M.H.A., O.M. No. 78/105/55-TS dated the 22nd December, 1955 read with G.I. Deptt. Of Pers. & A.R. Notfn. No. 4/2/72-Estt. (C)dated the 22nd November, 1972]

2.22 Competent authorities to reopen the cases of termination of services of the employees under Rule 5(2) of CCS (TS) Rules for review of the orders passed by the appointing authorities

The cases of termination of services of temporary Government servants under Rule 5(1) can be reviewed by the Central Government or by any other authority specified by the Central Government in this behalf or by a Head of Department if the appointing authority is subordinate to him. Ministries/ Departments of Government have been issuing orders under SR 2(10) specifying various authorities as Head of Departments from time to time. The time schedule fixed for reopening of the case and the scope of review has been laid down in Rule 5(2) of CCS (TS) Rules.

2.23 Reinstatement of a temporary employee under Rule 5(2) of CCS(TS) Rules cannot be conditional:

One Dayanand Misra was appointed as an L.D.C. in a temporary capacity in the office of Accountant General U.P. on 28-10-1967 as per recruitment rules *viz.* possession of education qualifications of High School and having typing speed of 30 words per minute. His services were later on terminated in September, 1975 on the ground that there was no proof of his having qualified the Typing test. On his representation, he was reinstated in service on 5-11-1977 under Rule 5(2) of CCS (TS) Rules with a rider that he would be required to appear at the typing test. He failed to qualify the said test and his services were once again terminated. The contention of the petitioner was that once having qualified the typing test before he was initially appointed in October, 1967, he cannot be asked to qualify that Test again. This case came up for consideration before Allahabad High Court which in its judgment dated 21-12-1982 observed as under:

> "This brings us to the contention of the petitioner that reinstatement cannot be conditioned. The order dated 5-11-1977 recites that the petitioner is reinstated to the post of the lower division clerk with effect from the date he resumes duty and that his further retention in service will be subject to his passing the prescribed typing test within a period of twelve months of his joining the duty. In view of the conditions imposed in the reinstatement order, the petitioner could not be retained on his failure to qualify the said test. We are unable to agree with this contention. There is no dispute that the order passed was of "reinstatement" and not of "reappointment". The expression 'reinstatement' means according to the Black Law Dictionary (5th Ed. (1979) at pages 1157) 'To reinstall; to re-establish; to place again in a former state or condition or office; to restore to a status or position from which the object or person had been removed'. Subsequent to his reinstatement, the petitioner was granted full pay and allowance for the period of termination which was also treated as on duty. Sub-rule (2) of Rule 5 of the

Central Civil Services (Temporary Service) Rules, 1965, empowers the appointing authorities to reopen the case and reinstate a Government servant in service. According to clause (b) of the proviso to Rule 5(2), the order of reinstatement shall specify (i) the amount or proportion of pay and the amount, if any, to be paid to the Government servant for the period of his absence from the date of termination of his service and the date of his reinstatement, and (ii) whether the said period shall be treated as a period spent on duty for any specified purposes or purpose. If it not without significance that the provision does not envisage the imposition of a new term of condition. On being reinstated, the petitioner could not be directed to reappear at the written test to enable appointing authority to reconsider whether he is fit to be taken in service. On parity of reasoning the position does not vary with reference to the type writing test either. "The petitioner was appointed on being adjudged duly qualified including in the matter of type-writing."

[*Dayanand Misra* v. *U.O.I.*, 1983 (2) SLJ All 159]

2.24 When the services of a temporary employee is terminated in an irregular manner before the stipulated fixed period of his employment, he can be reinstated in service to serve the remaining term of his employment

One Y.N. Pradhan was appointed as a driver under Sikkim Administration on a temporary basis for a period for six months. Before expiry of the said period, he was arrested on a charge of theft and his services were terminated on 18-8-1979 *i.e.,* 25 days before the said stipulated period of six months was to expire. The procedure laid down in Article 311 (2) of the Constitution was not followed in the case. Meanwhile, he was convicted of the charge but subsequently his conviction was set aside on appeal. He pleaded for reinstatement in service and the department revoked his order of termination on 31-5-1982 and was allowed to work for 25 days more *i.e.* for the period falling short of six months. He argued that he should be deemed to be in service during the entire intervening period even though his employment was only for six months. This case came before Sikkim High Court, which in its judgment dated 29-8-1983 observed as under:

"The claim of the petitioner that as the order of termination dated 18-8-1979 was revoked by order dated 31-5-1982, he must be deemed to have been in service during the entire intervening period, even though his employment was for 6 months only, cannot but be rejected as without any basis in facts or in law. His employment for a fixed term of six months was purported to be terminated 25 days before the expiry of the term and if the order of termination was ineffective in law, and, at any rate was revoked by a subsequent order, all that the petitioner could claim was employment for 25 days more. The petitioner having admittedly given the opportunity to be in service for 25 days more and having served accordingly, he could not have any further claim against the respondents."

[*Yok Narayan Pradhan* v. *General Manager, Sikkim, Nationalised Transport*, 1983 (2) SLJ 381]

2.25 An interim order passed by the court in a termination cases does not and cannot amount to a direction that the employee is entitled to be reinstated in service irrespective of the merits of the case when the writ is finally disposed of

One Arun Govil was appointed on contract on 20-8-1979 on the following terms and conditions:

"The appointment shall be on contract for a period of one year w.e.f. the date of assumption if it is not terminated earlier by giving one month's notice by the Hon'ble Governor or on paying one month's salary in lieu thereof or by giving one month's notice by the officer."

The period of the contract was extended from time to time till 30-8-1985. His services were eventually terminated on 29-3-1985. He filed a writ petition in the High Court which passed an interim order to keep the post vacant and make it available to the petitioner if he succeeds ultimately in the case. The question that arose for consideration was whether the interim order can reinstate him in service beyond the stipulated extended period of the duration of the post which was upto 30-8-1985 irrespective of the fact that no further extension beyond 30-8-1985 was accorded by the competent authority. He succeeded in the case. The question before the Supreme Court was whether the interim order can reinstate him in service beyond that extended period of appointment upto 30-8-1985 irrespective of the fact that no further extension beyond 30-8-1985 was accorded by Government. The query was answered in the negative.

[*State of Uttar Pradesh* v. *Ex. Pilot Officer Arun Govil*, 1990 (1) SLJ 56]

2.26 Reinstatement of a temporary employee after his acquittal in a criminal case is not automatic

It is open to the competent appropriate authority to take a decision whether a further departmental inquiry into his conduct is required to be done before directing reinstatement. In a case, the respondent was a temporary Government servant and he was accused of defalcation of public money. The competent authority had powers under Rule 5(1) of CCS (TS) Rules to terminate his services instead of conducting the inquiry or to continue him in service. Reinstatement in such a case would be a charter for him to indulge with impunity in misappropriation of public money.

[*U.O.I.* v. *Biharilal*, 1997 (4) JT 541]

Note.—There are large number of judgments on the subject which have been discussed elsewhere in the book which may also kindly be perused.

2.27 In cases where a *de novo* inquiry is ordered by the competent authority in a case of termination of services of a temporary employee, the order of termination is deemed to have been set aside

"Where after an order of termination of services of an Extra Departmental Agent, the appellate authority orders *de novo* inquiry (though without specific order setting aside the termination) the order of termination must be deemed to have been set aside."

[*Ram Chandra Pangrahi* v. *Supdt. of Post Offices*, 1985 (1) SLR 81 (Ori) DB]

2.28 The services of a temporary employee can be terminated on the ground of his physical unfitness without notice

Under Rule 6 of CCS (TS) Rules, the services of a temporary Government servant can be terminated at any time without notice on his being declared physically unfit for continuance in service by an authority which would have been competent to disclose him as permanently incapacitated for service had his appointment been permanent. The provisions of Rule 6 are, therefore, an exception to the provisions of Rule 5 in that no notice is required to be given to an employee for termination of his services on ground of physical unfitness.

2.29 Case law on the subject of termination of services of services of employees on medical grounds

The service of an employee were terminated on the ground that he was "colour blind". In the past, he had been medically examined by Civil Surgeon and found physically fit. It was held that his order of termination should not have been passed—

(i) without getting him examined by a Medical Board; or

(ii) without affording him an opportunity of being heard.

[*Tarlok Chand* v. *State of Punjab*, 1989 (6) SLR 285 (P&H)]

The services of a casual worker were discontinued on the ground that he was medically unfit. No supporting documents were, however, produced in evidence to substantiate it. The order was held illegal.

[*Chhagan Vila* v. *U.O.I.*, 1989 (7) SLR 131 CAT (Amd)]

Termination of services on medical ground does not attract Article 311.

[*Jagannath Ghosh* v. *D.F.O.*, 1976 (1) SLR 243]

In the case of a temporary employee, his services were terminated on medical grounds after he had completed training. The trainee was suffering from "high myopia" which was disqualification for appointment in the Electricity Board. It was held that contract of apprenticeship comes to an end after completion of training. After completion of training the candidate has only a right to be considered for employment. There is no obligation on the part of the authority to give employment even after successful completion of apprenticeship.

[*Deonarayan Deokumar Patil* v. *M.P. Electricity Board*, 1988 (4) SLR 307 (MP)]

Services of a probationer were terminated as he was a sickly person. The order was set aside by the U.P. Public Services Tribunal. On a writ petition filed by the employer corporation the High Court found that the employee had lost the confidence of employer. Hence without deciding the other issues, High Court accepted the writ petition subject to employer paying the employee Rs. 5,000 as compensation.

[*U.P. Hills Electronics Corporation Ltd.* v. *Kunwar Arun Kumar*, (1996) 7 SLR 66]

2.30 Terminal benefits available to a temporary employee whose services have been terminated under Rule 5(1) of CCS (TS) Rules

In addition to payment of pay and allowances in lieu of the notice period under proviso to Rule 5(1) of CCS(TS) Rules, a temporary employee is entitled to payment of cash equivalent to leave salary and also terminal gratuity. The relevant provisions of the rules in this regard are discussed below:—

(a) Where the services of a Government servant are terminated by notice or by payment of pay and allowances in lieu of notice, or otherwise in accordance with the terms and conditions of his appointment, he may be granted *suo moto* by the authority competent to grant leave, cash equivalent in respect of earned leave at his credit on the date on which he ceases to be in service subject to a maximum of 300 days, including the number of days for which encashment was availed along with LTC.

[Rule 39 (6)(a)(i) of CCS (Leave) Rules]

(b) *On resignation/quitting service.*—If a Government servant resigns or quits service, he may be granted *suo motu* by the authority competent to grant leave, cash equivalent in respect of earned leave at his credit on the date of cessation of service, to the extent of half of such leave at his credit, subject to a maximum of 150 days, including the number of days for which encashment was availed along with LTC.

[Rule 39 (6)(a)(ii) of CCS (Leave) Rules]

The cash equivalent payable under (a) and (b) above shall be calculated as follows, and it shall be payable in one lump sum as a one time settlement. No HRA or CCA shall be payable.

$$\text{Cash equivalent} = \frac{\text{Pay admissible on the date of cessation plus DA admissible on that date}}{30} \times \text{No. of days of unutilised earned leave for which encashment is admissible.}$$

[Rule 39(6)(b) read with 39(2)(b) CCS (Leave) Rules]

(c) *In case of death in service.*—In case a Government servant dies while in service, the cash equivalent of the leave salary that the deceased employee would have got had he gone on earned leave that would have been due and admissible to him but for the death on the date immediately following the death and in any case not exceeding leave salary for 300 days shall be paid to his family without any reduction on account of pension equivalent of death-cum- retirement gratuity. In addition to the cash equivalent of leave salary admissible under this rule, the family of the deceased Government servant shall also be entitled to payment of dearness allowance only as per orders issued in this behalf separately.

[Rule 39A of CCS (Leave) Rules]

In addition to the cash equivalent of leave salary in respect of earned leave, the family of the deceased Government servant is eligible for the payment of cash equivalent of leave salary in respect of half pay leave also at the credit of the deceased Government servant at the time of his death. However, pension equivalent of death-gratuity and family pension (including dearness relief thereon) will be deducted from the cash equivalent of leave salary for half-pay leave.

[G.I. Deptt. of Per. & Trg. O.M. No. 14020/2/93-Estt. (L) dated the 29th March, 1995]

(d) The provisions regarding payment of gratuity are mentioned in Rule 10 of CCS (TS) Rules, 1965.

Chapter 3

GROUNDS OF TERMINATION OF SERVICES OF TEMPORARY EMPLOYEES

The State is not a free master to "hire and fire" a temporary employee in any manner it likes in its absolute pleasure. The position of law is that if the hired employee even though temporarily employed can show that such a firing has left some scar on him, the firing would be declared unlawful unless the constitutional requirements of Article 311 are fulfilled.

SYNOPSIS

3.2 TERMINATION OF SERVICES OF EMPLOYEES ON GROUNDS OF THEIR UNSUITABILITY FOR THE SERVICE

3.2.1 Law on the subject

3.2.2 Termination of the services of a temporary employee on the ground of his unsatisfactory performance does not violate Article 311(2) of Constitution

3.2.3 The order of termination of services of an employee under Rule 5 of CCS(TS) Rules cannot be challenged if it is on the ground of his unsuitability for the post held by him

3.2.4 Orders of termination cannot be interfered with in cases where the competent authority is satisfied that there are grounds showing unsuitability of the employee for the post held by him

3.2.5 Services of a temporary employee can be terminated under Rule 5(1) of CCS (TS) Rules, 1965 in cases where a review has been undertaken to find out the desirability or otherwise of continuance of such employee for their further retention in service

3.2.6 The services of a temporary Government Servants can be terminated under Rule 5(1) of CCS (TS) Rules, 1965 even when he is under suspension and inquiry is made against him to find out the truth of allegations against him

3.2.7 The services of a temporary employee can be terminated under Rule 5 even when he is under suspension and criminal proceedings are pending against him if his services are found undesirable

3.2.8 The Petitioner cannot take advantage of the averments made in the counter affidavit about his unsuitability for the job to allege that the termination order simpliciter is penal in nature

3.2.9 Short notes on judgments of the courts relating to termination of services of employees on ground of unsatisfactory work / unsuitability for the job

3.3 TERMINATION OF SERVICES OF TEMPORARY EMPLOYEES ON THE GROUND OF WITHHOLDING OF VITAL INFORMATION BY THEM AT THE TIME OF THEIR APPOINTMENT

3.3.1 Propositions of Law

3.3.2 Services of a temporary employee can be terminated for hiding vital information in the Attestation form of character and antecedents

3.3.3 Punitive order of termination of services of an employee on the ground of adverse Police Report but couched in innocuous form is liable to be quashed

3.3.4 Termination of services of the holder of a civil post in a temporary capacity on the ground of adverse report from the Collector that he was involved in a criminal case, without hearing him, is liable to be set aside

3.3.5 The order of termination is liable to be set aside when no inquiry is made against the employee on the ground that he had suppressed material information at the time of his appointment

3.3.6 The order of termination of an employee is liable to be quashed when the nature of information suppressed is not vital but is of negative character

3.3.7 When there is no concrete proof that the employee himself had misled the department about his educational qualifications, this order of his termination is liable to be set aside

3.3.8 The contents of the adverse police report should be disclosed to employee concerned if punitive action is proposed to be taken against him on the said report. This is necessary in compliance with the requirements of Article 16 of the Constitution

3.3.9 The contents of the adverse police report are required to be disclosed to the temporary employee and his explanation obtained before resorting to termination of his services

3.4 TERMINATION OF THE SERVICES OF AN EMPLOYE WHO WERE WRONGY APPOINTED

3.4.1 Law on the subject

3.4.2 The services of an employee cannot be terminated if a mistake is made by the appointing authority itself in proper scrutiny of the educational certificates etc. submitted by the employee at the time of his selection

3.4.3 The services of a temporary employee can be terminated on the ground of his appointment being irregular

3.4.4 Interpretation of the term "Appointing Authority" in relation to termination of services of temporary employees

3.4.5 The order of termination of the services of a temporary employee can be issued either by the Appointing Authority or by another authority of the same rank

3.4.6 Short notes on the judgements of the Courts relating to termination of services of temporary employees by incompetent authorities, etc.

3.5 TERMINATION OF SERVICES OF EMPLOYEES ON ADMINISTRATIVE GROUNDS

3.5.1 Law on the subject

3.5.2 Termination of services of an employee by stating that the said order has been passed on "administrative" grounds without mentioning the specific reasons therefor is bad in law and liable to be quashed

3.5.3 Termination of services of a temporary employee on administrative grounds unconnected with conduct is valid

3.5.4 The services of a temporary employee responsible for loss of official documents due to negligence and carelessness cannot be dispensed with without complying with the requirements of Article 311(2) of the Constitution

3.5.5 Services of a temporary employee cannot be terminated merely on the dictation of higher authority

3.5.6 The services of a temporary employee holding "Anand Margi" ideology cannot be terminated under CCS (TS) Rules, 1965 without proof that he had indulged in subversive activities

3.5.7 The authorities should not take too technical a view about the fulfilment of the requisite qualifications for a post while terminating the services of a sportsman under Rule 5 of CCS (TS) Rules

3.5.8 The services of temporary employees can be terminated even before the qualified persons report for duty to replace them

3.6 TERMINATION OF THE SERVICES OF THE SENIORS WHILE THEIR JUNIORS ARE RETAINED IN SERVICE

3.6.1 Law on the Subject

3.6.2 The services of a senior temporary employee can be terminated while retaining his juniors in service only if it is shown that the juniors do not stand at par with him or that they have better service record than him

3.6.3 Where the services of a temporary employee are terminated on the grounds other than his unsuitability, unsatisfactory conduct or the like which put him a class apart from his juniors in the same service, it is a case of indiscrimination and the order of termination is liable to be quashed

3.6.4 The protection of Articles 14 and 16 of the Constitution is available even to a temporary Govt. servant if he has been arbitrarily discriminated against and singled out for harsh treatment in preference to his juniors similarly circumstanced

3.6.5 Short notes on the judgements of the courts in cases where services of senior persons were terminated while retaining juniors

3.9.5 **Courts can go into the causes of termination of service of a temporary employee even though the order issued is a simpliciter**

3.9.6 **Termination of the services of a temporary employee on the stated ground of overstayal of leave mentioned in the order of termination itself amounts to his "removal" from service and is illegal**

3.9.7 **When the order of termination of the services of a temporary employee is based on a report of misconduct, it attracts Article 311(2) of the Constitution**

3.9.8 **Services of an employee cannot be terminated under Rule 5 of C.C.S. (Temporary Service) Rules, 1965 on the ground of misconduct even if the order termination is innocuous and does no cast any stigma on the employee**

3.9.9 **The services of a probationer cannot be terminated through an order simplicitor if there are positive allegations against him**

3.9.10 **The services of a temporary employee cannot be terminated by termination simpliciter when the foundation is allegation of forgery, cheating, inefficiency against him**

3.9.11 **Termination of services of an employee by order simpliciter after making some sort of inquiry on charges of misconduct amounts to punishment and is violative of provisions of Article 311(2) of the Constitution**

3.9.12 **Can the services of an employee be terminated under Rule 5(1) of T.S. Rules, 1965 on the basis of a private complaint against him which was inquired into at his back?**

3.9.13 **The burden of proof to convince the Court that the termination simpliciter is actually an order of punishment lies on the employer**

3.9.14 **The burden of proving that the action of the employer in terminating the services of an employee is *mala fide*, rests on the employee himself**

3.9.15 **Short notes on judgments of courts relating to "Burden of Proof" in departmental inquiries**

3.9.16 **Short notes on judgments of courts in which it was held that Article 311(2) was applicable in cases of termination on the ground of misconduct**

3.9.17 **Short notes on judgments of courts in which it was held that inquiry under Article 311(2) was necessary before terminating the services of temporary employees on charges of misconduct**

3.1 TERMINATION OF SERVICES OF THE EMPLOYEES CONSEQUENT UPON ABOLITION OF THEIR POSTS

3.1.1 Law on the subject

It is now well-settled that an order terminating the services of a temporary Government servants and *ex facie* innocuous in nature that not cast any stigma on the Government servant or visits him with penal consequences, must be regarded as effecting a termination simplicitor but if it is discovered on the basis of the matter adduced that although innocent in its terms, the order was passed, in fact, with a view to punishing the Government servant, it becomes punitive order which can be passed only after complying with Article 311(2) of the Constitution.

[*Nepal Singh* v. *State of Uttar Pradesh*, AIR 1980 SC 1459]

The employees whose services have been terminated under Temporary Service Rules often agitate in the courts on the plea that their orders of termination are, in fact, orders of punishments and that a short cut had been applied in their cases by their employers to get rid of their services. The burden of proof to convince the Court that termination simplicitor is actually an order of punishment, however, lies on the employees only.

The employers have been issuing orders simplicitor on various grounds which are not disclosed in the orders of termination which become subject matter of adjudication by the courts. These grounds come to light only when the courts lift the veil and see for themselves what is hidden behind such innocuous orders of termination.

The case law on the subject is discussed below under various sub-heads dealing with different grounds for termination.

3.1.2 It is the inherent right of the Government to create or abolish any post

It has been held in various judicial pronouncements that Government has the absolute right to create or abolish any post within the provisions of the statute or in the interest of efficiency and economy. Abolition of the posts in good faith without any pretence to get rid of any inconvenience is valid. It may result in losing the job by some incumbent. Where a post is abolished *bona fide,* the *bona fide* of abolition and the consequent effects flowing therefrom such as termination of services etc. is not challengeable in courts as this does not amount to removal or dismissal from service and does not attract provisions of Article 311(2) of the Constitution.

The power to create or abolish a post is not related to the "doctrine of pleasures". The abolition of post is a matter of Governmental policy. Every sovereign Government has powers of abolition of post in the interest and necessity of internal administration. The creation and abolition of post is dictated by policy decision, exigencies of circumstances and administrative necessity. The creation and continuation of posts are all decided by Government in the interest of administration and general public. A Government servant cannot complain of violation of Article 19(1)(f) and Article 311 of the Constitution when a post is abolished as the right to hold a post comes to an end on the abolition of the post which he holds.

[*N. Ramanatha Pillai* v. *State of Kerala,* 1974 (1) SLR 225 SC]

"The Court would be least competent in the face of scanty material to decide whether in a particular case, Government acted honestly in creating a post or refusing to create a post or that its decision suffers from *mala fide,* legal or factual."

[*Dr. N.C. Singhal* v. *U.O.I.,* 1980 SCC (L&S) 269]

> "Whether a post should be retained or abolished is essentially a matter for the Government to decide. As long as such decision of the Government is taken in good faith, the same cannot be set aside by the Court. It is not open to the Court to go behind the wisdom of the decision and substitute its own opinion for that of the Government on the point as to whether a post should or should not be abolished. In case it is found on consideration of the facts of a case that the abolition of the post was only a device to terminate the service of an employee, the abolition of the post would suffer from a serious infirmity and would be liable to be set aside. The termination of a post in good faith and consequent termination of the services of the incumbent of that post would not attract Article 311".

[*State of Haryana* v. *Des Raj,* 1976 (1) SLR 191; *Ali Mohd.* v. *Chairman, TAC,* 1980 (3) SLR 546]

The appellant was suspended and served with charge sheet. However before this, a notice was served abolishing all posts in the Department. Disciplinary proceedings did not proceed further and after about two years, on the representation of the appellant, Government ordered that the disciplinary action against him would be treated as closed. It was held that the appellant was employed in a department which has since been abolished and with the abolition of the department; his claim to hold any post in the department must fail.

[*Gurdeep Singh* v. *Union of India*, 1982 (2) SLJ 380 (SC)]

"It is no doubt true that Article 38 and Article 43 of the Constitution insist that the State should endeavour to find sufficient work for people so that they may put their capacity to work into economic use and earn a fairly good living but these Articles do not mean that everybody should be provided with a job in the Civil Service of the State and if a person is provided with one, he should not be asked to leave it even for a just cause. The question whether a person who ceases to be a Government servant according to law, should be rehabilitated by giving an alternative employment, as the law stands today is a matter of policy on which the Court has no voice."

[*K. Rajindran* v. *State of Tamil Nadu*, AIR 1982 SC 1107]

3.1.3 Observations of the Supreme Court relating to termination of the services of the employees consequent upon abolition of the projects / schemes on which they are employed

When posts temporarily created for fulfilling the needs of a particular project or scheme which is limited in its duration come to an end because the need for the project is over either because the need was fulfilled or the project had to be abandoned wholly or partially for want of funds, the employer cannot be directed to continue employing such employees as have been dislodged, because such a direction would amount to requisition for creation of posts though not required by the employer and funding such posts though the employer does not have funds available for the purpose.

[*Rajindra* v. *State of Rajasthan*, 1999 (2) SCC 317]

> "The employees of the project of "Adult and Non-formal education", a temporary project which was time bound to last till 1990 are not entitled for regularisation of their services."
>
> [*Jaipal* v. *State of Haryana*, (1988) 3 SCC 354]

> "It is a common knowledge that the Government as a welfare State floats several schemes and projects generating employment opportunities, though they are short lived. The objective is to meet the need of the moment. The benefit of such schemes and project is that for the duration they exist, they provide employment and livelihood to such persons as would not have been able to secure the same but for such schemes or projects. If the workers employed for fulfilling the need of such passing phase projects or schemes were to become a liability on the employer - State by too liberally interpreting the labour laws in favour of the workmen, then the same may well act as a disincentive to the State for floating such schemes and the State may opt to keep away from initiating such schemes and projects even in times of dire need, because it may feel that by opening the gates of welfare it would be letting in onerous obligations entailed upon it by extended application of the labour laws."
>
> [*S.M. Nilaj Kar* v. *Telecom, District Manager, Karnataka*, JT 2003 (3) SC 436]

The nature of employment under Jawaharlal Nehru Rozgar Yojna came to be examined by the Supreme Court in *Delhi Development Horticulture Employees' Union* v. *Delhi Administration, Delhi*, (1992) 4 SCC 99: (1992) 1 SCR 565, and the Court found that the scheme under which the petitioners therein were employed was evolved to provide income for those who are below the poverty line and particularly during the periods when they are without any source of livelihood and therefore without any income whatsoever. Such schemes were further meant for the rural poor, for the object was not to provide the right to work as such even to the rural poor much less to the employed in general. The Union of India had filed a detailed affidavit showing the purpose and working of such schemes, which in their very nature could provide some employment to some people for some time and not an employment to all the employed for all times. The Court held: "if the resources used for the Jawaharlal Rozgar Yojna were in their entirety to be used for providing full employment throughout the year, they would have given employment only to a small percentage of the population in need of income, the remaining vast majority being left with no income whatsoever. No fault could, therefore, be found with the limited object of the scheme given the limited resources at the disposal of the State. Those employed under the scheme, therefore, could not ask for more than what the scheme intended to give them. To get an employment under such scheme and to claim on the basis of the said employment, right to regularization, is to frustrate the scheme itself. No Court can be a party to such exercise. It is wrong to approach the problems of those employed under such schemes with a view to providing them with full employment and guaranteeing equal pay for equal work. These concepts, in the context of such schemes, are both unwarranted and misplaced. They will do more harm than good by depriving the many of the little income that they may get to keep them from starvation. They would benefit a few at the cost of the many starving poor for whom the schemes are meant. That would also force the State to wind up the existing schemes and orbit them from introducing the new ones, for want of resources. This is not to say that the problems of the unemployed deserve no consideration or sympathy. This is only to emphasize that even among the unemployed a distinction exists between those who live below and above the poverty line, those in need of partial and those in need of full employment, the educated and uneducated, the rural and urban unemployed etc. The Court emphasized how a judicial sympathy with such workmen could boomerang upon the purpose of the schemes itself and thereby in the larger context, deny the limited benefit extended by the State to the unemployed which would not be available but for such schemes.

The Court held that the petitioners cannot be directed to be regularised on the only ground that they have put in work for 240 or more days, as such directions lead to pernicious consequences. Although there is the Employment Exchange Act which requires recruitment on the basis of registration in the Employment Exchange, it has become a common practice to ignore the Employment Exchange and persons registered in the Employment Exchanges and to employ and get employed directly those who are either not registered with the Employment Exchange or who though registered are lower in the long waiting list of the Employment Register. The Courts can take judicial notice of the facts that such employment is sought and given directly for various illegal considerations including money. The employment is given first for temporary periods with technical breaks to circumvent the relevant rules, and is continued for 240 or more days with a view to give benefit of regularisation knowing the judicial trend that those who have completed 240 or more days they are directed to be automatically regularised. A good deal of illegal employment market has developed, resulting in a new source of corruption and frustration to those who are waiting at the Employment Exchanges for years. Not all those who gain such back door entry in the employment are in need of the particular jobs. Though already employed elsewhere, they join the jobs for better and secured prospects. That is why many of the cases which come to the Courts are of employment in Government Department Public Undertakings or Agencies. Ultimately it is people who bear the heavy burden of the surplus labour. The other equally injurious effect of indiscriminate regularisation has been that many of the agencies have stopped undertaking casual or temporary work though they are urgent and essential for fear that if those who are employed on such works are required to be continued for 240 or more days they have to be absorbed as regular employees although the works are time bound and there is no need of the workmen beyond a completion of the works undertaken. The public interest are thus jeopardized on this counts."

3.1.4 There is no automatic termination of services of an employee consequent upon abolition of the post

Mere abolition of post does not automatically terminate the services of an employee. An employee is to be served a notice before such termination is effected. It is open to the appointing authority to offer any other post in lieu of the post abolished or even a lower post to its incumbent as envisaged in F.R. 22 which may be available at that time. The termination of services without following the prescribed procedure or non-compliance of the rules is invalid.

3.1.5 There is no cause of action when the services of a temporary employee are terminated consequent upon abolition of the post held by him

One Shuba Varma was appointed as a Senior Instructor (Library) in Bal Bhavan on 1-5-1965 in a temporary capacity and was put on probation for 2 years which she completed successfully. Thereafter, an Evaluation Committee was set up to study the activities of various departments of National Bal Bhavan and it recommended abolition of the post held by the Petitioner. She was not found fit to be absorbed in the new departmental set up recommended by the Committee and consequently, her services were terminated on 11-9-1969. She challenged her termination order on various grounds in Delhi High Court and the Court in its judgment dated 6-4-1981 observed as under:

> "The contention of the petitioner is that her work was admittedly satisfactory and that no opportunity had been given to her before the issuance of the letter dated 11th September, 1969. The fact that the petitioner's services were satisfactory is not denied. In view of the averments on record, it must be held that the literary section was closed. It was contended by the petitioner that the work being done by the literary section and the new section created was of a more or less similar nature. That may or may not be so. The fact, however, remains that the literary section having closed down, the petitioner's post came to an end. It would be recalled that her letter of appointment dated 27th April, 1965 makes it clear that the petitioner was appointed to a temporary post. The right of respondent to create and abolish cannot be denied. The right is contained in Regulations and Bye-laws of the Board, the validity of which has not been challenged. It is, true, that in the letter dated 11th September, 1969 it has been mentioned that the working committee had recommended "transfer" of the incumbents from the literary section to the new section. The use of the word "transfer", to my mind, is clearly a misnomer. It is evident that if a post is abolished, the incumbent has no right to be retained in the employment of that institute. In order, however, to provide an alternative employment, respondent did see the suitability of the incumbents of the literary section for being appointed

to the new section. The appointment to the new section would, in a way, be a fresh appointment. Even if it be regarded as a transfer, the petitioner cannot make a grievance that she was not heard. It has not been shown that the rules postulate the giving of an opportunity of being heard prior to a selection taking place. The petitioner can have no right of hearing before the respondents decided to abolish the post."

[*S. Varma (Mrs.)* v. *B.B. & N.C.M. New Delhi*, 1981 (2) SLJ 328]

3.1.6 No relief can be granted to an employee whose services are terminable on 24 hours notice when the post on which he was appointed was created for one year only and the project was closed

One F.R. Jesuratnam was appointed as Senior Research Assistant in I.I.T. Delhi in a temporary capacity subject to verification of his character and antecedents with the stipulation that his services were terminable on 24 hours' notice. It revealed later on inquiry that he was a dismissed Squadron Leader of Indian Air Force. His services were terminated by the Institute against which he filed an appeal in the Supreme Court in which he pleaded that the institute did not apply its mind to the facts of the case while deciding to terminate his services and in any event the appellant was entitled to an opportunity to be heard before his services could be terminated.

The Apex court in its judgment dated 22-7-1981 observed as under:

"It appears from the record before us that the appellant was appointed in the Institute in connection with the programme of writing a monograph undertaken by Prof. B. Karunesh. The appointment was temporary only and could be terminated on 24 hours notice. It is averred in the counter affidavit filed by the Institute that the post of Research Assistant, to which the appellant was appointed, was created for one year only. That being so, although according to the appellant the programme extended to two years, it was affirmed in the counter-affidavit that on the death of Professor Karunesh in June, 1978, the project in which he was engaged had been dropped and finally closed, and the period for which the appellant's post of Research Assistant was created has also expired. The order of termination is upheld."

[*F.R. Jesuratnam* v. *U.O.I.*, 1981(2) SLJ 239]

3.1.7 Where the project is closed and the services of the employees working in the project are not required, it is necessary to issue formal orders of termination of their services

One Assudani was appointed as Instructor in the Training Centre, C.W.P.C. (Water Wing) at Kota on 11-8-1961. The said Training Centre was closed on 15-9-1974 and he was declared surplus but no termination order as such was issued. He was, however, transferred to Salal Project and was paid T.A. advance and was also allowed joining time and adjusted against the post of supervisor. He superannuated on 31-7-1987. The Department allowed him only terminal gratuity for the period 1961 to 1974 and not pensionary benefits. An order was issued on 18-8-1987 *i.e.* after his superannuation terminating his services as Instructor retrospectively from 15-9-1974. The petitioner sought relief in the case and CAT (Principal Bench) held that in the circumstances the appellant is to be treated in service right from 11-8-1961 to 31-7-1987 and entitled to all retirement benefits including pension. The order dated 18-8-1987 has no legal effect.

[*T.S. Assudani* v. *U.O.I.*, 1989 (4) SLJ 489 CAT]

3.1.8 Termination of services of an employee consequent upon abolition of his post does not amount to his dismissal or removal from service to attract Article 311 of the Constitution

This proposition of law came up for consideration before the Supreme Court in *Ramanatha Pillai* v. *State of Kerala*, AIR 1973 SC 2641, which observed as under:

> "The abolition of a post may have the consequence of termination of service of a Government servant. Such termination is not dismissal or removal within the meaning of Article 311 of the Constitution. The opportunity of showing cause against the proposed penalty of dismissal or removal does not therefore arise in the case of abolition of post. The abolition of post is an executive policy decision. Whether after abolition of the post, the Government servant who was holding the post would or could be offered any employment under the State, would be a matter of policy decision of the Government because the abolition of post does not confer on the person holding the abolished post any right to hold the post."

A slightly different case came up before Bombay High Court in which the services of one Malani were terminated consequent to abolition of his post. The Hon'ble court in that judgment dated 23-6-1976 observed as under:

> "The petitioner's conditions of service do not show that his services were co-terminus with the post. On the contrary, the terms provide for the petitioner being liable to transfer. Under the circumstances, on the terms and conditions, the petitioner's services could be utilised inspite of the post of Deputy Director (Mechanical Engineer) having been abolished. In my view, abolition of the post in which the petitioner was working has nothing to do with the question of termination of the petitioner's services either under the Rules or under the Contract. The terms and conditions of his service do not provide for the petitioner's services with the Textile Committee coming to an end with the abolition of the post. The order of termination of the petitioner's services not having been made in accordance with the Rules by which the petitioner was governed, had to be treated as invalid and non-existing and by reason thereof, the petitioner has to be treated as if his services with the Textile Committee were not terminated and he has all along continued in their service."
>
> [*R.A.Malani* v. *Textile Committee*, (1977) SLJ 576]

3.2 TERMINATION OF SERVICES OF EMPLOYEES ON GROUNDS OF THEIR UNSUITABILITY FOR THE SERVICE

3.2.1 Law on the subject

The law relating to termination of services of temporary employees on the ground of their unsuitability for the service has now been well settled by a catena of cases decided by their Lordships of the Supreme Court. In the case of *Jagdish Mittar* v. *Union of India*, AIR 1964 SC 449, it was held that the appropriate authority may make an enquiry whether the temporary employee deserves to be continued. Such an enquiry is actuated solely by the desire to decide the simple question as to whether the temporary servant should be continued in service or not and is undertaken for that purpose alone without any desire to attach any stigma to him. An enquiry of this character must be distinguished from a formal departmental enquiry which is undertaken for the purpose of punishing an employee. In case, after such an enquiry, the authority decides to terminate the service of the temporary employee such termination would not amount to dismissal or removal, as no stigma attaches to it. The test in such cases must be: Does the order cast an aspersion or attach a stigma to the person when it purports to discharge him? If the answer to this question its in affirmative, then notwithstanding the form of the order of termination of service, must be held in substance to amount to dismissal. But if the answer is in the negative, then it is discharge simpliciter.

The following observations of Gajendragadkar J., as he then was, are worth reproducing:

> "It is true that the tenure held by a temporary public servant or by a probationer is of a precarious character. His services can be terminated by one month's notice without assigning any reason either under the terms of contract which expressly provide for such termination or under the relevant statutory rules governing temporary appointments or appointments of probationers. Such a temporary servant can also be dismissed in a punitive way; that means that the appropriate authority possesses two powers to terminate the services of a temporary public servant; it can either discharge him purporting to exercise its power under the terms of contract or the relevant rules, and in that case, it would be a straight forward and direct case of discharge and nothing more. In such a case, Article 311 will not apply. The authority can also act under its power to dismiss a temporary servant and make an order of dismissal in a straight forward way; in such a case, Article 311 will apply.

This simple position is sometimes complicated by the fact that even while exercising its power to terminate the services of a temporary servant, the authority may in fairness inquire whether the temporary servant should be continued in service or not. It is obvious that temporary servants or probationers are generally discharged, because they are not found to be competent or suitable for the post they hold. In other words, if a temporary servant or a probationer is found to be satisfactory in his work, efficient, and otherwise eligible, it is unlikely that his services would be terminated, and so, before discharging a temporary servant the authority may have to examine the question about the suitability of the said servant to be continued and acting *bona fide* in that behalf, the authority may also give a chance to the servant to explain, if any complaints are made against him, or his competence or suitability is disputed on some grounds arising from the discharge of his work; but such an enquiry would be held only for the purpose of deciding whether the temporary servant should be continued or not. There is no element of punitive proceedings in such an enquiry. The idea in holding such an enquiry is not to punish the temporary servant but to decide whether he deserves to be continued in service or not. If as a result of such an enquiry, the authority comes to the conclusion that the temporary servant is not suitable to be continued it may pass a simple order of discharge by virtue of the powers conferred on it by the contract or the relevant rule; in such a case it would not be open to the temporary servant to invoke the protection of Article 311 for the simple reason that the enquiry which ultimately led to his discharge was held only for the purpose of deciding whether the power under the contract or the relevant rule should be exercised and the temporary servant discharged."

3.2.2 Termination of the services of a temporary employee on the ground of his unsatisfactory performance does not violate Article 311(2) of Constitution

One V.K. Srimali was appointed as Assistant Boring Mechanic in a temporary capacity in Irrigation Department U.P. on 2-12-1965. His services were terminated by giving him one month's notice. He made inquiries from the authorities as to why his services were terminated and was informed that his performance was not found satisfactory and also because he was careless and negligent in his work. The adverse remarks contained in his Character Roll also disclosed the fact that his performance was not satisfactory. The petitioner challenged his order of termination on the ground that it was violative of Article 311(2) of the Constitution before Allahabad High Court, which in its judgment dated 3-1-1983 observed as under:—

> "The impugned order of termination of employment is an order simpliciter. It does not cast any stigma against the petitioner. He was informed orally that his services were terminated on the ground of his unsatisfactory work. That was the basis for it as was also evident from his Character

Roll entries and also the letter of warning administered to him. There is, therefore, no escape from the conclusion that the services of the petitioner were terminated on the ground of his unsatisfactory work and unsuitability and not with a view to impose any penalty on him or to punish him or to cast any stigma against him. Hence even if persons junior to him were retained in service, the termination order would not be violative of Article 16 of the Constitution. It is also not violative of Article 311(2) of the Constitution."

[*State of Uttar Pradesh* v. *Virendra Kumar Srimali*, 1983 (2) SLJ 283]

3.2.3 The order of termination of services of an employee under Rule 5 of CCS(TS) Rules cannot be challenged if it is on the ground of his unsuitability for the post held by him

One V.N. Rajan was appointed as a labourer on "casual basis" in I.N.S. Vendurathy for one month on 18-12-1961, He was subsequently regularized and promoted as Ammunition Repair Labourer Grade II on 2-3-1964 His services were terminated on 17-1-1967 under Rule 5. The petitioner challenged the order before the Supreme Court on the ground that termination of his services was violative of Article 16 of the Constitution. He also quoted various judgments of the Apex Court to plead that even temporary Government servants are entitled to the protection of Article 311(2) of the Constitution. The Hon'ble Court in its judgment dated 10-3-1981 observed as under:

"The respondent was only a temporary Government servant but even as a temporary Government servant, he is entitled to the protection of Article 311 (2) of the Constitution where termination involves a stigma or where it amounts to "punishment". We have looked into the file relating to the respondent ending with the order of termination of his service. We are satisfied that the decision to terminate the services of the respondent had been taken at the highest level on the ground of unsuitability of the respondent in relation to the post held by him and it is not by way of any punishment and no stigma is attached to the respondent by reason of termination of his service. In these circumstances we allow the appeal and confirm the order of termination."

[*Commodore Southern Naval Area* v. *V.N. Rajan*, 1981 (2) SLJ 48]

3.2.4 Orders of termination cannot be interfered with in cases where the competent authority is satisfied that there are grounds showing unsuitability of the employee for the post held by him

One Dalwadi was appointed as a watchman in Central Horticulture Station Godhra under I.C.A.R. on 9-12-1980 by an appointment letter dated 2-1-1981. In terms of the said letter, he was put on probation for an initial period of 2 years. His services were terminated under Rule 5(1) of CCS (TS) Rules, invoking condition No. 3 of the letter of appointment which gave the employers the right to terminate his services without assigning any reason by one month's notice on either side in the service.

The petitioner sought relief in the case before CAT. It was pleaded by the Department that there were allegations against him for producing bogus medical certificates and was also found sleeping while on duty. The case of the petitioner was that the Respondents were avoiding disciplinary proceedings and instead of inquiring into specific allegations against him, they were using the ground of unsuitability for getting rid of him. The Ahmedabad Bench in its judgment dated 5-7-1989 observed as under:

> "It is not necessary for us to go into the merits of such independent reasons because the respondent is competent to come to his own conclusion and it is only necessary to know whether there was some contemporaneous attempt on the part of the respondent to ascertain suitability of the petitioner or to caution and warn him and then to take necessary action against him. We find that this condition is fulfilled and in the circumstances of the case, it would be mistaken latitude on our part to allow the petitioner to continue in service. It cannot be said that because of specific allegation made against the petitioner the respondent cannot have separate reasons to come to a conclusion about his unsuitability".

[*Bhagwan Das M. Dalwadi* v. *U.O.I.*, 1989 (4) SLJ CAT (Ahmedabad Bench) 1005]

3.2.5 Services of a temporary employee can be terminated under Rule 5(1) of CCS (TS) Rules, 1965 in cases where a review has been undertaken to find out the desirability or otherwise of continuance of such employee for their further retention in service

In the case of *D.K. Gupta* v. *U.O.I.*, (1978) SLJ Raj 277, the petitioner was appointed as Assistant Medical Officer on *ad hoc* basis. He was not selected by U.P.S.C. for the post but was allowed to continue on the said post by extending his term from time to time. He was subsequently removed from service under Rule 5(1) of CCS (TS) Rules. He contended before Rajasthan High Court that his "termination" was actually "removal" from service and is bad in law being violative of Article 311 (2) of the Constitution. He further took the plea that he was unlawfully discriminated against other persons who were also not selected by U.P.S.C. but were allowed to continue on similar posts. The contention of the Department was that as a result of review of the performance of the persons working on the post of Assistant Medical Officer, the competent authority had found that the performance of the petitioner was unsatisfactory and his services were accordingly terminated not by way on penalty but purely for administrative reasons. In its judgment dated 28-3-1977, the Hon'ble High Court observed as under:

> "It is well settled that an order terminating the service of a temporary employee under the rules of employment or under the contract of service and without anything more will not attract Article 311. There is nothing to show that the termination of services of the petitioner was by way of punishment. In the present case it is a simple order of discharge without casting any aspersion against the petitioner or attaching any sigma to his character. If a screening was made by the authority concerned for the purpose of deciding the question of further retention of the petitioner in service and if, it was found on such screening that it was not desirable to continue him in further employment, then it can only be said that his termination was a discharge simplicitor. The unsatisfactory work of the petitioner may only be the motive for terminating his service but clearly it was not the foundation for the same."

3.2.6 The services of a temporary Government servants can be terminated under Rule 5(1) of CCS (TS) Rules, 1965 even when he is under suspension and inquiry is made against him to find out the truth of allegations against him:

In the case of *Dhananjay* v. *Chief Executive Officer, Zila Parishad, Jalna,* 2003 (2) SLJ SC 46, the petitioner was a temporary Government servant having been appointed for one year. While in service, he was placed under suspension on the allegation that he had made payment of Rs. 18,000 instead of Rs. 8,000 to a contractor. He was also prosecuted on the same charge in a court of law in which he was eventually acquitted. Subsequently, his services were terminated under Rule 5(1) of CCS (TS) Rules. He challenged his order of termination on the ground that regular departmental inquiry should have been held in the case before removing him from service and that his removal under CCS (TS) Rules is irregular. This case came up before Supreme Court in the abovementioned case which in its judgment dated 30.1.2003 justified the order of termination of his services under CCS (TS) Rules, 1965. In this connection, the Apex Court referred to its earlier judgment in the case of *U.O.I.* v. *Bihari Lal Sadhna,* (1997) 4 SCC 385, the operative part of which reads as under:

> "It is true that the respondent was acquitted by the criminal court, but acquittal does not automatically gives him the right to be reinstated in service. It would still be open to the competent authority to make decision whether the delinquent Government servant can be taken into service or disciplinary action should be taken under the Central Civil Services (Classification, Control and Appeal) Rules or under the Temporary Service Rules. Admittedly, the respondent had been working as a temporary Government servant before he was placed under suspension. The termination order merely indicated the factual position by mentioning that he was under suspension. It is only a way of describing of his status at that time that he was under suspension. The order came to be passed but that does not constitute any stigma. Mere acquittal of Government employee does not automatically entitle the Government servant to reinstatement. As stated earlier, it would be open to the appropriate competent authority to take a decision whether

the inquiry into the conduct is required to be done before directing reinstatement or appropriate action should be taken as per law if otherwise available. Since the respondent is only a temporary Government servant, the power being available under Rule 5(1) of the Rules it is always open to the competent authority to invoke the said power and terminate the services of the employee instead of conducting the enquiry or to continue in service a Government servant accused of defalcation of public money. Reinstatement would be charter for him to indulge with impunity in misappropriation of public money."

3.2.7 The services of a temporary employee can be terminated under Rule 5 even when he is under suspension and criminal proceedings are pending against him if his services are found undesirable

One Ashok Kumar, a security guard in A.I.R. Bhagalpur was involved in a case of assault on the appointing authority and was placed under suspension. His services were terminated under Rule 5(1) of CCS (TS) Rules. The petitioner challenged his termination of services in CAT (Patna Bench) which in its judgment dated 28-10-1986 observed as under:

"If in the order, it is simply stated that his services are terminated and no reasons have been given in the termination order then it is termination simpliciter and in such a case no notice to show cause either under Article 311(2) of the Constitution or on the principles of natural justice will be required. It is not disputed that no charges were framed against the petitioner and whatever be the motive for termination of the services of the petitioner, as the termination was termination simplicitor, there was no question of framing any charges against the petitioner. It cannot be denied that the services of the petitioner were terminated forthwith on 31-8-1982 and the judgment in the criminal case was delivered on 8-10-1982 and till then the petitioner was under suspension from 26-7-1979. Thus the termination of service was not connected with the criminal trial. The motive may be for termination as he was suspected to be involved somehow in the assault of the Station Engineer who was his appointing authority and so it was not considered desirable that he should be retained. Under such circumstances the termination of service of the petitioner while still under suspension and during the pendency of the criminal trial cannot be said to be illegal."

[*Ashok Kumar* v. *U.O.I.*, 1987 (1) SLJ 187 CAT]

3.2.8 The petitioner cannot take advantage of the averments made in the counter affidavit about his unsuitability for the job to allege that the termination order simpliciter is penal in nature

One Varish Bhan was appointed as a constable in Haryana Police on 1-10-1989. After watching his performance, the authorities came to the conclusion that he was not expected to become efficient Police Officer and his services were accordingly terminated on 12-12-1991 by termination simpliciter.

The petitioner submitted a representation to D.I.G. in this regard which was rejected by an order in which it was disclosed that the order of termination had been passed on the ground of grave misconduct of willful absence from duty. He challenged the order of his termination in Punjab & Haryana High Court which in its judgment dated 5-8-1998 observed as under:

"The petitioner cannot take advantage of the reasons given in the order of D.I.G. The said order was passed by an authority which was competent to go into the matter. Therefore, it cannot be said that the original order of discharge attaches stigma. It has been held by the Supreme Court in *State of Uttar Pradesh* v. *Krishan Kumar Sharma*, (1997) 2 SCC 437, that the averments in the counter affidavit do not alter the nature of the order of termination which was termination simpliciter in accordance with the Rules. It cannot, therefore, be said that the order of discharge amounts to a stigmatized order. One has to look at the order of discharge only whether it attaches any stigma. It is not disputed that the authority which passed the order of discharge was competent to pass such an order under rule 12.21 of the PP Rules. In this view of the matter I do not find any ground warranting interference with the impugned order. The writ petitioner fails and is accordingly dismissed."

[*Const. Varish Bhan* v. *State of Haryana*, 1998 (4) RSJ 204]

3.2.9 Short notes on judgments of the courts relating to termination of services of employees on ground of unsatisfactory work / unsuitability for the job

Petitioner was prosecuted for an alleged offence. During the pendency of the prosecution, his services were terminated. It was held that there was no rule that once departmental or criminal proceedings are initiated against a temporary employee, his services cannot be terminated if he is not found suitable to hold the post.

[*Sekhar Roy* v. *U.O.I.*, 1984 (3) SLR 588 Gau (DB)]

Services of a probationer were terminated one month prior to completion of probation period because of unsuitability. Order of termination set out reasons for regarding him as unsuitable for service. It was held that the order was not stigmatic and the termination was valid.

[*H.G. Raghu* v. *Superintendent of Police*, (1984) 1 SLR 695 (Karn)]

Under Byelaw 3(1) Haryana Harijan Kalyan Nigam Employees Services Byelaws, if the work or conduct of any person appointed to the service during probation is in the opinion of the appointing authority not satisfactory it may "dispense with his services". Petitioner was a probationer in the Corporation. He was removed for misconduct without inquiry. Removal was held proper.

[*Haryana Harijan Kalyan Nigm Ltd.* v. *H.K. Juneja*, (1991) 2 LR 41 (DB)]

The services of an employee were terminated on the ground that his work and conduct was not satisfactory. He was never informed about his deficiencies. It was held that non-communication thereof was indicative of the fact that the employee had completed successfully his probationary period. The order of termination was quashed.

[*Anil Kumar Verma* v. *Punjab State Warehousing Corporation, Chandigarh*, 1988 (4) SLR 228 (P&H)]

Services of a temporary employee were terminated after 9 years without assigning any reason on one month's notice. The action was taken on the basis of adverse reports for 2 years which however, were not communicated to the employee. It was found that he was also contributing to G.P.Fund as in the case of regular employees. Action was held illegal in those circumstances.

[*Hare Ram* v. *State of Haryana*, 1988 (1) SLR 738 (P&H)]

Petitioner's services were terminated on the ground of unsatisfactory work and absence from duty. It was held that mere notice to the petitioner indicating nature of the allegation levelled against her is not enough compliance with natural justice. Her failure to reply does not also amount to proof.

[*Vidya Rani* v. *State of Haryana*, 1996 (7) SLR 79 (P&H) (DB)]

3.3 TERMINATION OF SERVICES OF TEMPORARY EMPLOYEES ON THE GROUND OF WITHHOLDING OF VITAL INFORMATION BY THEM AT THE TIME OF THEIR APPOINTMENT

3.3.1 Propositions of Law

Termination of services of an employee for furnishing false information in the attestation form at the time of his appointment is invalid if no opportunity of "hearing" is given to such employee before his termination. Failure to communicate adverse police report to him violates the principle of *audi-alteram-partem*.

[*State of West Bengal* v. *Madan Mohan Beg*, 1977 (1) SLJ 677 (Cal)]

If the employee has suppressed certain vital facts relating to his involvement in a criminal case while filling up the attestation form meant for police verification, then the order of his termination from service is valid even if no hearing has been given to him.

[*Bhagirath Prasad* v. *U.O.I.*, 1989 (9) ATC 437]

An Inspector of Delhi Police failed to disclose information about his previous criminal conviction in writing at the time of his appointment though he had informally mentioned about his conviction to D.I.G. Police orally who was the Chairman of the Selection Committee. The order of termination of his service was set aside.

[*Jagdish Chand* v. *U.O.I.*, 1984 (3) SLR 382 (Del)]

In a case, the police report against the petitioner was that he had participated in an illegal or vicious activity. There was no other allegation. The termination order though innocuous in nature, was held illegal.

[*M. Venugopalan* v. *Government of India*, 1989 (7) SLR 670 CAT (Ernakulam)]

3.3.2 Services of a temporary employee can be terminated for hiding vital information in the Attestation form of character and antecedents

In the case of *Jagga Dutta Chatterjee* v. *U.O.I.*, 1990 (1) SLJ CAT 52, the services of a temporary driver were terminated under Rule 5(1), CCS (TS) Rules. In the counter-affidavit filed by the respondents, it was disclosed that motive for his removal from service was that he had suppressed material information relating to his previous criminal record in the Attestation form of character and antecedents filled by him at the time of his appointment. CAT (Calcutta Bench) in its judgment found that termination of services on the ground of hiding vital information was the "motive" and not the "foundation" of his termination and as such Article 311 (2) is not attracted.

3.3.3 Punitive order of termination of services of an employee on the ground of adverse Police Report but couched in innocuous form is liable to be quashed

One Gopa Ram was appointed as a temporary Assistant sorter in Postal Department on 14-5-1983. His services were terminated under Rule 5 CCS (TS) Rules on 9-8-1983 by an order simpliciter. He challenged the order on the ground that the foundation of the order is, in fact, punitive in nature since it is based on some adverse report received by the Department from the District Magistrate, Jodhpur about his character and antecedents. This case came up before CAT (Jodhpur Bench). [*Gopa Ram* v. *U.O.I.*, 1987 (1) SLJ 401 CAT]. The Tribunal called for the records of the case and after examining the same, observed as under in its judgment dated 6-11-1986:

> "Taking into consideration the facts and circumstances of case, it would appear to be safe to take the view that the report of the District Magistrate is the foundation of the impugned order and is not merely a motive as contended by the learned counsel for the respondents. The petitioner had averred that he had performed his duties sincerely and honestly and that there was no complaint against him in that

connection. Since the respondents have not denied the averments made by the petitioner, they are deemed to have accepted the same. In other words, the petitioner's contention that he had performed his duties sincerely and honestly stands established and the assertion of respondents that the petitioner was not found suitable for further retention is ill-founded.

The departmental nothings and the order made by the competent authority show in unmistakable terms that the services of the petitioner had been terminated on the basis of the adverse report of the District Magistrate which, in turn, was based on the adverse Police verification. The sequence of events including the timing thereof supports the view that the impugned order is in substance founded on the aforesaid adverse report. This is evident from the following factual data:

"The report of the District Magistrate dated July 30, 1983 was sent by hand on August 3, 1983. The case was submitted to the competent authority for perusal and orders on the same date, the competent authority made the order for terminating the services of the petitioner and the order is dated August 9, 1983."

It would bear repetition to state that the aforesaid facts and circumstances would support the view that the impugned order though couched in innocuous terms is in reality founded on the adverse report of the District Magistrate. In view thereof, the impugned order is unsustainable."

3.3.4 Termination of services of the holder of a civil post in a temporary capacity on the ground of adverse report from the Collector that he was involved in a criminal case, without hearing him, is liable to be set aside

One Lakshman Reddy was appointed as Extra-Departmental Postmaster in a temporary capacity against a permanent post. There was an adverse report against him from the Collector that he was involved in a criminal case before his appointment. His services were terminated on 19-4-1977 without issuing any show cause notice to him. He challenged his termination in the case *K. Lakshman Reddy* v. *Director of Postal Services*, 1980 SLJ 257 (AP) before Andhra Pradesh High Court which in its judgment dated 12-2-1979 observed as under:

"The petitioner was not served with any notice prior to the termination of services. The course adopted cannot be justified for it violates the principle of *audi alteram partem*. The respondents, however, relied on Rule 6 contained in the Posts and Telegraphs Manual, Volume III which reads as under:

"The services of an employee, who has not already rendered more than three years continuous service from the date of his appointment shall be liable to termination by the appointing authority at any time without notice for general work, or on any administrative ground unconnected with that conduct".

Rule 6 is an executive instruction. It cannot override a salutary principle as *audi alteram partem* which has now become a part of our jurisprudence. Even in cases where there are statutory Rules, it is said *audi alteram partem* operates. The order of termination is set aside."

3.3.5 The order of termination is liable to be set aside when no inquiry is made against the employee on the ground that he had suppressed material information at the time of his appointment

The petitioner was appointed as a clerk in District Cane Committee Muzffarnagar. After his appointment, it came to notice that he had suppressed the fact that he had been removed earlier on corruption charges in U.P. Roadways. He was issued a show cause notice and immediately on the receipt of his reply, his services were terminated on 28-10-1976. No regular inquiry in the case was held as envisaged under Regulation 68 of U.P. Cane Co-operative Service Regulations, 1975. This case came up before the Supreme Court which observed as under:

"The order of termination is not an innocuous order but an order which on the face of it casts stigma on the service career of the petitioner and it is in effect an order of termination on the charges of concealment of facts that he was removed from his earlier service under the U.P. Roadways on charges of corruption. The order is undoubtedly penal in nature having civil consequences and is *per se* illegal, arbitrary and in breach of mandatory procedure prescribed by Regulation 68 of U.P. Cane Cooperative Service Regulations, 1975. The order of termination is set aside."

[*Jagdish Prasad* v. *Sachiv Zila Ganna Committee*, AIR 1986 SC 1108]

3.3.6 The order of termination of an employee is liable to be quashed when the nature of information suppressed is not vital but is of negative character

The services of the petitioner were terminated on the ground that at the time of her appointment, she had suppressed the fact that she had undergone training at State Government expenses and had also executed a bond. No opportunity was given to her to show cause. It was held that execution of bond has only civil consequences. Information suppressed was merely of negative character. The order of termination was held illegal.

[*Usha Tiwari* v. *Ordnance Factory Itarsi*, 1989 (2) SLR 767 CAT (Jab)]

3.3.7 When there is no concrete proof that the employee himself had misled the department about his educational qualifications, the order of his termination is liable to be set aside

The services of the petitioner were terminated on the belief that he had made a false statement about his S.S.C. marks at the time of his appointment. However, there was no proof that petitioner himself had misled the department. At the most, it was only a suspicion. The order of termination was set aside.

[*Anil Jayantilal Vyas* v. *U.O.I.*, 1989 (3) SLR 303]

3.3.8 The contents of the adverse police report should be disclosed to employee concerned if punitive action is proposed to be taken against him on the said report. This is necessary in compliance with the requirements of Article 16 of the Constitution

One Madan Mohan Beg was appointed as a clerk on temporary basis in Directorate of Commercial Taxes, Government of West Bengal for a period of 3 months on 11-11-1970 on the following terms and conditions:

> "The appointment is subject to verification of his character and antecedents and medical examination of his health by the prescribed medical authority."

The appointment was continued upto 30-7-1971 when he received the following communication:

"Your appointment will not be renewed beyond 31-7-1971"

This action was taken against him on the receipt of the adverse police report that the person is unsuitable for appointment under Government . The contents of the report were not, however, disclosed to Shri Beg. He made a representation to the authorities that the adverse police report was due to jealousy of some persons. He sought relief in the case from Calcutta High Court which in its judgment dated 7-4-1977 observed as under:

> "It cannot be disputed that the appointment of the petitioner was temporary. The petitioner had no right statutory or otherwise to continue in his employment beyond the period he was allowed to function. The order or the communication informing the petitioner that his period of service would not be extended as noticed before does not contain any stigma. Where there are no express words in the order itself which would throw any stigma on the Government servant the Court cannot look into the background resulting in the passing of such order in order to discover whether some kind of stigma could be inferred.

There is, however, another aspect of the matter. Article 16 of the Constitution ensures equality of opportunity for all citizens relating to employment or appointment to any office under the State. The employment involved in the instant case is employment under the State. State authorities in respect of such public employment must act reasonably and not whimsically, must act *bona fide* and not *mala fide* and must act on relevant objectivity and not on subjective prejudices, and above all State authorities must act in respect of public employment fairly. In this case, it is indisputable indeed that it is the case of the State authorities, that the decision not to extend the appointment of the respondent/petitioner was taken as a result of the report of the police verification against the petitioner. An adverse police report on which action is taken would naturally disentitle the person concerned to public employment and also deprive him the chances of future employments. It, therefore, comes as serious prejudice to the person concerned. If the police report is incorrect or based on wrong data or material or erroneous or *mala fide* a person against whom such adverse report is made suffers greatly and equality in public employment guaranteed under Article 16 is jeopardized.

Further held that in our opinion the appropriate order would be to direct the State authorities to disclose to the petitioner the gist or extract of the police verification report so far as the same is against the petitioner. The petitioner would be at liberty to make a representation against such report and if he does, the State authorities will consider such representation in the matter of any fresh appointment of the petitioner."

[*State of West Bengal* v. *Madan Mohan Beg*, 1977 SLJ 677]

3.3.9 The contents of the adverse police report are required to be disclosed to the temporary employee and his explanation obtained before resorting to termination of his services

The services of a temporary employee were terminated on the ground that he had willfully suppressed information regarding criminal proceedings. No opportunity had been given to him to offer his explanation nor was any chance given to him to make a representation. His termination was held illegal and violative of Article 16. The case of the department was that according to the police verification Report, the petitioner had been convicted on a criminal charge and hence the termination was legal. It was held that this argument is misplaced. The question is not whether there was any reason to believe that the petitioner had withheld information or suppressed it but whether the respondents came to that conclusion after due scrutiny and application of mind in which opportunity had to be available to the petitioner to put forward his case..... "The respondents did not, in fact, had any representation of the petitioner before them and it is matter of hypothetical speculation how they would have viewed if it had been furnished to them at the appropriate stage."

[*Z.B. Zala* v *U.O.I.*, 1989 (3) SLR 311 CAT (Ahd)]

3.4 TERMINATION OF THE SERVICES OF EMPLOYEES WHO WERE WRONGLY APPOINTED

3.4.1 Law on the subject

If the appointment has been made by an incompetent authority and the same incompetent authority has terminated the services, there is no cause of action. In a case, the petitioner was appointed by the Principal, Industrial Training School although the competent authority was Director of Education. The services were terminated by the Principal. It was held that the petitioner cannot complain that the termination was by an authority not competent to appoint.

[*Santosh Jain* v. *State of Punjab*, 1985 (2) SLR 330 (P&H)]

The services of an employee cannot be terminated on the ground that he does not possess revised qualifications of the post prescribed for the post subsequently if he had been selected on the basis of the then essential prescribed qualifications of the post at the time of his appointment.

[*Pawan Kumar* v. *State of Punjab*, 1992 (5) SLR 423 (P&H)]

If a person is appointed to a post though not possessing the advertised qualifications, this mistake can be rectified. The matter is not merely between the appointing authority and the appointed. Unless, the qualifications are relaxable, it would amount to playing a fraud on the public to appoint such a person.

[*District Collector* v. *M. Trepura Sundari Devi*, 1990 (4) SLR 239 (SC)]

If a wrong appointment has previously been made, it would not justify to perpetuate the same mistake by misinterpreting the provisions of the Statute.

[*Sarabjit Singh* v. *Punjab University, Patiala*, 1988 (1) SLR 360]

An employee cannot claim to be retained in service if his appointment is made by an authority not competent to make the appointment.

[*Sheikh Alim Pasha* v. *U.O.I.*, 1989 (6) SLR 771 CAT (Jab)]

In case of invalid appointments, no right accrues to the appointees and it is open to the appointing authorities to cancel such appointments. Any invalid appointment will not give rise to promissory estoppel against the appointing authority.

[*D.G. of Police* v. *Ravishankar Vishwanath Singh*, 1988 (1) SLR 200 (MP)(DB)]

3.4.2 The services of an employee cannot be terminated if a mistake is made by the appointing authority itself in proper scrutiny of the educational certificates etc. submitted by the employee at the time of his selection

One Vijay Pal Singh was appointed as a constable in C.R.P.F. At the time of his selection, he produced a "Prathma Certificate" issued by Hindi Sahitya Samalan, Allahabad. The respondents found that this certificate is not equivalent to Matriculation which was the essential educational qualification for the post. His services were terminated on the ground of misconduct committed by him in this regard. The plea of the petitioner was that he never claimed that he was Matric and that it was only the respondents who had conceived Prathma certificate to be equivalent to Matric. This case came up before Delhi High Court in *Ex-constable Vijay Pal Singh* v. *U.O.I.*, SLJ (2003) Del HC - 221 Crl No. 4374 of 1992 which in its judgment dated 3-2-2003 observed as under:

> "We have given our careful consideration to the arguments advanced by learned counsel for the parties. There is no doubt that if the petitioner did not fulfil the eligibility conditions, his services could have been terminated. It is also a settled proposition of law that if mistake is subsequently found, that mistake can be rectified by the Appointing Authority. But we are not impressed by the stand of the respondent that it was the petitioner who had committed misconduct as alleged in the Article of charge. Respondent itself had misunderstood Prathma certificate as equivalent to Matriculation. There was no misconduct on the part of the petitioner. Charge of misconduct cannot be sustained in the eyes of law. If the petitioner had been removed for not having requisite qualifications or on account of his non-fulfilling the eligibility conditions, that case would have been different. But to remove the petitioner on the ground that the petitioner had produced Prathma certificate and had committed some misconduct, is totally perverse and untenable charge."

3.4.3 The services of a temporary employee can be terminated on the ground of his appointment being irregular

One Doddasiddiah was appointed as a part time casual labour in the Deptt. of Post on 27-9-1987. Later on, he was appointed as Extra-Departmental Mail Man on 2-9-1989. His services were terminated under Rule 6 of E.D.A. (Condition of Service) Rules, 1964 without assigning any reason. The applicant contended that his services should not have been terminated without affording him an opportunity of being heard and that Rule 6 was applicable only in cases of unsatisfactory service. This case came up for consideration before CAT (Bangalore Bench) in *Doddasiddiah* v. *U.O.I.*, SLJ 1993 (3) CAT 448 [OA No. 216 of 1992] which in its judgment dated 27-7- 1993 observed as under:

> "Admittedly, the appointment of the applicant as ED MM was irregular in the sense that it overlooked the claims of three more casual Mazdoors who were working prior to 7-5-1985 and the applicant was not sponsored by the Employment Exchange, thus as the applicant had rendered only 1 year and 6 months service and his appointment was irregular, it came to be terminated rightly by the authority concerned by invoking Rule 6 of the Rules. This was quite in accordance with law. Further, the applicant had neither alleged any *mala fide* against the authority who had terminated his services nor any attempt was made to show any bias on his part. Viewed from any angle, the action of the competent authority was quite in accordance with Rules and, therefore, there is no reason to interfere."

3.4.4 Interpretation of the term "Appointing Authority" in relation to termination of services of temporary employees

One Sant Lal was appointed as a Male Social Worker in Health Department U.P. on 1-2-1962 by Joint Director Medical Services, U.P. His services were terminated under Rule 3(1) of Temporary Government servants (Termination of Services) Rules, 1975 applicable to him by District Magistrate on 27-2-1976. Relevant rule 3(i) *ibid* reads as under:

> "3(1) *Termination of service.*—(1) Notwithstanding anything to the contrary in any existing Rules or orders on the subject, the service of a Government servant in temporary service shall be liable to termination at any time by a notice in writing either by the Government servant to the appointing authority, or by the appointing authority, to the Government servant."

The petitioner challenged his order of termination before Allahabad High Court. The contention of the petitioner was that since his appointing Authority was Joint Director, his services could have been terminated under Rule 3(1) only by that authority and not by the District Magistrate. The plea of the respondent, however, was that consequent upon the order issued by the Governor on 30-4-1969, the power of appointment of Social Workers were delegated to District Magistrate and that the order of termination of the services of the petitioner by the District Magistrate, cannot, therefore, be assailed. The Hon'ble High Court in its judgment on 1-3-77 observed as under:

> "In the present case, the appointing authority was the Joint Director Medical Services (U.P.). No powers were conferred on him to delegate that function to another. The subsequent order of the Government made the District Magistrate, the appointing authority for Health Assistant, and affected change in the appointing authority. Thus so far as old employees were concerned, the situation remained unaltered. We have already indicated our reasons for holding that the appointing authority, for the purposes of Rule 3, is the authority which appointed the employee, and not one on whom the power has been conferred subsequently."

[*Sant Lal* v. *State of Uttar Pradesh,* (1978) SLJ 217 All]

3.4.5 The order of termination of the services of a temporary employee can be issued either by the Appointing Authority or by another authority of the same rank

One Jarnail Singh was appointed as a Sub-Inspector by Assistant Inspector General of Police on 13-10-1969 against a temporary vacancy. It was mentioned in the said order that the provisions of Rule 12.8 (1) of the Punjab Police Rules will not be applicable to him and that he would be governed by the provisions of Central Civil Services (Temporary Service) Rules, 1965. On the same day, a certificate in Form No. 12.22 (1) was issued to him by the Superintendent of police by which he was appointed as a member of the Police Force under the Police Act No. 5 of 1861 and was vested with the powers, functions and privileges of a Police Officer. The said order was signed by Superintendent of Police for D.I.G. but due to typographical error, the word "or" was typed in place of "for".

The said certificate was, therefore, deemed to have been issued by the S.P. for himself and not for the D.I.G. The petitioner underwent the prescribed course of instructions and was declared qualified for the rank of Sub-Inspector by the Police Training College, Phillaur. By order dated 15th October, 1973, the Superintendent of Police of North District terminated the services of the petitioner under sub-rule (1) of Rule 5 of the Central Civil Services (Temporary Service) Rules, 1965. The petitioner challenged this order on the ground that his appointing authority was I.G. or at any rate D.I.G. and not S.P. and, therefore, his services could not be terminated by S.P. This case came up before Delhi High Court in *Jarnail Singh* v. *Superintendent of Police*, 1983 (2) SLJ 101, which observed as under:

> "It appears from the order of appointment that it was made by the Assistant Inspector General of Police. There is nothing on record to show that the appointment was made by the I.G. or D.I.G. or that the Assistant General of Police was only communicating the order made by them. There is no basis for such a contention. I have seen the file of recruitment. The petitioner was selected by a Board chaired by a D.I.G. but neither the Board nor the D.I.G. or I.G. had appointed or approved the appointment of the petitioner. The rank and grade of an Assistant Inspector General Police, Headquarters is equal to that of a Superintendent of Police and, therefore, if the petitioner's services were terminated by the District Superintendent of Police, it cannot be said that his services were terminated by an officer below the rank of the appointing authority."

3.4.6 Short notes on the judgments of the Courts relating to termination of services of temporary employees by incompetent authorities, etc.

An authority lower than appointing authority cannot terminate the appointment under Delhi Municipal Corporation Regulations. The appointing authority for terminal Tax Inspector in the Corporation is Commissioner. Hence, Deputy Commissioner cannot terminate the services of the Inspector.

[*MCD* v. *Om Parkash*, 1980 (2) SLR 253 (Del)]

Where the authority who appointed the petitioner was Senior Superintendent of Police exercising the powers of D.I.G., he cannot be dismissed by Superintendent of Police, being lower in rank.

[*Braham Singh* v. *U.O.I.*, 1988 (5) SLR 1260 CAT (Del)]

If the employee's services are terminated by an authority subordinate to the appointing authority, termination is illegal.

The defect cannot be cured by the mere fact that termination was confirmed by the Appellate Authority.

[*Niladri Chandra* v. *State of Orissa*, 1983 (3) SLR 310 (DB)]

The Managing Director of Haryana State Co-operative Labour and Construction Federation was appointed by Board of Directors. He cannot be removed by the State Government.

[*Mewa Singh Dattar* v. *State of Haryana*, 1991 (1) SLR 673 (P&H) DB]

Under the Rules of State Bank of Hyderabad, an officer competent to appoint an employee is competent to terminate his services. It is immaterial that the employee was appointed by a different authority.

[*P. Jayachandra Rao* v. *State Bank of Hyderabad*, 1991 (1) SLR 79]

Petitioner was appointed by Board of Directors of Haryana Agro Industries Corporation, a State owned Corporation. It was held that the Managing Director could not terminate his services. The Article s of Association gave powers only to the Board.

[*Daksh Kumar Sharma* v. *State of Haryana*, 1991 (2) SLR 354 (P&H)]

Respondent was appointed by District Council without approval of Governor, District Council terminated his services without approval of Governor. Held, the respondent cannot complain that his termination by the very Council without Governor's sanction is invalid.

[*H. Lyngdoh* v. *Cromlyn, Lyngdoh*, 1971 (2) SLR 330 (SC)]

An employee of National Insurance Co. Ltd. was removed from service by an authority subordinate to the appointing authority. It was held it was illegal. Even if provisions of Article 311 do not apply, the principle of natural justice would apply.

[*Chairman National Insurance Co. Ltd.* v. *S. Narayanakutty*, 1985 (2) SLJ 5]

The services of a temporary employee were terminated because he did not possess the qualifications prescribed in the advertisement. Juniors who possessed the requisite qualifications were retained. It was held that classification was on reasonable basis and there was no illegal discrimination.

[*Sudesh Vohra* v. *State of Punjab*, 1984 (1) SLR 71 (P&H)]

Services of petitioners were terminated by Government of Rajasthan. The ground given was that appointment had been made in violation of rules of recruitment. No notice was given to the petitioners. It was held that termination of services was illegal in the circumstances.

[*Nand Lal* v. *State of Rajasthan*, 1989 (1) SLR 364 Raj (DB)]

Where appointing authority is the Registrar of the Institute, the Deputy Registrar cannot issue the termination order.

[*Proshanta Guha* v. *I.I.T. Kharagpur*, 1995 (8) SLR 792 (Cal)]

Where the services of an employee are terminated on the ground that the appointment has been secured by fraud, the allegation must be established by proper fact finding inquiry.

[*Sheikh Anwar* v. *U.O.I.*, 1989 (7) SLR 79 CAT (Jab)]

The appointment order did not mention terms and conditions of appointment. Petitioner's services were terminated by one month's notice though the appointment order did not provide for a termination with notice. Order was set aside with consequential benefits and costs.

[*Col. Prithvi Singh* v. *State of Haryana*, 1996 (3) SLR 587 (P&H)]

Services of persons recruited to the armed police cannot be terminated on the ground that there are no vacancies. Procedural formalities are expected to be completed before appointments are made.

[*Mohinder Singh* v. *State of Haryana*, 1991 (1) SLR 527 (P&H)]

Petitioner's services were terminated on the belief of the department that he had made a false statement about his S.S.C. marks at the time of applying for the post. But there was no proof that the petitioner had himself misled the Department. At the most, it was a suspicion.

[*Anil Jayantilal Vyas* v. *U.O.I.*, 1989 (3) SLR 303]

3.5 TERMINATION OF SERVICES OF EMPLOYEES ON ADMINISTRATIVE GROUNDS

3.5.1 Law on the subject

There may be several reasons which may fall within administrative sphere for termination and it is, therefore, only the statement of reason which will make a person aware of the specific ground for termination of his service. Any person who is told that his services are dispensed with in administrative ground is not really told of the reason. It is as good as non-statement of any reason. It would be necessary to state what that administrative ground is for a person to understand why he is being shunted out. There is generally a specific challenge in every petition against the order of termination in which the action of the authorities is branded as arbitrary. That challenge calls for an answer, for, if any person is singled out for a treatment not generally meted out to all and that treatment is challenged as unfair, it is the duty of the authority which effects such treatment to place before the Court the circumstances under which and the reasons for which termination was resorted to. Of course, if the reason is found to be relevant and if the Court finds that there was some material to support such a reason, the Court may not sit in judgment over the ultimate decision.

3.5.2 Termination of services of an employee by stating that the said order has been passed on "administrative" grounds without mentioning the specific reasons therefor is bad in law and liable to be quashed

Rule 6 of Extra Departmental Agents (Conduct and Services) Rules, 1964, reads as under:

> "The services of an employee shall be liable to termination by the appointing authority at any time without notice for generally unsatisfactory work within 3 years from the date of appointment or on any administrative ground unconnected with his conduct."

The import of this rule came up for consideration before Andhra Pradesh High Court in *E. Kunhiraman Nair* v. *Superintendent of Post Offices, Cannanore Division*, 1984 (1) SLJ 157. In this case, the services of the petitioner who was an Extra Departmental Branch Post Master had been terminated on "administrative" ground without giving any specific reason. The High Court in its judgment dated 16-8-1984 observed as under:

> "The order challenged is arbitrary, in as much as the administrative ground which is said to have prompted the passing of that order is not disclosed, no attempt has been made in the counter-affidavit to explain or indicate the administrative reason which weighed with the authority in passing the order of termination. There is only reiteration that the termination was on administrative ground. That would not satisfy the requirement of Rule 6 and therefore the plea of

discrimination must succeed. In this view the order of termination is quashed and the petitioner is found entitled to the benefit of service as if the order had not been passed."

A similar view was also taken earlier by the same High Court in *A.K. Sethi* v. *Senior Superintendent of Post Offices*, 1973 KLJ 501 in which facts were similar to the one in *Kunhiraman Nair's* case.

3.5.3 Termination of services of a temporary employee on administrative grounds unconnected with conduct is valid

One Biswal was appointed as Extra-Departmental Branch Post Master. After joining his services, he absented himself for some days and his services were terminated under Rule 6 of E.D.A. (C&S) Rules, 1964, which were applicable to him. It was alleged by him that he was restrained by certain anti-social elements from attending to his duties. He challenged the order of termination of his services before CAT (Cuttck Bench), which in its judgment dated 18-11-1986 observed as under:

"During the course of argument, it was submitted before us that petitioner could not join his duties because he was physically obstructed by some persons who resented his appointment. Being obstructed, he could not join his duty and for which First Information Report was also lodged by him at the Police Station and a criminal case is pending against those anti-social elements. We have gone through the relevant Rules. The competent authority has the right to terminate the services of a particular employee on administrative grounds unconnected with his conduct. In our opinion, the competent authority has exercised his powers vested in him under the law and we would refrain ourselves from making any comment on the truth or otherwise of the allegation of the petitioner since a criminal case is pending between the two parties and therefore, any opinion expressed by us one way or the other may adversely affect the case of the either parties. That apart, we are not concerned with the truth or otherwise of the matters involved in the criminal case as to whether the petitioner had absented himself from duty after being obstructed. The competent authority having exercised his discretion vested in him under the law, we find no reason to interfere, even conceding for the same of argument that the reasons assigned by the petitioner preventing him from joining his duty may be true. Hence, we find no merit in the contention of the petitioner that the discretion vested in the authority under the law has been illegally exercised."

[*Sankarsan Biswal* v. *U.O.I.*, 1987 (1) SLJ 271 CAT]

3.5.4 The services of a temporary employee responsible for loss of official documents due to negligence and carelessness cannot be dispensed with without complying with the requirements of Article 311(2) of the Constitution

One Kanhiya Lal was found to be *prima facie* responsible for the loss of some documents from the judicial records and his services were accordingly terminated under Temporary Service Rules by the District Judge. In the Civil Appeal No. 141/1983, the Hon'ble Supreme Court observed as under:

"It is clear on the facts of the present case and particularly from the order passed by the Administrative Judge on November 20, 1980 while disposing of the representation of the appellant that the only reason why he was discharged from service was that he was "*prima facie* responsible for the loss of some documents from the judicial record on account of his negligence and carelessness." The order of discharge passed against the appellant was, therefore, clearly penal in character and there can be no doubt that even if he was a temporary servant, he was entitled to the protection of Article 311(2) of the Constitution and hence no penal order could be passed against him without complying with the requirements of that Article. Since admittedly the requirements of Article 311(2) were not satisfied in the case of the appellant before terminating his service, we are of the view that the order passed by the learned District Judge terminating the service of the appellant must be held to be void."

[*Kanhia Lal* v. *District Judge*, 1983 (2) SLJ 528 (SC)]

3.5.5 Services of a temporary employee cannot be terminated merely on the dictation of higher authority

One Gowri Kutty was appointed as Extra-Departmental Post Master on 23-5-1991 by the competent appointing authority. His services were terminated under orders of Post Master General without any reasons whatsoever. This case came up before CAT Ernakulam Bench, which in its judgment dated 23-8-1993 observed as under:

> "Decision in this case was not based on any rule or reason. It was based on the unlimited discretion of the Post Master General. The appointing authority had acted under dictation without application of mind and without any valid reasons. No rule was violated in making selection. Therefore the decision to revoke the appointment which was made according to Rules, could not be justified in law. Hence the notice for termination of service is quashed."

[*T.G. Gowri Kutti* v. *Superintendent of Post Office*, SLJ 1993 (3) CAT 483]

3.5.6 The services of a temporary employee holding "Anand Margi" ideology cannot be terminated under CCS (TS) Rules, 1965 without proof that he had indulged in subversive activities

One Dipti Singh was appointed as a Technical Assistant in I.C.A.R. on 12-9-1979 in a temporary capacity. Earlier, he was working in the Ministry of Planning. While working in that Ministry, he had been detained under MISA from 30-10-1976 to 21-3-1977. His services had been terminated but was reinstated in service. After his appointment in I.C.A.R., a report was called from the Police about his character and antecedents. It was stated in the Report that he was an active member of Anand Margis and had taken part in a demonstration on 27-3-1977. He was arrested at that time and lodged in the jail for about 7 days. The fact about his detention under M.I.S.A. was also mentioned. After the receipt of the said Police Report, the Assistant Administrative Officer I.C.A.R. submitted a report to the Director that the petitioner was not a desirable person to continue in the service of the Institute since he was an adherent of Anand Margi ideology. His services were terminated on 20-8-1982 under Rule 5 of CCS (TS) Rules, 1965, without assigning any reason. The petitioner sought relief in the case before Delhi High Court, which in its judgment dated 11-3-1983 observed as under:

> "The action of the Director, I.C.A.R. is plainly in contravention of Articles 14 and 16 of the Constitution

because the petitioner is being discriminated against on the ground of his opinion, his way of thinking and his doctrine because he accepts and conforms to a particular 'ideology'. Because he is an advocate or adherent of a particular system, a body of ideas on which that system is based. He is a mere theorist, a person occupied with ideas. The manner or the content of his thinking is characteristic of an Anand Margi. This is all. But no man can be tried for his thoughts. No punitive action can be taken because an individual subscribes to a particular school of thought, religious or secular."

3.5.7 The authorities should not take too technical a view about the fulfilment of the requisite qualifications for a post while terminating the services of a sportsman under Rule 5 of CCS (TS) Rules

One Uma Shankar was appointed an Inspector of Central Excise under the Sports quota on temporary basis on 12-12-1975. The condition for eligibility for the candidate was his representation in the university in Inter University tournament Meet conducted by Inter-University Sports Board. Later on his services were terminated on 16-6-1975 on the ground that though he had been selected to represent Mithila University he actually could not participate in the said tournament due to his illness. He moved the Supreme Court for relief which in its judgment dated 17-4-1980 observed as under:

"Having given the matter our careful consideration, it seems to us that the respondents have proceeded on a technical view of the matter wholly unjustified by the intent behind the condition of eligibility. The condition required that the appellant should have been a sportsman who had represented his university in an Inter-University Tournament conducted by the Inter-University Tournament Board. He had been selected, for representing the Mithila University in the Inter-University Tournament at the Banaras Hindu University in the year 1972. All that remained was that he should have participated in the tournament. Unfortunately, for him, he fell ill and was unable to do so. The fact that he fell ill, and for that reason was unable to represent his University, is not disputed. There is nothing to show that but for that illness he would not have actually taken part in the tournament. It seems to us that on a reasonable view of the facts, the appellant should be taken to have fulfilled the condition of eligibility. The terms and conditions of service are intended to be construed reasonably, and too technical a view can defeat the essential spirit and intent embodied in them. The intention was to appoint meritorious sportsman to the posts, and that object is served if a person who had qualified and was selected for representing his university in an Inter-University Tournament conducted by the Inter-University Sports Board is appointed, notwithstanding that he was actually prevented from participating because of reasons beyond his control."

[*Uma Shankar* v. *U.O.I.*, 1981 (1) SLJ 154]

Under the rules of Panchayat, employees were required to pass the departmental test in specified attempts. In one examination, petitioner was unable to appear on account of his illness. The authorities terminated his services on the ground of his failure to pass. It was held that a person who fails to appear on account of illness cannot be said to have attempted the examination. Termination was set side.

[*J.M. Shukla* v. *A. Myanger, DDO Bulsar*, 1986 (1) SLR 514 (Guj)]

3.5.8 The services of temporary employees can be terminated even before the qualified persons report for duty to replace them

Certain persons were employed on temporary basis as a stop-gap arrangement for the period till the approved candidates qualified for the posts are appointed and report for duty. The services of those temporary persons were terminated after the period for which they were appointed was over but before the qualified persons had actually joined. The aggrieved persons approached Kerala High Court for relief which in its judgment dated 16-11-1983 observed as under:

"The petitioner has contended that until and unless a person recommended by the Public Service Commission reports for duty, the petitioners' service, even after the period for which they were appointed, could not have been terminated. It is true that a person appointed shall be replaced as soon as possible by a member of the service or an approved candidate qualified to hold the post; that does not, however, mean that unless such candidate reports for duty, the service of the temporary hand employed to meet the emergency and as a stop gap arrangement, could not be terminated even after the lapse of the period for which he or she was appointed in terms of the appointment order issued to him or her. In this view the writ appeal is without merit, and is, accordingly dismissed."

[*Lower Division Typists in Munsiff's Courts Haripad* v. *State of Kerala*, 1984 (1) SLJ 181]

Where the appointment is temporary or stop gap till qualified person join, it can be terminated even if qualified approved candidate is not appointed.

[*Remulah* v. *State of Kerala*, 1984 (1) SLR 476]

3.6 TERMINATION OF THE SERVICES OF THE SENIORS WHILE THEIR JUNIORS ARE RETAINED IN SERVICE

3.6.1 Law on the Subject

"The rule of natural justice is that the services of a senior employee cannot be terminated while his juniors have been retained in service. It is only in special and exceptional circumstances that such terminations can be resorted to by the competent authorities. This is not to say that these authorities have no right whatsoever to terminate the services of a senior temporary employee. The only limitation is that there should be no hostile discrimination on the part of such authorities in such cases against the senior employees whose services have been terminated. There is always some reason or cause for terminating the service of a temporary Government servant. It is not necessary to state reasons in the order of termination communicated to the employee concerned. But where there is a specific charge of arbitrary discrimination or some hostile motive is attributed to the authority terminating the service of a senior person, it is incumbent on the authority making the impugned order to explain the same by disclosing the reason for impugned action. If the authority withholds that information from the court, the conclusion of the court will be that the respondent was picked out for the impugned action, whimsically without any special reason which could have put him in a class separate from that of his juniors, who have been retained in service. The protection under Articles 14 and 16 (i) will be available to such a temporary Government servant."

3.6.2 The services of a senior temporary employee can be terminated while retaining his juniors in service only if it is shown that the juniors do not stand at par with him or that they have better service record than him

One Ajay Mohanty was appointed as a temporary U.D.C. in the office of A.G. Orissa on 9-2-1973. His services were terminated under Rule 5(1) of CCS (TS) Rules on 2-4-1974. He challenged the order of his termination before Orissa High Court on the ground that it was violative of the equality clause under Articles 14 and 16 of the Constitution because five persons junior to him were retained in service while his services were terminated and it was not shown that these five persons had better service record than him. The petitioner referred to the judgment of the Hon'ble Supreme Court in *Manager, Government Branch Press* v. *D.B. Belliappa*, 1979 SLJ 233 (SC) wherein it was held that even in case of temporary employees, if juniors are retained and a senior, although temporarily employed, is thrown out by taking recourse to the terms of employment, there would be an infraction of Articles 14 and 16 of the Constitution. The department, too, relied upon this decision in support of their contention that there would be no infraction of Articles 14 and 16 if it can be shown the petitioner's service was terminated because his work was found to be unsatisfactory. In order to fortify their stand, the respondents produced at the time of hearing, the relevant files relating to the case of termination of the petitioner's service. From the notes and orders recorded therein, it appeared that the petitioner's service was terminated on the following grounds—

(a) That he was most irregular in attending office and was absenting from office without any prior intimation;
(b) That he was involved in some criminal cases; and
(c) That he was persuing his studies in a law college without permission of the authorities.

Having regard to what has been stated above, the Orissa High Court in its Judgement dated 15-12-1980 [*Ajay Mohanty* v. *U.O.I.*, 1981 (1) SLJ 552] observed as under:

"It was incumbent on the Department to show that the petitioner stood as a class by himself. There was absolutely no allegation that the petitioner was considered unsuitable or that his services were found to be unsatisfactory. In course of hearing of this writ application when the decision of the Supreme Court in *Belliappa's case* was cited on behalf of the petitioner, the respondents finding themselves in an uncomfortable position tried to impress upon us by producing their office file to prove that the petitioner's service was terminated on account of negligence of duty and misconduct. The respondents did not however, produce any material to show that persons junior to the petitioner had better service records than the petitioner. Since no material with regard to their records of service was produced, we are not in a position to accede to the contention that the petitioner stood as a class by himself. We hold that the equality clause enshrined in Articles 14 and 16 of the Constitution has been contravened. We have no doubt that the impugned order is founded on allegation of misconduct and negligence of duty. These are positive allegations, which, if established, would justify removal of a Government servant from service. These allegations could not form the basis of the impugned order unless the petitioner had been given a reasonable opportunity of being heard, which was obviously not afforded. The provisions of Article 311 of the Constitution were clearly attracted and it was not open to the authorities to have terminated the service by giving the order a cover of termination simplicitor. The order, must, therefore, be struck down for non-compliance with the requirements of Article 311 of the Constitution."

3.6.3 Where the services of a temporary employee are terminated on the grounds other than his unsuitability, unsatisfactory conduct or the like which put him a class apart from his juniors in the same service, it is a case of indiscrimination and the order of termination is liable to be quashed

One Kewal Krishan was working as a temporary employee for 11 years and his services were terminated by an order simplicitor while retaining his juniors. This case came up for consideration before Punjab and Haryana Court in *Kewal Krishan* v. *State of*

Punjab, 1987 (1) SLJ 243 (P&H) which in its judgment dated 26-5-1986 observed as under:

The Court quoted with approval the judgment of the Supreme Court in the case of Manager, *Government Branch Press* v. *D.B. Belliappa*, 1979 SLJ 233 (SC) in a similar case which reads as under:

> "If the services of a temporary Government servant are terminated in accordance with the conditions of his service on the ground of his unsatisfactory conduct on his unsuitability for the job and/or for his work being unsatisfactory, or for a like reason which marks him a class apart from other temporary servants who have been retained in service, there is no question of the applicability of Article 16 . Conversely, if the services of a temporary Government servant are terminated arbitrarily and not on the ground of his unsuitable, unsatisfactory conduct or the like which would not put him in a class apart from his juniors in the same service, a question of unfair discrimination may arise, notwithstanding the fact that in terminating his service, the appointing authority was purporting to act in accordance with the terms of his employment."

Applying the aforesaid judgment to the case under reference, the High Court observed as under:

> "In the present case, the petitioner has been serving as a temporary employee for about 11 years and his services were terminated without a finding that he was unsuitable for the job. As more than 60 persons appointed after him have been retained in service, the order of termination has to be held arbitrary...... The petition is allowed with costs and the impugned order quashed."

3.6.4 The protection of Articles 14 and 16 of the Constitution is available even to a temporary Government servant if he has been arbitrarily discriminated against and singled out for harsh treatment in preference to his juniors similarly circumstanced

One Balliappa was appointed as a temporary Junior Compositor in Government Branch Press, Mercara. On 29-12-1966, he was served with a notice stating that he had taken outside the Press some copies of the ballot papers relating to the Director's election of Coorg Cardamon Co-operative Societies, Mercara. He was required to show cause before 2.00 P.M. of 30-12-1966 as to why disciplinary action should not be taken against him as per Rules. It was further stated in the said notice that his failure to comply with the notice will result in his suspension and also disciplinary action against him. Thereafter on 3-1-1967, an order was served on him terminating his services which read as under:

> "As per instructions contained in Head Office order No. 570/66-67, dated 3-1-1967 Shri D.B.Belliappa, Junior compositor of this office is hereby informed that your appointment is purely temporary and terminable at any time without any previous notice and without reasons being assigned. Therefore, your services are hereby terminated with immediate effect."

Shri Belliappa challenged the order of his termination in judicial courts on the ground that he was meted out hostile discrimination in as such as three of his juniors were retained in service. It was pleaded on behalf of the Department that Belliappa had been appointed in a temporary capacity and that his services could be terminated at any time without notice. It was further pleaded that Articles 14 and 16 of the Constitution are not attracted in a case where the services of a temporary employee are terminated in accordance with the conditions of his service. It was further argued by the department that the principle of 'first come and last go' applies only when there is a general retrenchment and not in cases where there is some special reason for terminating the services of an employee while continuing his juniors in the temporary service. It was maintained that the show cause notice which was served on him on 29-12-1966 furnishes the motive or the cause for terminating his services while retaining his juniors in service. Although his services could be terminated without assigning any reason in accordance with the conditions of his service, it was spelt that the real cause for terminating his service was his unsuitability for the job and for his unsatisfactory conduct.

This case eventually came up for consideration before the Supreme Court, which in its classic judgment dated 30-11-1978 observed as under:

"Power of termination of services of a temporary employee without assigning any reason is not absolute when charge of unfair discrimination is levelled or where improper motives are imputed to the authority. It is the duty of the authority to dispel that charge by disclosing to the court the reason or motive which impelled it to take action. In this particular case although a show cause notice was served on the petitioner but the same was not relied upon by the department in the court.

The protection of Articles 14 and 16 will be available even to a temporary Government servant if he has been arbitrarily discriminated against and singled out for harsh treatment in preference to his juniors similarly circumstanced. It is true that the competent authority had the discretion under the conditions of service governing the employee concerned to terminate the latter's employment without notice. But, such discretion has to be exercised in accordance with reasons and fair play and not capriciously. Bereft of rationality and fairness, discretion degenerates into arbitrariness which is the very antithesis of the rule of law on which our democratic policy is founded............

In the absence of any information from the department indicating that Balliappa was marked off for discharge on the basis of an intelligible differentia having a reasonable nexus with the object of maintaining the efficiency and integrity of the public service, we are constrained to hold that the impugned order suffers from the vice of unfair discrimination and is violative of Articles 14 and 16 (1) of the Constitution."

[*Manager Government Branch Press* v. *D.B.Balliappa*, AIR 1979 SC 429.

3.6.5 Short notes on the judgments of the courts in cases where services of senior persons were terminated while retaining juniors

The fact that the services of temporary Government servants are terminated, either in accordance with the conditions of their appointment or of their service rules, while their juniors are retained in service *per se* would not prove unequal treatment for them nor would it be violative of Articles 14 and 16 of the Constitution but if in a given case, the temporary Government servant is able to show that the simple order of termination of service in accordance with the terms of his appointment or of his service rules was actuated by improper motive or on the charge of unfair discrimination specifying the facts in that regard and those facts are either not controverted or stand proved, then that simple order of termination of services may be quashed by a Court of law".

[*Krishan Chand Goyal* v. *Punjab State*, 1980 (2) SLR 623]

It is well settled that if there are a number of posts in a cadre and some of the posts are abolished, it is not the incumbent of the post which is abolished who is liable to be reverted but the axe would fall ordinarily on the junior most in the cadre. This is because the rule of "Last come, first go" does not apply strictly to the service under the State and even though ordinarily the State may follow such a wholesome practice, it may, for good reasons, decide to retain the junior most in preference to the comparative senior one if there are valid administrative grounds such as competence, record of service etc. which may justify such a departure.

[*Kuldeep Chand Sharma* v. *Delhi Administration*, 1978 SLJ 461]

In a case, persons junior to applicant were kept in service on the abolition of the post, the order of termination was arbitrary and, violative of Article 16 of the Constitution but he never pleaded any other ground of unfair indiscrimination or improper motive for the termination of his services, it was held that his suit was liable to be dismissed.

[*Union of India* v. *Prakash Lal*, 1980 (2) SLR 596 (P&H)]

"A temporary employee's service can be dispensed with under the terms of contract of employment although his juniors may be retained if it can be shown that the juniors were not similarly placed as the person whose service has been dispensed with on account of misconduct or inefficiency or since he was standing as a class by himself but in such cases, however, it would be incumbent upon the authority to satisfy the Court that persons junior to the person, whose services have been terminated, do not stand at par with or have better service record than, the person impugning the order of termination."

[*Subhash Chandra Chaudhary and Jamuna Ram* v. *Bihar State Warehousing Corporation*, 1980 (2) SLR 760]

A full bench of Punjab and Haryana High Court in *Y.K. Bhatia* v. *State of Haryana*, 1977 (1) SLR 85, held that the termination of the services of a temporary Government employee does not offend Article 16(1) of the Constitution merely because his juniors are retained in service. Of course, it will be open to the persons effected in individual cases to establish discriminatory treatment which cannot be explained except on the basis of 'malice in law' or 'malice in fact'. Without any suggestion of 'malice in law' or 'malice in fact', there can be no question of invoking the aid of Article 16(1) of the Constitution against an order of termination of service or reversion of a temporary employee merely because juniors are continuing.

3.6.6 The order terminating the services of a senior can be challenged only on the ground of hostile discrimination against the competent authority

It is now well established by the rulings of the Supreme Court that where the relevant service rules empower the appointing authority to terminate the service of a temporary Government servant by notice given in the manner provided therein, without assigning any reason, an order of termination passed under such rule will not be regarded as discriminatory merely because the employee, whose service was terminated, was not the junior most in the concerned category. Rule 5(1)(a) of the Rules empowers the appointing authority to terminate the service of a temporary servant at any time by notice in writing given in the manner prescribed therein regardless of his seniority in the particular category. Inasmuch as the constitutional validity of this rule has been upheld by the Supreme Court there is no scope at all for any challenge being raised against an order passed in the exercise of the power conferred by this rule complaining of infringement of Article 16 of the Constitution merely on the ground that while dispensing with the service of the temporary employee concerned some persons junior to him were retained in service. When the validity of an order passed under Rule 5 is challenged before the Court on the ground of violation of Article 16, except in cases where *mala fides* is clearly alleged, the Court would not go into the reasons which prompted the appointing authority to terminate the service of the employee. When the termination of the service of a temporary employee is not on the ground of retrenchment no question of offending Article 14 or 16 of the Constitution will arise from the mere fact that he was not the junior most in the particular category of temporary employee at the time of the action impugned. Once it is held that the Court will not investigate in the grounds that weighed with the appointing authority in terminating the service of the employee it must necessarily follow that there is no legal obligation for the appointing authority to plead and establish before the Court grounds in justification of the action taken by it to terminate the service of senior temporary employee while retaining junior hands.

3.6.7 Observations of the Supreme Court in the case of *Champak Lal Shah* v. *U.O.I.*, AIR 1964 SC 1854 relating to retention of juniors while terminating the services of seniors

"A reference was made in the plaint to a number of Assistant Directors whose services were not dispensed with even though they were junior to the appellant and did not have as good qualifications as he had. We are of opinion that there is no force in this contention. This is not a case where services of a temporary employee are being retrenched because of the abolition of a post. In such a case a question might have arisen as to who should be retrenched when one out of several posts is being abolished in an office. In those circumstances, qualifications and length of service of those holding similar temporary posts may be relevant in considering whether the retrenchment of a particular employee was as a result of discrimination. The present case is, however, where the appellant's services were terminated because his work was found to be unsatisfactory.

The position is now well-settled that Rule 5 of T.S. Rules in so far as it empowers the appointing authority to terminate the service of a temporary Government servant at any time by a notice in writing whenever the Government thinks it necessary or expedient to do so for administrative reasons, is perfectly valid and constitutional and that no violation of Articles 14 or 16 of the Constitution is involved in the exercise of the said power. The contention that Rule 5 confers an arbitrary and unguided discretion on the Government has been expressly negatived by the Supreme Court as being totally devoid of merit. When

Rule 5(1) confers on the appointing authority the power to terminate the service of a temporary Government servant irrespective of any consideration as to his position in the seniority list and the said provision has been expressly held to be constitutionally valid and not violative of Article 14 or Article 16, we fail to see how an order passed in the *bona fide* exercise of the power conferred by the said rule can be called in question on the ground of infringement of Articles 14 and 16 of the Constitution. Once it is recognised that there is a valid power vested in the appointing authority to terminate at any time the service of any temporary Government servant, irrespective of his position in the seniority list, by a notice in writing given in accordance with the provisions contained in Rule 5, there is no longer any scope for basing a plea of arbitrary discrimination on the mere fact that the person whose services were terminated was not the junior most in the concerned category. Inasmuch as the rule confers the power on the appointing authority to terminate at any time the service of any temporary Government servant the exercise of the said power will not be interfered with by the Court unless it be very clearly made out that the action impugned was taken *mala fide*. Thus except in cases where there are clear and specific allegations of *mala fides* into which an investigation is considered necessary by the court will not delve into the reasons which prompted the appointing authority to terminate under Rule 5(1) of the Rules the service of a temporary Government servant.

3.6.8 Observations of the Supreme Court in the case *Manager, Government Branch Press* v. *D.B. Belliappa*, 1980 SLJ 233 (SC) about rights of temporary employees in cases of retention of juniors while dispensing with the services of the seniors and other allied matter

Extracts from this classic judgment have been reproduced earlier at various places. The reader will not mind its repetition since it is now being reproduced in a comprehensive manner in this sub-head.

There is always some reason or cause for terminating the services of a temporary employee. It is not necessary to state that reason in the order of termination communicated to the employee concerned. But where there is a specific charge of arbitrary discrimination, or some hostile motive is attributed to the authority terminating the service, it is incumbent on the authority making the impugned order to explain the same by disclosing the reason for the impugned action. In the instant case, the authorities intransigently withheld that information from the court. There is no escape from the conclusion that Belliappa was picked out for the impugned action, whimsically without any special reason which could put him in a class separate from that of his three juniors who have been retained in service.

The contention of the department is that Articles 14 and 16(1) of the Constitution have no application, whatever to the case of a temporary employee whose service is terminated in accordance with the terms and conditions of his service because the tenure or the duration of the employment of such an employee is extremely precarious being dependent upon the pleasure and discretion of the employer State. In our opinion, no such generalisation can be made. The protection of Articles 14 and 16(1) of the Constitution will be available even to a temporary Government servant if he has been arbitrarily discriminated against and singled out for harsh treatment in preference to his juniors similarly circumstanced. It is true that the competent authority had the discretion under the conditions of service governing the employee concerned to terminate the latter's employment without notice. But, such discretion has to be exercised in accordance with reason and fair play and not capriciously. Bereft of rationality and fairness, discretion generates into arbitrariness which is the very antithesis of the rule of the law on which our democratic policy is founded. Arbitrary invocation or enforcement of a service condition terminating the service of a temporary employee may itself constitute denial of equal protection and offend the Equality clause in Articles 14 and 16(1).

It is now well-settled that the expression "matters relating to employment" used in Article 16(1) is not confined to initial matters prior to the act of employment, but comprehends all matters in relation to employment both prior and subsequent, to the employment which are incidental to the employment and form part of the terms and conditions of such employment, such as, provisions as to salary, increments, leave, gratuity, pension age of superannuation, promotion and even termination of employment. It is further well established that Articles 14, 15(1) and 16(1) form part of the same constitutional code of guarantees and supplement each other.

In the view we take, we are further fortified by a decision of the Constitution Bench in *Champaklal Shah* v. *U.O.I.*, 1964 (5) SCR 190. That was a case of temporary Government servant. Rule 5 governing a temporary Government servant, which came up for consideration in that case, gave power to the Government to terminate the service of a temporary Government servant by giving him one month's notice or on payment of one month's pay in lieu of notice. This rule was attacked on the ground that it was hit by Article 16. In the alternative it was urged that even if rule 5 is good, the order by which the appellant's services were dispensed with, was bad because it was discriminatory. Reference was made to a number of persons whose services were not dispensed with, even though they were junior to the appellant and did not have as good qualifications as he had. Wanchoo; J. (as he then was) speaking for the court, repelled the alternative argument in these terms:

> "We are of the opinion that there is no force in this contention. This is not a case where service of a temporary employee are being retrenched because of the abolition of a post. In such a question, a question may arise as to who should be retrenched when one out of several temporary posts is being retrenched in an office. In those circumstances, qualifications and length of service of those holding similar temporary posts may be relevant in considering whether the retrenchment of a particular employee was as a result of discrimination. The present however is a case where the appellant's services were terminated because his work was found to be unsatisfactory. (In such a case) there can, in our opinion, be no question of any discrimination. It would be absurd to say that if the service of one temporary servant is terminated on the ground of unsatisfactory conduct, the services of all similar employees must also be terminated along with him, irrespective of what their conduct is. Therefore even though some of those mentioned in the plaint by the appellant were junior to him and did not have as good qualifications as he had and were retained in service, it does not follow that the action taken against the appellant terminating his services was discriminatory, for that action was taken on the basis of his unsatisfactory conduct.

> A question of discrimination may arise in a case of retrenchment on account of abolition of one of several temporary posts of the same kind in one office but can in our opinion never arise in the case of dispensing with the services of a particular temporary employee on account of his conduct being unsatisfactory".

The principle that can be deduced from the above analysis is that if the services of a temporary Government servant are terminated in accordance with the conditions of his service on the ground of unsatisfactory conduct or his unsuitability for the job and/or for his work being unsatisfactory or for a like reason which marks him off a class apart from other temporary servants who have been retained in service, there is no question of applicability of Article 16.

Conversely, if the services of a temporary Government servant are terminated, arbitrarily, and not on the ground of his unsuitability, unsatisfactory conduct or the like which would put him in a class apart from his juniors in the same service, a question of unfair discrimination may arise not withstanding the fact that in terminating his service the appointing authority was purporting to act in accordance with' the terms of the employment. Where a charge of unfair discrimination is levelled with specificity, or improper motives are imputed to the authority making the impugned order of termination of the service, it is the duty of the authority to dispel that charge by disclosing to the Court the reason or motive which impelled it to take the impugned action. Excepting, perhaps, in cases analogous to those covered by Article 311(2); Proviso (c), the authority cannot withhold such information from the Court on the lame excuse that impugned order is purely administrative and not judicial, having been passed in exercise of its administrative discretion under the rules governing the conditions of the services. The giving of reasons, as Lord Denning put it in *Green* v. *Amalgamated Engineering Union*, 1971 (1) All LR 114 "is one of the fundamental of goods administration and to recall the words of this court in *Khudi Ram* v. *State of West Bengal*, 1975 (2) SCR 832 (845), in a Government of laws there is nothing like unfettered discretion immune from judicial reviewability". The executive not less than the judiciary is under a general duty to act fairly. Indeed, fairness founded on reason is the essence of the guarantee epitomised in Articles 14 and 16(1).

Another facet of department contention is that Shri Belliappa had voluntarily entered into a contract of service on the terms of employment offered to him. One of the terms of the contract, embodied in the letter of his appointment was that his service was purely temporary and was liable to termination at the will and pleasure of appointing authority without reason and without notice. Having willingly accepted the employment on terms offered to him, he cannot complain against the impugned action taken in accordance with those mutually agreed term. The argument is wholly misconceived. It is borrowed from the archaic common law concept that employment was a matter between the master and servant only. In the first place, this rule in its original absolute form is not applicable to Government servants. Secondly, even with regard to private employment, much of it has passed into the fossils of time. This rule held the field at the time when the master and servant were taken more literally than they are now and when as in early Roman Law, the rights of the servant, like the rights of any other member of the household were not his own but those of his pater familias." But that philosophy is incompatible with these days of large impersonal, corporate employers. To bring it in tune with vastly changed and changing social economic conditions and chores of the day, much of this old antiquated and unjust doctrine has been eroded by judicial decisions and legislation, particularly in its application to persons in public employment, to whom the constitutional protection of Articles 14, 15, 16 and 311 is available."

3.7 TERMINATION OF SERVICES OF TEMPORARY EMPLOYEE ON THE GROUND OF THEIR ABSENCE FROM DUTY OR OVERSTAYAL OF LEAVE

3.7.1 Law on the subject

Absence without leave constitutes misconduct and it is not open to the employer to terminate the services of a temporary employee without notice or inquiry or at any rate without complying with the minimum principles of natural justice.

[*Ram Kishore Pandey* v. *U.O.I.*, 1982 Lab IC 281]

In a case a temporary employee was transferred but he did not join his new place of duty and applied for leave. Without proceeding to take disciplinary action, his services were terminated. It was held violation of Article 311(2) of the Constitution.

[*N. Yellaih Swamy* v. *Director of Industries*, 1971 (1) SLR 730 (AP)]

Services of an employee cannot be terminated straightaway on account of absence from duty without taking disciplinary proceedings contemplated under the Rules.

[*Bahadur Singh* v. *State of Haryana*, 1988 (1) SLR 650 (P&H)]

The removal of Government servant from service for overstaying leave without opportunity to show cause is illegal even though it is provided by the service regulations that any individual who absents himself without permission after the end of the leave would be considered to have sacrificed his appointment and may be reinstated only with the sanction of the competent authority.

[*Jai Shankar* v. *State of Rajasthan*, AIR 1966 SC 492]

Overstayal of leave without reasonable cause or absenting without leave will not result in automatic discharge from service. Reasonable opportunity must be given to show cause why he be not discharged.

[*Mafatlal Narain Dass Barat* v. *J.D. Rathod*, 1967 (2) SLJ 64]

In the case of an employee governed by Industrial Dispute Act 1947, whose services were terminated on account of overstayal of leave it was held that this amounts to 'retrenchment'. Retrenchment in violation of section 25 of the Act is illegal.

[*Mohd. Abdul Khadar* v. *A.P.R.T.C.*, 1983 (3) SLR 562 AP (DB)]

Applicant was 'censured' for his long absence from duty because of illness. "Censure" was made basis for termination. There was nothing also unsatisfactory on record against him. Termination was quashed. It attracted Article 311(2).

[*Dhrubchand Jha* v. *U.O.I.*, 1988 (7) SLR 66 CAT (Pat)]

Termination of service for overstayal of leave, ordered without framing a charge and without giving reasonable opportunity of being heard is illegal and violative of Rule 311(2).

[*Radha* v. *Station Director*, 1985 (1) SLR 349 (Ker)]

Termination of service for overstayal of leave is punitive and attracts Article 311(2).

[*Tarsem Kumar Sood* v. *Chief Engineer H.P.*, 1984 (2) SLR 437]

Services of a doctor were terminated as per terms and conditions of the order of his appointment but it was because of his alleged absence without getting leave sanctioned. It was held such termination casts a stigma and principles of natural justice ought to have been observed.

[*Baljit Singh* v. *State*, 1989 (2) SLR 135 (P&H)]

The employee had served for 9 years. Owing to overstayal of leave, his services were regarded as automatically terminated. It was held that such a provision was unconstitutional.

[*Kamla Devi* v. *U.O.I.*, 1989 (7) SLR 147 CAT (Del)]

Where the charge against the employee is overstayal of leave, his services cannot be terminated on the basis of absence from departmental inquiry.

[*Tarsem Kumar* v. *Chief Engineer Himachal Pradesh*, 1984 (3) SLR 820 (HP) DB]

3.7.2 When a temporary employee has resigned with due notice, he cannot be treated to be on unauthorized absence after he has vacated the office

One Padmalochan Das was appointed as a temporary Assistant in Postal Department. He resigned from the post under Rule 5 of CCS (TS) Rules, 1965 by giving one month's notice, which expired on 7-6-1978. No reply was given to the notice submitted by the petitioner. However, on 7-6-1978 he handed over the keys of the cash safe and other documents to his superior officer. Later on, he was charge sheeted for unauthorized absence from 8-6-1978 and after holding the inquiry, he was removed from service. He challenged the order of his removal from service before CAT (Cuttak Bench) in *Padmalochan Das* v. *U.O.I.*, 1987 (1) CAT 273, the Tribunal held that his removal from service was perverse as the petitioner had observed all the rules.

3.8 TERMINATION OF SERVICES OF TEMPORARY EMPLOYEES ON THE GROUND OF "LOSS OF CONFIDENCE" IN THEM

3.8.1 Law on the subject

"Loss of Confidence" of the employer is a valid ground of termination of services of an employee if the same is *bona fide* and not a cover of victimization. For instance if the Chief Cashier had furnished guarantee for the Asstt. Cashier at the time of appointment and later on the Chief Cashier withdraws such guarantee of good conduct, the Asstt. Cashier may be discharged from service. It is a case of "Loss of Confidence". Another instance could be when an employee secretly runs a parallel business, that is a ground for loss of confidence and the employer can discharge him for loss of confidence. However, in *Chandulal* v. *Management,* (1985) 51 FLR 142 (SC), the Supreme Court has held that the termination for loss of confidence casts a stigma on the employee. So according to the latest view of the Supreme Court, for termination of an employee on the ground of loss of confidence, the enquiry must precede such termination for loss of confidence. So the earlier view that there was no need of enquiry for discharge for loss of confidence has been drastically changed. When an organization terminates the service of an employee by stating in the order that it has lost confidence in the employee, it is not conclusive and the Tribunal can go behind the order and see whether it is motivated by victimization or based on misconduct. However, in order to discharge an employee for loss of confidence it is to be established that the employee was holding a post of confidence. A chowkidar holds a post of confidence. So, if he sleeps during duty hours he can be discharged for loss of confidence. A darwan also holds the post of confidence. A compounder-in-charge of medicine holds the post of confidence. But a lower division clerk cannot be an employee of confidence. Also a Librarian does not hold the post of confidence. A bank employee cannot be discharged for loss of confidence for his negligence in dealing with the affairs of a Co-operative Housing Society because there was no nexus between he work of the Bank employee with the work of Secretary of the Co-operative Housing Society.

If the services of the General Manager of a nationalized Bank are terminated for "loss of confidence", it does not necessarily mean that there is no stigma. Form of the order is not decisive. Courts can go behind it.

[*S.Amarjit Singh* v. *P.N. Bank,* 1986 (2) SLR 121 Del (DB)]

When the services of a workman were terminated on the loss of "loss of confidence" on grounds of his involvement in the act of smuggling, it amounts to stigma and warrants inquiry proceedings as contemplated under law. Disciplinary proceedings were necessary as a condition precedent to the passing of order of termination as a measure of punishment against the employee.

[*Chandulal* v. *Management P.A.W. Airways Inc.*, AIR 1985 SC 1128]

3.8.2 The ground for "loss of confidence" for terminating the services of an employee must flow logically in the facts and circumstances of the case

One Michel was an employee of M/s. Johnson Pumps Ltd. It was suspected that the workman had been indulging into secrets of business. But the employer did not disclose the grounds on which the suspicion arose. In fact, he was given two increments in appreciation of his work. However his services were terminated on the ground that the employer had lost confidence in the workman. The Supreme Court held that action of termination of the worker by order simplicitor was not *bona fide.*

[*L.Michel* v. *Johnson Pumps Ltd.*, 1975 SLJ 369]

3.8.3 The services of an employee can be terminated by the employer without holding the enquiry when he has lost confidence in him in certain exceptional circumstances

One Rebellow was an employee of Air India Corporation. The management had strong suspicion against him that his private conduct and behaviour with air hostesses was not above board. Instead of holding an enquiry into his conduct the management terminated his services under Regulations 48. Regulation 48 in its plain language does not lay down or contemplate any defined essential pre-requisite for invoking its operation. Action under this regulation can be validly taken by the employer at his sweet will without assigning any reason. He is not bound to disclose why he does not want to continue in service any particular employee.

Rebellow approached the Labour court against his termination. The Labour court decided in his favour. It held that the dismissal was not a discharge simpliciter but in breach of the provisions of section 33 of the Industrial Disputes Act. The Air India Corporation took the matter in appeal to the Supreme

Court under Article 136 of the Constitution. The Supreme Court set aside the order of the Labour Court and held that the Labour Court was not right in holding that Rebellow was guilty of misconduct and that his services could not have been terminated by order simpliciter. Speaking for the court Dua, J said:

> "The complainant, it may be remembered had to deal with air hostesses in the performance of his duties and if the appellant was not fully satisfied beyond suspicion about his general conduct and behaviour while dealing with them it cannot be said that loss of confidence was not *bona fide* . Once *bona fide* loss of confidence is affirmed, the impugned order must be considered to be immune from the challenge. The opinion formed by the employer about the suitability of his employee for the job assigned to him even though erroneous, if *bona fide,* is in our opinion final and not subject to review by the industrial adjudication. Such opinion may legitimately induce the employer to terminate the employee's services; but such termination can on no rational grounds be considered to be misconduct and must, therefore, be held to be permissible and immune from challenge."

The order does not suggest any misconduct on the part of the complainant and indeed it is not possible to hold this order to be based on any conceivable misconduct.

[*Air India Corporation Bombay* v. *V.A. Rebellow,* AIR 1972 SC 1343]

3.8.4 Pre-requisite for termination of services of an employee on the ground of "loss of confidence" in him

For invoking the aforesaid principle, it must be pleaded and proved that—

(i) the employee was holding a position of trust and confidence;

(ii) by abusing such power, he committed acts which resulted in forfeiture of the same; and

(iii) to continue him in service would be embarrassing and inconvenient to the employer or would be detrimental to the discipline or security of establishment.

[*Kanhiyalal Agarwal* v. *Factory Manager, Gwalior Sugar Company Ltd.,* 2001 (7) JT 571 SC]

3.9 TERMINATION OF SERVICES ON CHARGE OF MISCONDUCT

3.9.1 The law on the subject

The rules empowering the appointing authority to terminate the services of a temporary Government servant are couched more or less in a uniform or say, in hackneyed manner stating that subject to the provisions contained in the appointment letter or in any agreement between the Government and the temporary Government servant, shall be liable to termination at any time by notice in writing by either party. The expression 'termination' may include termination for misconduct. But in the light of the judicial pronouncements, on the subject, the meaning of the word 'termination" has been restricted to 'contractual termination unconnected with any idea of punishment for misconduct.

3.9.2 The innocent looking order of termination of services of an employee can be screened and x-rayed to ensure that public authority does not misuse its authority

One B.R. Rathode was serving as a Bus Conductor in State Transport Corporation,. Gujarat for 10 years and had unblemished record of service. He was holding a permanent post. While on duty on 8-6-1978 in the bus which was bound for Mitha Ghoda, a girl named Shankuntla boarded the bus at Sanand and she was to alight at Khoraghoda. Due to some confusion, she could not get down at her proper destination and was stranded when the bus stopped at the terminus. The passengers present in the bus helped her and she stayed for the night at the house of the village sarpanch. Next day, she boarded the same bus and reached her destination. On 14-6-1978 a sensitive news was splashed in "Jai Hind daily" under the caption "If true, shameful". On the basis of the report, a departmental preliminary enquiry was conducted and the statement of the bus conductor was recorded on 20-6-1978. The Divisional Director of S.T.C. Raj Guru who happened to visit the office while the statement of the bus conductor was recorded, passed an order there and then discharging the delinquent bus conductor from services with immediate effect as per provisions of Regulation 61 of S.T.C. Regulations. The petitioner challenged this order in Gujarat High Court, and the court in its judgment dated 8-12-1980 observed as under:

> "The respondent has time and again stated in his reply that his action was rooted in the State Transport Employees Regulations, Regulation 61 and that the services of the petitioner were terminated as his services were not found to be "satisfactory, trustworthy and useful in the interest of the Corporation". He denied that the order was passed by way of punishment on the petitioner for the alleged incident but on the ground that his services of the petitioner were not "useful to the Corporation" and therefore the impugned order was passed.

The Court went on to recall that Supreme Court has time and again insisted that such innocent looking orders in the facts and circumstances of the case can be screened and X-rayed so that a public authority does not abuse its powers. The petitioner's statement was that he was a permanent employee of the S.T. Corporation and not having at his back any bad record as far as his service was concerned. There is no denial of the fact that a news item was flashed in the Jai Hind Daily on 14-6-1978 attributing the possible outraging of the modesty of the girl Shakuntala at the hand of the conductor of the S.T. Corporation. Raj Guru, the Divisional Director, STC does not dispute the fact that he had got held an *ex parte* preliminary inquiry into the alleged incident nor did he dispute the fact that on 20th June, 1978 he had summoned the petitioner to his office to have his personal say in the matter. The order of termination of services came to be passed immediately. Can it be said in this background that the petitioner's services were really not needed by the State Transport Corporation? A man who had been serving the Corporation for 10 years past and was a permanent employee of the Corporation was overnight found to be a useless person. Why his services were not required should have been elaborated. The respondent simply banked on Regulation 61 of the State Transport Employees Regulations. In my view the power reserved by the said Regulation 61 has been abused by the respondent under the guise of exercising that power. He wanted to visit this petitioner with punishment for his alleged worthlessness and alleged unworthiness and his alleged unsatisfactory performance or character.

In my view, the case of the State Transport Corporation is absolutely defenceless. I am surprised that not only the order had come to be passed but it has been sought to be stuck to. It is really unfortunate that even public officers like the Divisional Director of the State Transport Corporation did not know the limitations on his public powers and that is why he has tried to justify an action which is *ex facie* untenable in the facts and circumstances of the case. The petition, therefore, is allowed. It is declared that the order passed by the Divisional Director of the State Transport Corporation terminating the services of the petitioner is bad at law and petitioner continues in the employment of the respondent State Transport Corporation. The Corporation is hereby directed to reinstate the petitioner in service with full back wages with continuity of service and all other benefits, if any."

[*Bhavanish Rajsingh Rathod* v. *S.T.C. Ahmedabad*, 1981(2) SLJ 648]

3.9.3 Order of termination of a temporary public servant on the ground of insubordination and misbehaviour is treated as an order of dismissal and it can be effective only if it has been passed after full compliance of Article 311(2) of the Constitution

One Padam Prasad Sharma, a temporary driver under Sikkam Administration was removed from service by an order dated 13-6-1979 which read as under:

> "The services of Driver Padam Prasad Sharma, Temporary Driver, is hereby terminated with immediate effect on account of his insubordination and misbehaviour with the Transport Officer, Siliguri in Jalpaiguri Court on 29-5-1979."

This order was contested by the petitioner in the Sikkim High Court, which in its judgment dated 30-5-1980 observed as under:

> "On a plain construction of the above order, the inference is obvious that it is based on the misconduct of the petitioner and has been passed as a measure of punishment on account of his improper and rude behaviour with a senior officer. There are clear imputations of misconduct and moreover a stigma against the petitioner flows from this order. The order, if read in a reasonable way, would carry the implication that the public servant was found to be undesirable and this in turn would import an element of punishment as the basis of the order. In the situation, the only plausible conclusion is that the impugned order would be treated to be one of

dismissal and it could be only effective if it had been passed after full compliance of Article 311(2). It is not in dispute that no inquiry within the meaning of Article 311(3) was held. In this situation, the order cannot be upheld as it is violative of the constitutional guarantee. In the result, the petition is allowed and the impugned order is set aside."

[*Padam Prasad Sharma* v. *S.N.T.*, 1982 (1) SLJ 431]

3.9.4 If the order mentions that services of an employee stand terminated 'before office hours'. It is *prima facie* penal in nature and liable to be quashed

One N.M. Khan was appointed as a stenographer in a temporary capacity on 23-3-1978. His services were terminated on 2-4-1979 by an order which read as under:

"The services of N.M. Khan, stenographer, are terminated before office hours on 2-4-1979."

The petitioner challenged the order of his termination before Gujarat High Court, which in its order dated 13-4-1981 observed as under:

"The impugned order deserves to be set aside on the short ground that *ex facie,* the order appears to be penal and does not speak of the services having been put an end to, because of his performance being found unsatisfactory. Quite often, we come across orders passed by experienced officers of the Sachivalaya, from which we can say that if the services are terminated because of the unsatisfactory performance during probation if any, they invariably mention that fact expressly. It appears that because of petitioner's long spell of leave enjoyed by him and because of his alleged sickness, which he has asserted and which has not been controverted, he was not regular in attendance. His services have been put an end to on the ground of his irregular attendance and his prolonged leave period. It therefore, in the facts and circumstances of the case, can be said to be penal order passed because of his alleged proceeding on leave at time without prior permission and at times after getting the leave sanctioned some time after the period of absence. On the above stated ground, the impugned order is set aside and the petitioner is directed to be reinstated in service."

[*N.M. Khan* v. *State of Gujarat*, 1981 (1) SLJ 277]

3.9.5 Courts can go into the causes of termination of service of a temporary employee even though the order issued is a simpliciter

One Pradeep Deb was working as a Computer Operator in the office of Census Operation, Arunachal Pradesh. Departmental proceedings were initiated against him on certain allegations of misconduct which were not concluded. His services were however terminated in the meanwhile under Rule 5(1) of CCS (TS) Rules without assigning any reasons. It was contended by the petitioner that the order of termination was, in fact, an order of punishment since departmental proceedings on allegations of misconduct were, in fact, continuing when the order of termination was issued. This action was taken by the authorities as a short cut. This case came up for consideration before CAT (Guwahati Bench), and the Tribunal in its judgment dated 17-9-1986 observed as under:

> "On consideration of the facts and circumstances of the case, we have no hesitation to come to the conclusion that the impugned orders were passed by way of punishment on the basis of certain allegations of misconduct for which the petitioner was not given any opportunity to prove his innocence. Further in passing the impugned order, the authority had violated the principle enshrined in Articles 14 and 16 of the Constitution, in as much as 12 of his juniors were retained in service and the petitioner was singled out for discrimination by discharging him from service without any reasonable cause. The authority did not disclose any reason as to why the petitioner was thus visited with such harsh treatment which was demonstrably a case of flagrant discrimination. The order of termination is set aside."
>
> [*Pradeep Deb* v. *Director Census Operation, Arunachal Pradesh*, 1987 (1) SLJ 469 CAT]

3.9.6 Termination of the services of a temporary employee on the stated ground of overstayal of leave mentioned in the order of termination itself amounts to his "removal" from service and is illegal

One Mangal Singh was appointed as a Mason in the Ground Water Department on 14-8-1969 "for one month or till the famine operations are over". His services were continued from time to time which were eventually terminated on 12-8-1974 under Temporary Rules applicable to him. He sought relief in the case before Rajasthan High Court, which in its judgment dated 27-2-1989 observed as under:

> "It cannot be denied that the respondent was a Government servant. It further appears that the order of termination of his services is not innocuous inasmuch as it is apparent from the very language of the notice that his services were terminated on account of his overstaying the leave and not joining the duty at his place of posting. Thus, it was not a termination pure and simple but a stigma is attached to the respondent by the very language of the order. Thus, it appears to us that though the order has been termed as one of termination, it is, in fact, an order of removal. If that is so, we think, there is no escape from the conclusion that a show cause notice or an opportunity of being heard against the action proposed should have been given to him, under Article 311 of the Constitution even though he was temporary employee. The notice of one month relied upon by the learned Additional Government Advocate is not a show cause notice, but it is only to the effect that the order of termination will come into operation after the expiry of one month from the date of the order. In our opinion, the respondent was entitled to an opportunity to show cause against the proposed removal from service for his overstaying his leave and for not joining duty and as no such opportunity was given to him the impugned order of termination of service is illegal."

[*State of Rajasthan* v. *Mangal Singh,* 1981 (1) SLJ 173]

3.9.7 When the order of termination of the services of a temporary employee is based on a report of misconduct, it attracts Article 311 (2) of the Constitution

One Kondu Reddy was appointed as a temporary clerk in Postal Department in March, 1975 on the basis of a "Community" Certificate issued by the Tahsildar claiming that he belonged to a Scheduled Tribe. The certificate on verification was found to be tampered with and his services were terminated on 2-2-1978 under Rule 5(1) of CCS (TS) Rules through an order simplicitor without attaching any stigma. Subsequently, the applicant faced criminal prosecution on the charge of producing the bogus certificate and cheating the Department in which he was exonerated. He prayed for his reinstatement to which he did not get any response from the Department. He approached CAT (Madras Bench) for relief and the Tribunal in its judgment dated 4-8-1986 observed as under:

> "In the instant case though the order of termination issued under Rule 5(1) of the Temporary Services Rules is termination simplicitor and does not cast any stigma on the applicant, it has to be viewed in the context of the background for such termination *viz.* subsequent happenings leading to a criminal charge against the applicant on the charge of bogus community certificate and his acquittal therefrom. The background of the case as revealed from perusal of records shows that the Revenue Divisional Officer, Sivakasi had written to the Respondent on 23-1-1978 stating that the applicant's community certificate issued by the Tahsildar, Aruppukkottai was tampered with and that the applicant did not belong to the Konda Reddy Scheduled Tribe and that he really belongs to Ganjamma Reddy community which is not classed as Scheduled Tribe. On receipt of this communication, the respondent invoked Rule 5(1) of the Temporary Service Rules and terminated the service of the applicant. But for the said communication from the Revenue Divisional Officer, the service of the applicant would not have been terminated. Apart from the fact that the applicant was acquitted by the Magistrate, when the whole matter was viewed in the context of the R.D.O.'s communication and the subsequent trial in the Criminal Court, it leaves no doubt in our minds that the termination of the service of the applicant was due to his allegedly having cheated the Postal Department by producing the bogus Community Certificate which was alleged to have been tampered with. Termination of service under these circumstances would fall within the meaning of Article 311(2) of the Constitution. As this was not done in this case, we quash the order dated 2-2-1978 of the Respondent, and direct the respondents to take back the applicant into service. However, as the termination of service was done on 2-2-1978 and the applicant had moved the court seeking remedy only

in January, 1984, after a delay of 6 years we cannot completely absolve the applicant of some share of his being guilty of laches. Therefore, we order that the respondents need not pay back wages to the applicant for the period he was out of service. The period from 2-2-1978 to the date of his reinstatement will be treated as dies-non with past service counting as Qualifying Service for retirement benefits."

[*Kondu Reddy* v. *P.M.G. Madras*, 1987 (1) SLJ 22 (CAT)]

3.9.8 Services of an employee cannot be terminated under Rule 5 of C.C.S. (Temporary Service) Rules, 1965 on the ground of misconduct even if the order of termination is innocuous and does not cast any stigma on the employee

In the case of *Director, Directorate of Economics and Statistics, NCT, Delhi* v. *Shalid Khan*, 2003 (3) SLJ 248 Del, the respondent was appointed as Statistical Investigator on 1-7-1998. He gave an undertaking that if anything was found adverse against him in the Police Verification (character and antecedents) Report, he would not claim any salary or other benefits. It was revealed subsequently that a F.I.R. had been lodged against him on 10-2-1998 under various sections of I.P.C. His services were terminated under Rule 5 of CCS (TS) Rules, 1965 without assigning any ground for his termination. This case came up for consideration before Delhi High Court which in its judgment dated 16-8-2002 observed that having regard to the fact that the respondent's services were terminated on the ground of commission of misconduct, it was obligatory on the part of the Petitioners to have initiated departmental proceedings against him. However, there cannot be any doubt whatsoever that the petitioner herein would be entitled to initiate appropriate action against the respondent accordingly.

3.9.9 The services of a probationer cannot be terminated through an order simpliciter if there are positive allegations against him

One Mamtani was appointed as a Foreman in I.I.T. Delhi on 5-12-1966 on probation for a period of one year which was extended from time to time till 2-1-1972 when his services were terminated. In the intervening period, a charge sheet had been issued to him on certain reports of misbehaviour made against him by his colleagues and superiors but which was later on dropped. It was contended by the petitioner that he had been confirmed and has a right to continue in service till his superannuation. He had also been allowed to subscribe to Provident Fund account. He sought relief in the case before Delhi High Court which in its judgment dated 5-5-1977 observed as under:

> "It is true that the impugned order is *ex facie* an innocent order in that it does not carry a stigma on the face of it. It is, however, well settled that in determining whether an order of termination is punitive in nature, the Court is entitled, as indeed bound, to examine not only the order but the circumstances anterior or posterior to it to determine if the order had its genesis in any prejudicial material against a public servant. There is clear reference in the records that the petitioner was not found fit to be retained in service because of persistent reports of his misbehaviour towards his colleagues and superiors and the termination of the service of the petitioner pursuant to this adverse material brought the order within the mischief of the rule of "foundation" without being a mere "motive". There is no force in the contention of the Institute that, while basing the order on the allegations of misbehaviour, the authorities were within their rights and were merely exercising their power to consider whether the petitioner had given satisfactory performance in his job and, therefore, deserved to be confirmed or that his services were no longer required. The exigencies of administration and the failure of a public servant to give satisfaction are conceptually different from positive allegations of objectionable conduct, like misbehaviour towards the colleagues and the superiors. Such allegations do not partake of the character that is attributed to them. These are positive allegations, which, if established, would certainly justify removal of a public servant from service. These allegations could not, therefore, form basis of the impugned order unless the petitioner had been given reasonable opportunity of being heard, which was obviously not afforded to the petitioner. The nature of the tenure of the petitioner, to my mind, would not make any difference because even a probationer is entitled to be heard before his services are

terminated on ground of misconduct because such adverse action against a public servant does not merely deprive him of the service but stigmatizes the public servant thereby prejudicing his chances of future employment.

In the result the petitioner succeeds. The impugned order terminating the services of the petitioner are quashed. The petitioner is restored to the position in which he was in relation to the service before these impugned orders were made. The authorities would, however, be entitled to consider and decide the question, after giving the petitioner a reasonable opportunity of being heard, if the petitioner is liable to be removed from service on account of the foresaid allegations or any other allegations which may justify his removal from service."

3.9.10 The services of a temporary employee cannot be terminated by termination simpliciter when the foundation of allegation is forgery, cheating, inefficiency against him

The services of one Jeevarathnam were terminated by termination simpliciter. He alleged that his order of termination was really an order of punishment since there were allegations of misconduct against him. He challenged the order before CAT (Hyderabad Bench) which in its judgment dated 25-11-1988 observed as under:

"We have called for the file relating to his termination and found that his services were sought to be terminated on various grounds as contained in the note dated 18-6-1984 which reads as under:

"......... He is unbecoming Government servant due to the fact mentioned above. Also he has displayed his misbehaviour/misconduct as revealed from the replies and explanations given by Shri A.S.J. Rathnam and also displayed indiscipline and misbehaviour and cheating by putting frivolous blames on office to cover up his weakness and lapses in response to this office memorandum No. 5-12/82 PG dated 7-6-1984 and dated 13-6-1984 as the same do not hold correct position and truth with reference to the rules and regulations and records available in the office. Besides his replies and explanations are of complete impoliteness, rudeness arrogance and hence contrary to the conduct rules.

Keeping in mind the above his carelessness, negligence, misconduct and misbehaviour, he is not worthy for keeping further more in service at the station and he deserves for stern action *i.e.* termination of his service in the interest from the post of Store Keeper as per terms and conditions stipulated in proviso 2 and 3 of his offer of appointment issued *vide* this office memorandum No. 5-12/81 PF dated 20/22-10-81-PF and as per Government of India decision No. 3 *i.e.* non-applicability of Rule 5 for termination of services in the case of probationers/persons on probation mentioned in page No. 13 of Central Civil Services (Temprory Service) Rules, 1965 corrected upto 1st December, 1977."

The file, therefore, discloses that the termination of the applicant was due to various acts of misconduct, cheating, negligence, etc. apart from sending seeds to one of the customers giving rise to loss of 493 to Government. From the reasons given above, it would follow that the order of termination of the applicant is in substance punitive though couched in innocuous termination is, therefore, quashed and set aside. The applicant will be reinstated in service forthwith with all consequential benefits of arrears of salary etc. from the date of termination till the date of reinstatement in accordance with the rules that he has not kept himself engaged in any others occupation during the intervening period. It is open to the respondents to take disciplinary action if desired in accordance with the procedure prescribed.

[*A.S. Jeevarathnam* v. *Director, Sh. K.N. Arora,* 1990 (1) SLJ 129 CAT]

3.9.11 Termination of services of an employee by order simpliciter after making some sort of inquiry on charges of misconduct amounts to punishment and is violative of provisions of Article 311(2) of the Constitution

One Naik was working as a Lecturer in a Government College, Daman. There was some conflict between him and the college Principal and in one of his representations, he used the word "Proved Liar" against the Principal. Some sort of inquiry was held against him by the Collector, Daman on the complaint made by the Principal. In the said inquiry, the petitioner justified the use of the word "Proved Liar" against the Principal. The Report of the inquiry was submitted by the Collector and the services of Naik were terminated. He contended before Bombay High Court that the impugned order of termination has been made by way of punishment in violation of the provisions of Article 311(2) of the Constitution. The court in its judgment dated 8-8-1983 observed as under:

> "Administrator, who is the disciplinary authority has not come forward to say that he did not accept the conclusion arrived at by the Collector on the inquiry or that he was unable to make up his mind one way or the other. It is, therefore, not possible to say that the alleged misconduct inhered in the state of mind which is not discernible. On the other hand in the absence of denial of all the allegations of the petitioner that the impugned order was based or founded on the report of the Collector, it can be said that the respondent accepted the conclusion arrived at by the Collector and the said conclusion or decision, that making the alleged misconduct as foundation for the impugned order. If that is so, there is no difficulty in holding that the impugned order has been passed in violation of the provisions contained in clause (2) of Article 311 of the Constitution inasmuch as the petitioner had not been given a reasonable opportunity of being defended before the order of termination, which amounted to removal or dismissal, was passed. We find that the impugned order has to be struck down."
>
> [*Ishwar Lal J. Naik* v. *S.C.Arya, Principal, Government Arts & Science College, Daman*, 1984 (1) SLJ 1]

3.9.12 Can the services of an employee be terminated under Rule 5(1) of T.S. Rules, 1965 on the basis of a private complaint against him which was inquired into at his back?

This interesting question of law arose in the case of *Dr. (Mrs.) Esmina Gomes Matins* v. *U.O.I.*, 1977 SLJ 415 before the Court of Judicial Commissioner, Goa, Daman & Diu. The petitioner was Health Officer in Goa Administration after having been selected by U.P.S.C. and was under probation. She was having some problem with her superiors for which adverse remarks had been communicated to her on which certain inquiries had been held at her back which were evidently not complimentary to her. Her services were terminated under Rule 5 without holding any inquiry. The main point for decision for the court was whether the facts and circumstances of the case could be construed as "misconduct" on her part and in that case, inquiry ought to have been held in accordance with provisions of Article 311 of the Constitution. The operative part of the judgment is reproduced below:

> "Misconduct denotes something more than negligence. Misconduct is not necessarily the same thing as conduct involving moral turpitude. In order to enable a master to take disciplinary action against his servant it is not a condition precedent that misconduct on the part of the servant must arise within his employment and not outside his employment. The test in each case will be whether the servant is conducting himself in a way inconsistent with the faithful discharge of his obligations undertaken by him either expressly or impliedly in accepting the service. The inconsistency may arise on account of any act of the servant, either in the course of his employment or outside it which injures or has the tendency to injure his master's business or interests or reputation. In the circumstances, I hold that the termination of services of the petitioner casts a stigma on the character of the petitioner and acts as a punishment. Termination of her services under Rule 5(1) of the Rules is not possible. The respondents had to give to the petitioner an opportunity to answer the charges made against her and after a proper inquiry take the steps that they deemed fit."

3.9.13 The burden of proof to convince the Court that the termination simpliciter is actually an order of punishment lies on the employer

It is now well settled that even a temporary Government servant is entitled to the protection of Article 311(2) of the Constitution where termination involves a stigma or amounts to punishment. However, where the decision to terminate the services of the servant has been taken on the ground of unsuitability of the servant in relation to the post held by him and it is not by way of any punishment and stigma, such termination cannot be said to be vitiated by non-observance of Article 311(2) of the Constitution *Commodore Commanding, Southern Naval Area, Cochin* v. *V.N. Rajan*, 1981 (2) SLJ 48 (SC).

The matter was also examined by the Supreme Court in *State of Maharashtra* v. *Veerappa R. Saboji*, 1979 SLJ 621 (SC) wherein Hon'ble Mr. Justice R.S. Pathak made the following observation:

> "The law, it seems to me, is that where the services of a temporary Government servant or a probationer Government servant are terminated by an order which does not *ex facie* disclose any stigma or penal consequences against the Government servant is merely a termination order simplicter there is no case ordinarily for assuming that it is anything but what it purports to be. Where, however, the order discloses on the face of it that a stigma is cast on the Government servant or that it visits him with penal consequences, then plainly the case is one of punishment. There may still be another kind of case where although the termination of services is intended by way of punishment, the order is framed as a termination simpliciter. In such a case, if the Government servant is able to establish by material on the record that the order is, in fact, passed by way of punishment, the innocence of the language in which the order is framed will not protect it as the procedural safeguards contemplated by Article 311(2) of the Constitution have not been satisfied. In a given case, the Government servant may succeed in making out a *prima facie* case that the order was by way of punishment but an attempt to rebut the case by the authorities may necessitate for the official records for the purpose of determining the truth. It is in such a case generally that the official records may be called for by the court. It is not open to the court to send for the official records on a mere allegation by the Government servant that the order is by way of punishment. For unless there is material on the record before the Court in support of that allegation, an attempt by the Court to find out from the record whether the termination of service is based on the unsuitability of the Government servant in relation to the post held by him or is in reality an order by way of punishment will in affect be an unwarranted attempt to delve into the official records for the purpose of determining the nature of the order on the basis of a mere allegation of the Government servants. On a sufficient case being made out on the merits before the Court by the Government servant it is open to the Court to resort to

scrutiny of the official records for the purpose of verifying the truth."

3.9.14 The burden of proving that the action of the employer in terminating the services of an employee is *mala fide*, rests on the employee himself

The services of one P.K. Chatterjee, a Tracer in the consolidation department were terminated on 3-4-1975 by an order simpliciter. The case of the employee was that he was President of the District Union of class IV employees and in that capacity he had staged hunger strike before Shri Mam Raj Singh. Even though Shri Mam Raj Singh conceded the demands of the employees and agreed that he would not take revengeful action, yet he nurtured ill-will against the petitioner. He was in the look out and was trying to find some opportunity to punish the petitioner. Accordingly, he made an inspection and made a report against him which led to termination of his services. The petitioner contended that these facts having not been denied by Shri Mam Raj Singh should be accepted as correct and they fully make out a case of *mala fides* against him.

This case came up before Allahabad High Court which in its judgment dated 11-11-1976 observed as under:

> "We are unable to accept this submission. A perusal of the allegations show that petitioner's assertion that Shri Mam Raj Singh bore ill will against him and was in the look out to find some reason to punish him is based only on two objective facts *viz.* that the petitioner who was the President of the Union of class IV employees of District Varanasi had resorted to hunger strike and that Mam Raj Singh had carried out an inspection and made a written report against him on 20-3-1975. In our opinion, neither fact relied upon by the petitioner is such on which an inference can be drawn that Shri Mam Raj Singh while making the impugned order was actuated by oblique motive. It may be that as the petitioner had gone on hunger strike, Shri Mam Raj Singh did not like this action and was for that reason not happy with him. Merely because Shri Mam Raj Singh was not happy with the petitioner it does not mean that in terminating petitioner's service, he was actuated by *mala fide* or that he did so for oblique motive. There is nothing on the record to indicate that

the petitioner's service was terminated in order to victimize him for having gone on hunger strike. Instead, the inspection note prepared by Shri Mam Raj Singh and the report submitted by the Consolidation Officer show that considering the manner in which the petitioner had been acting *vis-a-vis* other employees and was doing his own work, the respondent thought that it was not in public interest to retain him in service. Whenever service of a temporary Government servant is sought to be terminated because of misconduct or inefficiency, it would always be that the officer terminating his service is not pleased with the Government servant, but merely because the officer terminating the service of the Government servant was not happy with him, it does not mean that he was actuated by *mala fide*. We are, therefore, of opinion that the objective facts stated by the petitioner are not such which can reasonably lead to an inference that while terminating petitioner's service Shri Mam Raj Singh was either actuated by *mala fide* or by oblique motive."

[*Priya Kumar Chatterjee* v. *State of Uttar Pradesh*, (1977) SLJ 563]

3.9.15 Short notes on judgments of courts relating to "Burden of Proof" in departmental inquiries

"Burden of proof - in a departmental or disciplinary inquiry:

(a) There is no absolute burden of proof,

(b) The burden of proof depends upon – (i) nature of the charge, (ii) nature of the explanation given by the delinquent."

[*Orissa Mining Corporation* v. *Ananda Chandra Prusty*, 1997 (1) SLR 286 (SC)]

The burden of proof that the order of termination is punitive is on the petitioner.

[*J.B. Sharma* v. *State of Madhya Pradesh*, 1988 (1) SLR 620 (SC)]

3.9.16 Short notes on judgments of courts in which it was held that Article 311(2) was applicable in cases of termination on the ground of misconduct

The services of a temporary employee of a Central Co-operative Bank were terminated by an order. On employee's challenging the order in appeal before the Registrar of Co-operative Societies, the Bank highlighted some of the acts of misconduct and mal-performance of the employee. It was held that this did not make the order penal in character.

[*Mohindergarh Central Co-operative Bank* v. *State of Haryana*, 1984 (3) SLR 401 (P&H)]

Where certain charges were framed against a temporary servant of a Central Cooperative Bank but later on, to avoid stigma, the inquiry was stopped and services terminated simplicitor the order was held legal.

[*Central Cooperative Bank* v. *Shibbulal Monga Singh*, 1980 (1) SLR 198 MP; *Jagdish Mitter* v. *U.O.I.*, AIR 1964 SC 449 followed]

"Order did not cast any stigma on appellant's character or integrity nor did it visit him with any civil consequences. Article 311 is not attracted. It is immaterial that the order was preceded by an information enquiry with a view for ascertaining whether he should be retained in service."

[*Ram Gopal Chaturvedi* v. *State of Madhya Pradesh*, AIR 1970 SC 159]

Petitioner's services were terminated by order simpliciter. He alleged that termination was on the basis of alleged negligence on his part. But his explanation had not been called nor was any inquiry instituted. Termination was held non-punitive on the facts and circumstances of the case.

[*Pramath Kumar Pradhan* v. *State of Orissa*, 1988 (6) SLR 252 Ori (CAT)]

3.9.17 Short notes on judgments of courts in which it was held that inquiry under Article 311(2) was necessary before terminating the services of temporary employees on charges of misconduct

Services of a doctor were terminated on the ground of alleged immoral conduct. He was a temporary employee but had put in 2 years service. The termination was held illegal.

[*Dr. Jain Singh Malika* v. *State of Haryana*, 1987 (1) SLR 263 (P&H)]

A temporary employee was charge-sheeted on 21-8-1981 to which he replied on 7-9-1981. His services were terminated by an order which did not refer to the charges mentioned in the charge-sheet. The termination order was held as punitive.

[*O.P. Goel* v. *H.P. Tourism Development Corporation*, 1991 (2) SLR 798]

The services of a temporary employee were terminated on the basis of a confidential inquiry relating to certain allegations of misconduct. No show cause notice was afforded to the employee. Termination order was held void.

[*Rajinder Kaur* v. *State of Punjab*, 1986 SCC 785 (L&S)]

Termination of services of a temporary employee on the basis of pendency of a criminal case is punitive and attracts Article 311(2). It also attracts principles of natural justice.

[*N.V.Prasonnon* v. *U.O.I.*, ATR 1990 (1) CAT 343 (Ernakulam)]

Respondent was appointed as a Secretary of a Bank on probation. He was placed under suspension and charge sheeted. He submitted his explanation. Thereafter his services were terminated without inquiry. It was held that his termination was punitive in nature and illegal as no inquiry had been held.

[*Ambala Central Co-operative Bank Ltd.* v. *Presiding Officer Labour Court Ambala*, 1990 (4) SLR 527 (P&H)]

Where disciplinary proceedings have started but not concluded, the termination on the ground that services are not required is not tenable.

[*Badri Narain Singh* v. *S.D.O. Basra*, 1991 (1) Lab IC 737 (All)]

A temporary employee took a loan of Rs. 10,000 for purchase of a house but did not utilise this amount for that purpose. His services were terminated without inquiry. It was held that this was illegal.

[*Ambala Central Co-operative Bank Ltd.* v. *State of Haryana*, 1991(2) SLR 395 (P&H)]

The services of a Probationer in National Institute of Ayurveda (Rajasthan) were terminated after an *ex parte* report by Vigilance Committee about submission of false certificate of experience by him. No opportunity was afforded to the employee to give his explanation. Termination was held illegal.

[*Kailash Chandra* v. *Director National Institute of Ayurveda*, 1986 (2) SLR 209 (Raj)]

The foundation of the order termination simplicitor was misappropriation and forgery. Termination held void since provisions of Article 311(2) were complied with.

[*State of Madhya Pradesh* v. *Raghunath Singh*, 1985 (2) SLR 72]

When a probationer has successfully completed the period of probation, then the termination of his services on the basis of adverse remarks contained in his C.R. attracts Article 311(2) of Constitution.

[*Narottam Kumar* v. *Chief Secretary*, 1989 (2) SLR 111 (P&H)]

Where a probationer had successfully completed the period of probation, there was no adverse report. Charge-sheet was issued subsequently but withdrawn. Thereafter his services were terminated. It was held that it was a clear case of punishment as no inquiry was held before passing the punitive order.

[*Dr. V.S. Dhaka* v. *State of Haryana*, 1989 (5) SLR 102 (P&H)]

Even in the case of a daily rated employee, though Article 311 is not attracted, his services cannot be terminated on the charge of negligence without giving him reasonable opportunity to defend.

[*Kuldip Singh* v. *State of Himchal Pradesh*, 1990 (2) SLR 93 HP (DB)]

The applicant participated in illegal or vicious activity. The termination by order simpliciter was held illegal since no inquiry was held.

[*N.Venugopalan* v. *U.O.I.*, 1989 (7) SLR 670 CAT (Ernakulam)]

Petitioner's services were terminated on the ground that she had been absent without leave for more than 15 days and under BHEL Rules, she was presumed to have left the service of the company on her own accord. Applicant disputed about her absence. It was held that even if the allegation was true, she should have been heard before her services were terminated.

[*Kamlesh Sharma* v. *U.O.I.*, 1990 (3) SLR 616 (Del) (DB)]

The termination of services of an employee on the ground that he had misled the Service Commission regarding his qualification is penal in character and attracts Article 311(2).

[*S.R.Patel* v. *State of Gujarat*, 1984 (1) SLR 238]

When departmental inquiry has been initiated and finding of guilt recorded, his services cannot be simply terminated. Compliance of Article 311(2) is a must.

[*Pashupati Dayal* v. *State of Uttar Pradesh*, 1988 (3) SLR 16 (All)]

An order of termination which is made effective from the date of suspension is not termination simpliciter but is punitive in nature and attracts Article 311(2). If there is doubt whether the impugned order (by referring to suspension) casts a stigma, the doubt should be resolved in favour of the Petitioner.

[*Rati Ram Durga Prasad* v. *Regional Settlement Commissioner*, AIR 1960 MP 230; Wang Tshering Ta, 1983 (1) SLR 230]

The termination of services of an officer cannot be ordered on the vague allegation that he has a "notoriety" for corruption. The "notoriety" must be based on some thing more than a mere allegation. Any statutory employer must take care when terminating a career on the ground of unsuitability, to ensure that its order is founded on definable material objectively assessed and relevant to the ground of termination.

[*Nepal Singh* v. *State of Uttar Pradesh*, 1984 (3) SLR 126 SC]

The services of a lady constable were terminated under Punjab Police Rules by an apparently innocuous order. However, it was found that behind her back an enquiry was made about her having spent two nights with a constable and that order was based on these allegations. The order of termination was held illegal.

[*Rajinder Kaur* v. *Punjab State*, 1986 (3) SLR 78 SC]

The services of an officer in Haryana Civil Medical Service were terminated which was apparently as per terms and conditions of his appointment but it was really because of his alleged absence without leave having been sanctioned. It was held that such termination cast a stigma on the employee and natural justice ought to have been observed.

[*Balbir Singh* v. *State of Haryana*, 1989 (2) SLP 135 (P&H)]

The order of termination of service of even an *ad hoc* employee though apparently innocuous, was held illegal because there were certain allegations of embezzlement and adverse remarks.

[*Jarnail Singh* v. *State of Punjab*, AIR 1986 (2) SC 193]

Chapter 4

CIRCUMSTANCES IN WHICH COURTS MAY CALL FOR THE RECORDS OF THE CASE TO LIFT THE VEIL FROM INNOCUOUS ORDER OF TERMINATION TO SEE WHAT IS HIDDEN BEHIND IT

"There is always some reason or cause for terminating the services of a temporary employee. It is not necessary to state that reason in the order of termination communicated to the employee concerned. But where there is a specific charge of arbitrary discrimination, or some hostile motive is attributed to the authority terminating the service by the employee, it is incumbent on the authority making the impugned order to explain to the court the reason for the impugned action."

(Supreme Court)

SYNOPSIS

4.1 Law on the subject

4.2 To what extent, a Government servant is entitled to information from official records forming basis of the order of his termination

4.3 Observations of Justice Pathak of the Supreme Court on the rights of the Government servants to information from official records forming the basis of the orders terminating their services

4.4 The order of termination of services under Rule 5(1) of CCS(TS) Rules can be assailed by the Petitioner only if he is able to show that the foundation of passing the order was to punish him

4.5 The onus to prove that the order of termination of a temporary employee is camouflaged lies on the employee concerned

4.6 An order camouflaged as Termination Simpliciter with a view to avoiding inquiry under Article 311(2) of the Constitution is liable to be quashed

4.7 The Courts can look into facts and circumstances of the cases of termination of services of temporary employees to ensure that the decision is not arbitrary or capricious

4.8 Gist of the judicial judgements on the subject of lifting of veil from the innocuous order of termination by courts to see what is hidden inside

4.1 Law on the subject

Judicial opinion is divided on the subject as to whether or not the courts should delve into official records to find out the real reasons behind an apparently innocuous order of termination *i.e.* whether the courts should call for official records from the departmental authorities to lift the veil and see for itself as to what is actually hidden behind those innocent looking orders of termination. This proposition of law was discussed at great length in the case of *State of Maharashtra* v. *Veerappa R. Saboji,* 1979 SLJ 621. Justice Untwalia and Justice Pathak both legal illuminaries had divergent opinions on the subject which are discussed below.

4.2 To what extent, a Government servant is entitled to information from official records forming basis of the order of his termination

The law on the subject has been discussed at great length in *State of Maharashtra* v. *Veerappa R. Saboji,* 1979 SLJ 621. Saboji was appointed as a civil judge in December, 1960 on probation and was continued in service. His services were terminated in December, 1971 by a simple order of termination. It was alleged by Saboji that both the District Judge (K.N. Wahi) and the Inspecting District Judge (D.G. Karnik) bore ill-will against him and had made certain inquiries against him and reported the matter to the High Court and as a result of which some adverse remarks were given to him and his services terminated. When this case came up before Supreme Court, Justice Untwalia in his judgment dated 6-9-1979 observed as under:

> "I find that respondent had made only general allegations of *mala fides* against his superior officers. No specific allegations were, however, made against them that they had made reports against them to the High Court due to any ulterior motive. Merely to say, that their action was not justified and it was out of bias that they took the action, will not, in the least, constitute any allegation of *mala fide.* If it were to be permitted in such cases to examine all these

reports in detail to find out whether the reports were justified or not and then to draw an inference of *mala fide,* on that basis, where will it lead to? Then in every case the reasons for termination of service will have to be scrutinized thread bare to arrive at a conclusion that the order passed was not *mala fide.* On his own showing the respondent had earned adverse remarks before his service was terminated which clearly showed that his record was not satisfactory. The High Court, therefore, recommended to the Government that the services of respondent be terminated. The Government accepted the recommendation of the High Court and terminated his services. No allegation whatsoever of any hostile discrimination was made in the Writ Petition against the High Court or the Government, not even against the Chief Justice or any Judge of the High Court who might have dealt with the matter. Nor was any such allegation made against the Law Secretary or the Chief Secretary or any Minister of the Government. After all when the orders were passed against the respondent, the High Court must have examined the matter carefully and found that it was not desirable to allow respondent to continue in the service and must have found further that the facts did not warrant or make it expedient to hold any regular enquiry against the respondent and to remove him from service by way of punishment. I may add that the High Court file containing the recommendation in case of respondent was ready in the High Court to be shown to the Division Bench which heard the Writ Petition. But the learned Judges refused to see it because the State Counsel was not prepared to show it to respondent. Obviously it could not be shown to him. Otherwise he would have come out with a plea, right or wrong, that the order was made against him by way of punishment. This is the delicate area where the Government and the State Counsel find themselves in a peculiar and delicate position. Mr. Phadke also informed us that the High Court file was ready with him and if we liked we could see it. On the facts and in circumstances of this case we did not think it necessary to see and, therefore, we did not see....... Sh. Saboji has been unable to make out any case at all that the impugned order is by way of punishment. It is evident from the material before us. No occasion arises in such a case for scrutinizing the official records."

4.3 Observations of Justice Pathak of the Supreme Court on the rights of the Government servants to information from official records forming the basis of the orders terminating their services

"The law, it seems to me, is that where the services of a temporary Government servant or a probationer Government servant are terminated by an order which does not *ex facie* disclose any stigma or penal consequences against the Government servant is, merely a termination order simplicter there is no case ordinarily for assuming that it is anything but what it purports to be.

Where, however, the order discloses on the face of it that a stigma is cast on the Government servant or that it visits him with penal consequences, then plainly the case is one of the punishments.

There may still be another kind of case where although the termination of services is intended by way of punishment, the order is framed as a termination simpliciter. In such a case, if the Government servant is able to establish by material on the record that the order is in fact passed by way of punishment, the innocence of the language in which the order is framed will not protect it if the procedural safeguards contemplated by Article 311(2) of the Constitution have not been satisfied. In a given case, the Government servant may succeed in making out a *prima facie* case that the order was by way of punishment but an attempt to rebut the case by the authorities may necessitate for the official records for the purpose of determining the truth. It is in such a case generally that the official records may be called for by the court. It is not open to the court to send for the official records on a mere allegation by the Government servant that the order is by way of punishment. For unless there is material on the record before the Court in support of that allegation, an attempt by the Court to find out from the record whether the termination of service is based on the unsuitability of the Government servant in relation to the post held by him or is in reality an order by way of punishment will in affect be an unwarranted attempt to delve into the official records for the purpose of determining the nature of the order on the basis of a mere allegation of the Government servant. On a sufficient case being made out on the merits of the case by the Government servant, it is open to the Court to resort to scrutiny of the official records for the purpose of verifying the truth. I am unable to see why the Court should decline to peruse the official records in an appropriate case and why, where considerations of privilege and confidentiality do not suffer, the information set forth in the records should not be made available to the Government servant. The mere possibility that the official records could confirm what the Government servant had set out to prove and *prima facie* had, indeed, proved should not shut out disclosure of the information.

· What I say here in no way detracts from what this Courts has laid down in *State of Uttar Pradesh* v. *Ram Chandra Trivedi,* (1969) 3 SC 603. The court did deprecate in that case the act of the High Court in probing into the departmental correspondence that passed between the superiors of the Government servant for the purpose of determining whether the impugned order was passed by way of punishment. But it does not appear from the tests recited in that case that the Government servant had made out any case that the impugned order had been made by way of punishment and that on the claim being disputed by the State it was necessary to ascertain whether the case sought to be proved by the Government servant stood rebutted or confirmed by the departmental correspondent. I am unable to spell out from the judgment any absolute rule enunciated by this Court that where the order terminating the services of a temporary or a probationer Government servant is barred from establishing that it is in fact an order by way of punishment, and that on the Government servant succeeding in establishing it to be so the court is prohibited from examining the official records for the purpose of verifying the true position.

The question of scrutinizing the official records arises where a Government servant is entitled to show that although the order impugned by him purports to be an order of termination simpliciter it is in fact an order made by way of punishment. In regard to that right this Court specifically referred in

Ram Chandra Trivedi, (1969) 3 SC 603, to the decisions in *Union of India* v. *R.S. Dhaba* and *R.S. Sial* v. *The State of Uttar Pradesh*, (1974) 3 SCR 734 and observed:

> "The form of the order, however, is not conclusive to its true nature. The entirety of circumstances preceding or attendant on the impugned order must be examined by the court and the over-riding test will always be whether the misconduct is a mere motive or is the very foundation of the order."

In *Shamsher Singh* v. *State of Punjab*, 1975 (1) SCR 814, decided by a Bench of seven Judges of this Court, it was observed as under:

> "No abstract proposition can be laid down that where the services of a probationer are terminated without saying anything more in the order of termination it can never amount to a punishment in the facts and circumstances of the case. If, however, a probationer is discharged on the ground of misconduct, or inefficiency or for similar reason without a proper inquiry and without his getting a reasonable opportunity of showing cause against his discharge it may in a given case amount to removal from service within the meaning of Article 311(2) of the Constitution."

In the same case, it was observed further:

> "Where a departmental enquiry is contemplated and if an enquiry is not in fact proceeded with, Article 311 will not be attracted unless it can be shown that the order though unexceptionable in form is made following a report based on misconduct."

It seems clear that if a Government servant is able to establish that, although the impugned order is innocent *ex facie*, it was made on the ground that he was guilty of misconduct and, therefore, the order was intended by way of punishment. The law still is that an order, although framed in terms which do not cast an aspersion against the character and integrity of the Government servant or visit him with evil consequences, may still be proved to be in fact one by way of punishment. It is true that in *S.P. Vasudeva* v. *State of Haryana*, 1976 (2) SCR 184 this Court laid down that ordinarily the courts should not go behind an order of reversion of a person who had no right to the post, if *ex facie* it did not cast any stigma on him. But the words advisedly used were:

> ".... The Courts will normally go behind that order to see, if there were any motivating factors behind that order."

No definite principle as a rule of law appears to have been laid down in that case on the point and the Court has merely suggested that the question whether it should be open to the courts in such cases to go behind the order should be examined *de novo,* and it recommended that an order reverting a probationer from a higher to a lower post, or discharging a probationer, or discharging a temporary servant from service should not be questioned except on the basis of *mala fides* in making the order. From the further comments of the Court, it appears that the observation was made with a view to lightening the burden of the Court having regard to the heavy load of work presently occupying it. Until the day, that the recommendation is accepted, I believe it to be true that the jurisdiction of the courts extends to examining and scrutinizing the official records in the circumstances which I have specifically adverted."

4.4 The order of termination of services under Rule 5(1) of CCS (TS) Rules can be assailed by the petitioner only if he is able to show that the foundation of passing the order was to punish him

One Jarnail Singh was serving as a Sub-Inspector in Delhi Police as a temporary employee since 13-10-1969. On 11-10-1973, an F.I.R. was lodged under section 376/342/506/34 IPC against him by one Ms. Rani. The petitioner was arrested and was later on released on bail. On 16-10-1973, a report appeared in the "Indian Express" that Jarnail Singh, Sub-Inspector has been sacked, for allegedly raping the wife of a tea vendor of Chandni Chowk. It was alleged that he had gone to her house in plain clothes to check a complaint against her husband who was not present in the house. The "Patriot" of the same date also reported that Jarnail Singh was served with a notice terminating his services for allegedly raping a woman. The alleged incident as appearing in the newspapers gave variety of versions. In the criminal charge of rape, the petitioner was ultimately acquitted on 27-1-1975 because prosecutrix Rani refused to recognize him.

The services of the petitioner were terminated by an order issued under Rule 5(1) of CCS (TS) Rules, which was challenged by the petitioner in Delhi High Court in *Jarnail Singh* v. *Superintendent of Police*, 1983 (2) SLJ 101 on the ground that the said order though on the face of it innocuous, was in reality an order of punishment and that provisions of Article 311(2) of the Constitution are attracted. The case of the respondent was that the services of the petitioner were not dispensed with on account of the alleged offence. As a matter of fact when his chance came for being declared as quasi permanent, he was passed over twice on account of his unsuitable and undesirable conduct. The respondents contended that the services of the petitioner were dispensed with on account of unsuitability.

The Hon'ble High Court in its judgment dated 1-9-1982, observed as under:

> "The perusal of the records of the case show that the termination was not at all in relation to the alleged occurrence. Therefore, it cannot be said that the said occurrence was the foundation of the impugned order. The Government may have been motivated by the said occurrence but the order was not made in order to cast any stigma or impose punishment on the petitioner, rather it was done with a view to give him a chance to make good in other walks of life. In *Shamsher Singh* v. *State of Punjab*, 1974 (2) SLR 701, it was observed that an innocuous order may involve infraction of Article 311(2) where the facts and circumstances establish that an inquiry into misconduct resulting in stigma has preceded the order. No inquiry of any kind was made in this case. Hence, there is no need to tear the veil and see the hidden face of the order. The facts stated in the publication of the news in the national dailies were not the foundation of the termination. Press in India enjoy great freedom in this country and I am further of the view that if they or the Government give publicity to such news, it serves a great public purpose as deterrence is one of the commendable motives for any effective and purposeful government. If the Government is not allowed to dispense with its temporary servants who bring bad name to it, then, it is to ask it to carry an unwanted weight until an enquiry is held. What has been

worrying the courts is that stigma or blame may not be apparent but it be the real motive or the base of the order. In such cases, it has been held that if it is a motive, it is wholly irrelevant and the Court need not question it. If certain complaints or circumstances are taken into account for the purpose of considering the suitability of the employee for his continuing in service or if the impugned order is made in the background of the allegations, then a departmental inquiry is not necessary. It is only when they form the foundation of termination, then the question of punishment may arise. The facts alleged in this case, even if they formed the motive, were not the foundation of the order. The order in question, therefore, cannot be held to be punitive in nature."

4.5 The onus to prove that the order of termination of a temporary employee is camouflaged lies on the employee concerned

One Dutta was appointed as constable in the Police Force of Tripura by the Superintendent of Police, Agartala on 18-4-1954. The employment was temporary and was liable to be terminated on one month's notice. On 6-12-1957, the Superintendent of Police acting under Rule 5 of the Central Civil Services (Temporary Service) Rules, 1949, informed Dutta that his services "will be terminated w.e.f. January 6, 1958". He presented an appeal to the Chief Commissioner against the order of termination. By letter dated April 11, 1958, he was informed that since he was "an ex-convict for theft, nothing can be done for him". In reply to another application addressed to Chief Commissioner the respondent was informed by letter dated May 26, 1958 that he has already been informed in reply to his previous appeal that being "an ex convict in a case of theft", he, "cannot be re-employed by the Administration". Dutta filed a petition praying for writ declaring the order of the Superintendent of Police terminating his service as illegal. The Judicial Commissioner of Tripura held that he was a temporary employee, but the order terminating his services was invalid for it infringed the constitutional guarantee of protection of public servants under Article 311, which applied to temporary employees as well as to permanent public servants. The Union Territory of Tripura filed an appeal before the Supreme Court which reversed the judgment of the Judicial Commissioner and held that it cannot be assumed that the order *ex facie* of termination of employment of a temporary employee was intended to be one of dismissal. The onus to prove that such was the intention of the authority terminating the employment must lie upon the employee concerned. On facts it was held that there was no ground for inferring that the Superintendent of Police was seeking to camouflage an order of dismissal of a temporary police constable by giving it the form of termination of employment of the contract of service in exercise of the authority under Rule 5 of the Central Civil Services (Temporary Service) Rules.

[*Union of Territory Tripura* v. *Gopal Chandran Dutta Choudhary*, AIR 1963 SC 601]

4.6 An order camouflaged as Termination Simpliciter with a view to avoiding inquiry under Article 311(2) of the Constitution is liable to be quashed

One Uttam Mandal was appointed as a temporary Child Development Project Officer. A Memo was issued to him alleging that he failed to maintain absolute integrity and devotion to duty in certain matters. His reply was considered but was not found satisfactory and his services were terminated. He challenged the order alleging that this was nothing but a camouflage with a view to avoid inquiry. This case came up for consideration before Gauhati High Court in *Uttam Mandal* v. *State of Tripura*, 1993 (3) SLJ 163 in which it was held as under:

"It was found that a number of allegations were brought against the petitioner and his explanation was also called for. In the counter affidavit, it has also been averred that there were serious complaints against the petitioner by the local public and that during enquiries it was found that those allegations were true. The order of termination also shows that this order of termination was passed after hearing the petitioner. It is, therefore, evident that the authority was not satisfied with the explanation submitted by the petitioner and hence the order of termination was passed. In the circumstances it has to be held that it was the alleged acts of indiscipline and negligence in performance of duties were the basis and foundation for terminating the services of the petitioner. Therefore, the order was nothing but a camouflage with a view to avoiding an inquiry warranted by Article 311(2) of the Constitution and is, therefore, quashed."

4.7 The Courts can look into facts and circumstances of the cases of termination of services of temporary employees to ensure that the decision is not arbitrary or capricious

The services of one Y.N. Reddy, a Field Publicity Assistant were terminated under Rule 5(1) without assigning any reason. This was challenged by the petitioner in the Andhra High Court in *Y.N. Reddy* v. *U.O.I.*, 1983 (2) SLJ 700, on the ground that the order was violative of Articles 14 and 16 of the Constitution. He pleaded that in view of the judgment of the Supreme Court in *Manager, Government Branch Press* v. *D.B. Balliappa,* AIR 1979 SC 429, his services could not have been terminated arbitrarily and that it was necessary for the Government to explain the circumstances and reasons which induced it to put an end to the services of the petitioner. The case of the respondent was that the petitioner had also been absenting himself from duty even without leave on more than one occasion. The Hon'ble High Court in its judgment dated 31-8-1982 observed as under:

"The order under which he was removed does not by itself cast a stigma on the petitioner. An examination of the facts and circumstances would reveal that the termination of the services of the petitioner is wholly justified. The department has ample evidence that he is not suitable for discharging the duties of the post given to him. The order was neither capricious nor arbitrary. Even in those circumstances, it would have been better for the department to have given notice to the petitioner and hold a summary enquiry. But in view of the fact that these facts are admitted by the petitioner himself and are not denied, I do not propose to take that default of the department into account in this case."

4.8 Gist of the judicial judgments on the subject of lifting of veil from the innocuous order of termination by courts to see what is hidden inside

"The circumstances preceding and attendant on the order of termination of service have to be examined in each case.

On such an examination, it should be found out whether the termination was essentially one based on unsuitability of the person to the service, or whether its real basis was punishment."

[*State of Punjab* v. *Sukh Raj Bahadur*, AIR 1968 SC 1089]

"No such rigid principle has ever been laid down by this Court that one has only to look to the order' and if it does not contain any imputation of misconduct, or words attaching a stigma to the character or reputation of a Government Officer, it must be held to have been made in the ordinary course of administrative routine, and that Court is debarred from looking at, all the attendant circumstances to discover whether the order had been made by way of punishment. The form of the order is not conclusive of its true nature, and it might merely be a cloak or camouflage for an order formed on misconduct......... The entirety of circumstances preceding or attendant on the impugned order must be examined..."

[*State of Bihar* v. *S.B. Mishra*, 1970 SLR 863]

In the case of *K.H. Phadnis* v. *State of Maharashtra*, 1971 (2) SLR 345, a Division Bench Judgement of 5 Hon'ble Judges of the Supreme Court, delivered in March, 1971. Termination of services of the Government servant was held to be violative of the provisions of Article 311 of the Constitution, even though the impugned order did not contain any express words of stigma. The Hon'ble Supreme Court went behind the form of the impugned order, and looked at the attendant circumstances, and discovered that the order had been made by way of punishment without following the procedure....."

"The mere form of the order in respect of even a temporary, or officiating Government servant is not decisive..... If the order involves a penalty, even if on the face of it the order does not bear any such impress (of stigma), the officer prejudiced by the making of that order, is entitled to prove that he has been denied the protection of the guarantee under Article 311 of the Constitution of India."

[*Jagdish Prasad Shastri* v. *State of Uttar Pradesh*, 1970 SLR 938]

The services of a probationer were terminated by passing a simple order of a termination. There were, however, serious allegations against him for which no inquiry had been conducted. It was held that form of order cannot be regarded as decisive but its substance has to be seen.

[*Ram Saran Das* v. *State of Punjab*, 1967 SLR 771]

"The form of the order in such cases is not conclusive and the tribunal (Court) can go behind the order to find the reasons which led to the order and then consider for itself whether the termination was a 'Colourable Exercise of Power'. If it (*i.e.* the Court) comes to the conclusion that the termination was a 'Colourable exercise of the power' or was a result of victimization......... it would have the jurisdiction to intervene and set aside such termination."

[*Michael* v. *Johnson Pumps Ltd.*, 1975 SLJ 369]

"An order terminating the services of a temporary servant or a probationer, if it is by way of punishment, will attract Article 311 of the Constitution; the form of the order is not conclusive, it is the substance of the matter that has to be looked into. Whether or not an order of termination is by way of punishment would depend on the facts and circumstances of each case.

[*State of Punjab* v. *Prakash Singh Cheema*, 1975 SLJ 449]

"If the facts and circumstances of the case indicate that the substance of the order is that the termination is by way of punishment, then a probationer is entitled to the protection of Article 311. The substance of the order, and not the form would be decisive."

[*Shamsher Singh* v. *State of Punjab*, AIR 1974 SC 2192]

"A.A. Singh was the Principal of a College. While reading the Annual Report, he made certain aspersions against some members of teaching staff. Thereafter, an enquiry was made pursuant to the demand of some of the parents of the students. Two Deputy Directors made an enquiry. At the enquiry, Shri Singh was neither given copies of statements recorded, nor was he allowed to cross-examine the witnesses. The State contended that it was a preliminary confidential enquiry into the affairs of the College, and after the inquiry, the department decided that Singh has no right to continue in Class-I appointment where he was only officiating. The High Court held that the order of reversion was not by way of punishment, but only because the person reverted was not found suitable to hold the post. The enquiry was only to find out the state of affairs of the normal functioning of the College. The Supreme Court, however, held that the enquiry by the Deputy Directors was to investigate allegations against the Principal and the Deputy Directors had recommended exemplary punishment to Singh. Therefore, the order amounted to "reduction in rank" and since no enquiry regarding disciplinary proceedings was held, the order was in violation of the provisions of Article 311."

It is pertinent to point out here that Shri Singh first succeeded at the hands of a single judge in the High Court; and thereafter lost in the "Letters Patent Appeal" before the Division Bench in the High Court; and at last he succeeded once again in the Supreme Court. The Apex Court held:

"In deciding whether an order is passed by way of punishment, the form in which it is expressed is not decisive. When the antecedent enquiry is not only to find out the suitability of employee, but with a view to investigate the allegation against the employees, then action will be punitive."

[*Appar Apar Singh* v. *State of Punjab*, (1970) 3 SCC 338]

"If a Minister states, in answer to a Legislative Assembly Question, that the services of a particular Government servant were not satisfactory, and if the services are terminated without any enquiry being held, then in that event, this fact would inevitably lead the public to believe that his services had been terminated on account of inefficiency or misconduct; and this does cast a stigma on his character. In this circumstance, the Supreme Court held that the provisions of Article 311(2) of the Constitution were not complied with."

[*Madan Mohan Prasad* v. *State of Bihar*, 1973 SLJ 349]

"If the action of terminating the service of a temporary, probationary officiating civil servant is taken 'not in the usual course of Administration', but as a 'measure of Punitive Action' against the civil servant, either on consideration of some complaints against him, or on finding about his inefficiency, that will be subject to the provisions of Article 311(2). Either the adverse order itself may show its punitive nature, or the facts and circumstances prior and leading to that order may disclose that, not the disguised form of the order itself, but the substance of the matter will determine the character and nature of the order. "

[*Shiv Bhikshuk Mishra* v. *State of Bihar*, AIR 1966 Pat 364]

In a decision taken by the Delhi High Court, the employee Shri Samar Singh, whose services were terminated under Rule 5 of the C.C.S. (TS) Rules, 1965, without assigning any reason, ultimately succeeded, because the Court went behind the form of the order and ascertained the true nature of the order which was indeed an order of punishment without complying with the provisions of Article 311 of the Constitution.

[*Samar Singh* v. *The Comptroller & Auditor General of India*, 1976 SLR 266]

In a case, the services of 5 employees were terminated forthwith in pursuance of the proviso to Sub-rule (1) of Rule 5 the Central Civil Services (TS) Rules, 1965 without assigning any reason. Even then the High Court of Kerala went behind the form of the order, and found out that the termination of services was not in usual course, nor for any administrative reason, but was as and by way of punishment without holding an inquiry. Therefore, the Hon'ble Court allowed he petition, after relying upon the principles emerging from the judgment of the Supreme Court, in AIR 1971 SC 1011, and AIR 1964 SC 1854.

[*Gangadhara Kurup* v. *Deputy Accountant General*, 1976 KLT 268]

In a case, a probationer was discharged from service with a 'simple order' of termination. The impugned order was innocuously worded, and it was made to appear that it was a discharge simpliciter. Even then the High Court of Karnataka went behind the order and found out that Order was by way of punishment without holding an inquiry; and, there allowed the writ petitioner.

[*K.S. Raghuramaiah* v. *Deputy General Manager & Divisional Controller, Karnataka State Road Transport Corporation*, 1980 SLJ 353]

In a case, the impugned order of purported termination read, as if it was a simple order of termination under Rule 5. But on an examination of the circumstances preceding the order of termination of service, it was found out that:

(a) the termination was not one based on unsuitability of the person to the service; but

(b) its real basis was punishment.

[*Director, Defence Research & Development Laboratories, Hyderabad* v. *C. Pandu, Instrument Mechanic*, AIR 1977 AP 4]

In a Division Bench decision of the Madhya Pradesh High Court, it went behind the order of the termination, and found that though the order of termination does not contain express words of stigma to the character or conduct of the petitioner, the said order was punitive in nature the said order was passed as and by way of punishment for some alleged misconduct, for which no proper enquiry was held. For this reason, the petition was allowed.

[*A.M. Rode* v. *Principal, Government Degree College, Chhindwara*, 1973 MP LJ 666]

For determining whether the order terminating the services of a temporary Government servant has been occasioned because of departmental exigency or is by way of punishment, the Court is entitled to look into the surrounding circumstances; the language in which the order is couched is not conclusive.

[*Sushma Rai* v. *The State*, 1976 LIC 1292]

In a case, the termination of services was done without holding inquiry; and the termination was during the probation-period, and the same was on the report of misconduct. It was held that:

> "the order of termination is a termination simplicitor, but by way of punishment. The order of termination being violative of Article 311(2) was to be quashed."

[*H.K. Srivastva* v. *Meerut University*, 1977 LIC 176]

In a case, an order of termination of service did not contain any reason and purported to have been passed in accordance with the service-conditions of the petitioner, he being a temporary employee. The attending circumstances and the sequence of events preceding the impugned order left no room for doubt that it was not a termination simpliciter occasioned by departmental exigencies but an order of punishment because of the adverse remarks against him in the inspection note. No regular inquiry was instituted after the petitioner denied the charges against him. In this case, it was held:

> "that the impugned order could not be upheld as the petitioner had been denied the protection contained in Article 311(2)"

[*Jagdish Prasad Pandey* v. *Collector, Deputy Director of Consolidation*, 1975 LIC 858: (1975) 1 All LR 62]

In a case, the petitioner was holding a temporary appointment. An enquiry about his alleged misconduct was held, and the disciplinary proceedings were abandoned and an 'innocuous order' of termination of his services was made, relying on service conditions. The High Court held that:

> "the simple order of termination was, in reality and truth, an order of punishment without holding proper inquiry."

[*Prasan Kumar Sadangi* v. *State of Orissa*, 1974 SLJ 667]

In a case an inquiry was made, and in the inquiry the statement of the petitioner was recorded; and on receiving the report of the Inquiry, the services were terminated by a 'simple order' of termination. The High Court, therefore, took into consideration, the surrounding circumstances to find out the real nature of termination order, and quashed the termination order.

[*Sarju Singh* v. *Additional District Magistrate, Faizabad*, Short Note No. 14 of 1973 SLJ]

Chapter 5

RELEVANCE OF 'MOTIVE' AND 'FOUNDATION' IN PASSING ORDERS OF TERMINATION OF SERVICES OF EMPLOYEES

"If the material against the Government servant on which the superior authority has acted constitutes the "motive" but not the "foundation", the order of termination cannot be held to be illegal. The function of the Court is to discover the nature of the order by attempting to ascertain what was the motivating consideration in the mind of the authority which prompted the order".

(Supreme Court)

SYNOPSIS

5.1 Distinction between "Motive" and "Foundation" in relation to orders of termination of services passed by the competent authority

This point came up for consideration before Delhi High Court in *U.O.I.* v. *B.C. Gupta*, 1980 SLJ 316 and the Hon'ble Court in its judgment dated 4-1-1980 observed as under:

> "It will be difficult to lay down or enunciate as to under what circumstances it can be said that an act of misconduct is the foundation or the motive of the order. It is obvious that before any order is passed terminating the services of a temporary employee, some reasons must necessarily be recorded for taking such an action. If no reasons are found on the files, an aggrieved employee would be justified in challenging the same as being arbitrary.

In our opinion, if a specific incident of misconduct alone is gone into and action is taken terminating the services of a temporary employee on the basis of that incident then, it could be justifiably said that the incident of misconduct is the foundation for the said action. In such a case there would be no other reason for taking action against a temporary employee.

If on the other hand, such an incident of misconduct is one of the factors which is taken into consideration along with a number of other facts and an overall view is then formed to terminate the services of a temporary employee then in those circumstances it cannot be said that the said incident was the foundation of the order of termination."

5.2 The order of termination of services of a temporary employee cannot be challenged if the motivating factor in mind of the competent authority is not to impose a punishment

One Nepal Singh was a temporary Sub-Inspector of Police. He was proceeded against departmentally for having contracted a second marriage while his first wife was alive. Later on, the proceedings were dropped. I.G. of Police under whom Nepal Singh was working issued a circular letter to all S.Ps. under his jurisdiction to submit a list of all Sub-Inspectors whose reputation and integrity were low or who were generally involved in scandalous conduct, drinking, immorality or other acts nefarious to the reputation of the Police or who were involved in encouraging crime. The name of Nepal Singh figured in that list and his services were terminated without assigning any reason. The petitioner challenged the order of termination in the Supreme Court in *Nepal Singh* v. *State of Uttar Pradesh*, 1980 SLJ 711 (SC), which observed as under:

> "In the present appeal, the appellant was a temporary Government servant. The question whether he should be retained in service was a matter which arose directly during the drive instituted by the Inspector General of Police in March, 1970, for weeding out police officers who were unsuitable or unfit to be continued in service. The Superintendents of Police prepared a list of Sub-Inspectors functioning within their jurisdiction, and included the name of the appellant in that list. The material which was considered was sufficient to lead to the conclusion that the appellant, who was a temporary Government servant, was not suitable for being retained in service. His general character and conduct led to that impression. There is nothing to show that the impugned order was made by way of punishment. The circumstances that disciplinary proceeding had been instituted against him earlier does not in itself lead to the inference that the impugned order was by way of punishment. As we have observed, that is a conclusion which must follow from the nature of the intent behind the order. That intention can be discovered and proved, like any other fact, from the evidence on the record. In this case, it is not proved that the impugned order was intended by way of punishment."

5.3 Even if misconduct, negligence, inefficiency may be the motive or the inducing factor which influences the authority to terminate the services of the employee on probation, such termination cannot be termed as penalty or punishment

One P.S. Bhatt was appointed as an Announcer in All India Radio on 29-5-1972 and he was subsequently promoted as a Producer on probation on 7-7-1975. While on probation, a Memo dated 1-12-1976 was issued to him which reads as under:

> "It has been brought to my notice that Shri P.S. Bhatt, Producer (Women and Children) has conducted himself in a manner not conducive to the discipline of the office by indulging himself in loose talk in the studios on 16-11-1976. A serious view is being taken of such an irresponsible lapse on his part. He is severally warned of such misdemeanour."

Subsequently, he was reverted to the post of Announcer *vide* order dated 28-1-1977 which reads as under:

> "Shri P.S. Bhatt, Producer (Women and Children), All India Radio, Vijayawada is informed, that during his probation period in the present post, he has not been found suitable for the post of Producer. It has therefore been decided by the Directorate to revert him back to the post of Announcer with immediate effect *i.e.* from the afternoon of 28th January, 1977."

This case came up before Supreme Court in *U.O.I.* v. *P.S. Bhatt*, 1981 (1) SLJ 212 which in its judgment dated 11-2-1981 observed as under:

> "On a proper consideration of the facts, in our opinion, it cannot be said that the impugned order was passed by way of punishment; and in that view, the High Court was in error in arriving at the finding that the impugned order was by way of punishment. The report of the Station Director had influenced the Director General to pass the said order. Loose talks and filthy and abusive language which had been used against the Station Director and the other officers may legitimately, in the facts and circumstances of the case, lead to the formation of a reasonable belief in the minds of the authorities that the person behaving in such fashion is not a suitable person to be employed as a Producer. This undesirable conduct on the part of Shri Bhatt might have been the motive for terminating the employment on probation and for reverting him to his previous post of Announcer. Even though misconduct, negligence, inefficiency or other disqualification may be the motive or the inducing factor which influences the Government to take action under the terms of the contract of employment or the specific service rule, nevertheless, if a right exists, under the contract or the rules, to terminate the services the motive operating on the mind of the Government is wholly irrelevant."

5.4 The mere fact that because a preliminary inquiry in the case was held can not be a ground to hold that it was the foundation of the order of termination if overall service record of the petitioner had been taken into account while ordering termination of services

One B.C. Gupta, a temporary employee was put on probation for a period of two years. During the said period of probation, his services were terminated under Rule 5(1) of TS Rules, without assigning any reason. He assailed the order of termination on the ground that it was, in fact, an order of penalty since it is connected with an incident dated 23-6-1978 in which he was involved in some controversy with his superior officer. A preliminary inquiry in the said case had been conducted in which he had been held guilty. According to the petitioner, the incident of 23-6-1978 was the foundation of the order of his termination and bad in law. This case came up for consideration before Delhi High Court which in its judgment dated 4-1-1980 observed as under:

> "It may be that the question as to the retention of B.C. Gupta came up for consideration as a result of the said incident but the decision to terminate his services was taken by taking into consideration his overall performance, conduct and behaviour. The very fact that his conduct since 1976 was commented upon by the officer conducting Preliminary inquiry clearly shows that he was commenting on the performance of B.C. Gupta by taking his entire service into consideration and not merely the single incident of 23rd June, 1978. We are, therefore, of the opinion that the incident of 23rd June, 1978 may have been the motive for passing the impugned order but was certainly not the foundation of the said order. The order of termination of service is upheld."

[*U.O.I.* v. *B.C. Gupta*, 1980 SLJ 316]

5.5 An *ad hoc* employee cannot be reverted without issuing charge sheet when the foundation of the said order is on the ground of his misconduct

One Jethani Mohan Chanchaldas was appointed as a civil Judge on *ad hoc* basis on 16-4-1975. He was reverted to his previous post of Assistant Public Prosecutor on 6-4-1979 without assigning any reason. He challenged the order of his reversion in

Bombay High Court. On perusal of the records of the case, the court found that the judge had misconducted himself in a suit filed by his own mother in his own court against an Income Tax Officer. The Court observed:

> "We feel that the order of reversion passed against the petitioner was clearly founded upon misconduct alleged against the petitioner. The said papers disclose that an inquiry was in fact contemplated but it was not held. It appears, therefore, clear to us that the said misconduct of the petitioner was the basis or foundation of the order and not merely a motive for doing so. In our view, therefore, that the said order of reversion against the petitioner was clearly by way of punishment and since it was made without giving the petitioner an opportunity of being heard, the said order was vitiated and was liable to be set aside."

[*Jethani Mohan Chanchaldas* v. *U.O.I.*, 1984 (1) SLJ 76]

5.6 Gist of judicial judgments on the subject of relevance of Motive/Foundation in orders of termination passed by authorities

It will be case of "Motive" if the master, after gathering some *prima facie* facts, does not really wish to go into their truth but decides merely not to continue dubious employee. But if he conducts inquiry only for the purpose of proving the misconduct and the employee is not heard, it is a case where inquiry is the "foundation" and the termination will be bad.

[*Radhey Shyam Gupta* v *U.P. State Agro Industries Corporation Ltd.*, 1999 (1) SLR 44].

If findings are arrived at in the inquiry as to misconduct behind the back of the officer or without a regular departmental inquiry, then simple order of termination is to be treated as "founded" on allegation and will be bad but if the inquiry was not held, no findings were arrived at and the employer was not inclined to conduct an inquiry but at the same time, he did not want to continue the employee against whom there were complaints, it will only be a case of "motive" and the order will not be bad.

[*Dipti Prakash Bannerjee* v. *Satvendra Nath Bose, National Centre for Basic Sciences, Calcutta,* AIR 1999 SC 983]

If the material against the Government servant on which the superior authority has acted constitutes the "motive" and not the "foundation", then the order of termination cannot be held "to be illegal". The application of the test is not always easy. In each case, it is necessary to examine the entire range carefully and consider whether in the light of those facts, the superior authority intended to punish the Government servant or having regard to his character , conduct and suitability in relation to the post held by him, it was simply intended to terminate his services. The function of the Court is to discover the nature of the order by attempting to ascertain what was the motivating consideration in the mind of the authority which prompted the order.

[*Nepal Singh* v. *State of Uttar Pradesh*, AIR 1980 SC 1459]

Note—There are large number of other judgments of the courts as well on the subject-matter of relevance of "Motive/ Foundation" on the part of the competent authorities in passing orders of termination which are discussed else where in the book under appropriate heads which may be referred to while studying the chapter.

Chapter 6

ROLE OF THE COURTS IN SAFEGUARDING THE INTERESTS OF THE TEMPORARY EMPLOYEES AGAINST MISUSE OF PROVISIONS OF CCS (TS) RULES BY THEIR EMPLOYERS IN TERMINATION CASES

"Master and servants cannot be permitted to play hide and seek with the law of termination. The courts will find out from other proceedings or relevant documents what the true ground of termination is i.e. whether the order of termination has punitive fervour or that it is just an innocuous order of termination."

(Supreme Court)

SYNOPSIS

6.1 Does the law of termination of services put a premium concealment of truth?

6.2 The writ petitions seeking relief from the courts must be filed within a reasonable time from the date of the impugned orders

6.3 The services of the employees cannot be terminated on the basis of stay orders passed by the courts in writ petitions unless there are specific directions to that effect in the orders of the courts

6.4 Instances of the cases where the courts have shown compassion in dealing with hard cases of termination of services of the employees

6.5 The Courts do not give relief to persons who were appointed only as a stop-gap arrangement to meet emergent situations since they have no vested right to hold the posts

6.1 Does the law of termination of services put a premium concealment of truth?

It is well settled for about a half of a century now since the decision of the Supreme Court in *Parshotam Lal Dhingra's* case, AIR 1958 SC 36 which has been described by the Supreme Court itself as "the Magna Carta of the Indian Civil Servants" that employment of a temporary Government servant can be terminated under the terms of the contract of employment or under the rules of service governing him by a simple order of discharge without disclosing any reason and without casting any aspersion against him or attaching any stigma on his conduct or character. But if it is shown that the order of termination casts or purports to cast some aspersion or imputation or stigma against the temporary servant then even though, it is justified under the relevant facts or circumstances, such termination would amount to dismissal under Article 311 of the Constitution and cannot be effective without complying with the provisions of the said Article. Thus, even in the matter of temporary appointments, the State is not a free master to hire and then to fire an employee in any manner it likes in its absolute pleasure, because the position in law is that if the fired employee; though employed temporarily, can show that such firing has left some scar on him, the firing would be declared unlawful, unless the constitutional requirements of Article 311 are fulfilled. However, one may criticise this state of law as it is interpreted today. The fact remains that if an employer finds his temporary employee to be absolutely unsuitable or undesirable or inefficient and terminates his employment expressly and avowedly on such ground, the employer gets himself caught in the coils of law. But if the employer is cautious or clever enough to conceal the truth and takes care not to call a spade a spade and terminates the temporary employment by just an order of termination simpliciter, his order is unscrutable and immune from all judicial scrutiny. The employers have rightly been advised to remember the good old precept.... *'Satyam Bruyat, Priyam Bruyat, Na Bruyat Satyam Apriyam'* ... *i.e.* tell the truth, but only the pleasant truth and never the unpleasant truth, even though one might wonder as to whether the law intends to put a premium on concealment of truth.

6.2 The writ petitions seeking relief from the courts must be filed within a reasonable time from the date of the impugned orders

The services of one Goyal who was a member of Rajasthan Higher Judicial Service were terminated on 4-5-1975. He filed a writ petition in Rajasthan High Court under Article 226 of the Constitution against the order of his termination, which was rejected on the ground of delay alone in approaching the Court. Explaining the scope of the term "delay", the court observed:

"We have heard the appellant at length and have considered the cases cited by him. In *P.S. Deodhar* v. *State of Maharashtra*, AIR 1974 SC 259, it was observed that the rule which says that a Court may not enquire into belated or stale claims is not a rule of law but a rule of practice based on sound and proper exercise of discretion, and there is no inviolable rule that whenever there is delay, the Court must necessarily refuse to entertain the writ petition. The question is one of the discretion to be followed on the facts of each case. These observations were also subsequently also adopted in *Jogindernath* v. *Union of India*, SLJ 1975 SN 42 where the writ petition filed even after two years was not thrown out, as the filing of the writ petition was not considered designedly delayed. In *P.S. Sadasivaswamy* v. *State of Tamil Nadu*, 1975 SLJ 80, the Supreme Court did, no doubt, purport to say that a person should approach the Court within 6 months or at the most a year of such orders but the High Court can refuse to exercise its extraordinary powers under Article 226, in case of persons who do not approach expeditiously for relief and put forward stale claim and try to unsettle settled matters. The learned Single Judge did rightly observe that there is no hard and fast rule regarding the time within which a writ petition must be filed and yet considering the responsible and important nature of the post, the delay of one year disentitled the petitioner from making the petition. The only explanation which the petitioner had to offer for delay in the case was that, in the first instance, he filed a representation, but the learned Single Judge considered that such a representation, which is not provided for by the Rules, was a mere exercise in futility. We are in entire agreement with these observations of the learned Single Judge. The writ petition cannot be entertained being belated."

[*Ram Charan Lal Goel* v. *State of Rajasthan*, 1977 SLJ 601]

6.3 The services of the employees cannot be terminated on the basis of stay orders passed by the courts in writ petitions unless there are specific directions to that effect in the orders of the courts

One Narinder Kumar and others were appointed as Peons/ Sewadars/Chowkidars on regular basis on the recommendations of D.P.C. Earlier, they had been working on contract basis. They were, however, relieved of their regular postings after about three months in view of the *ex parte* interim orders passed in other writ petitions filed by other interested employees. No inquiry was instituted nor any notice or opportunity of hearing was given to the aggrieved employees. There were no directions from the court about the termination of their services. This case came up before the Punjab and Haryana High Court which in its judgment dated 4-5-1998 quashed the concerned order and allowed the petitioners to resume their respective duties with all consequential benefits.

[*Narinder Kumar* v. *State of Punjab*, 1998 (4) RSJ 493]

6.4 Instances of the cases where the courts have shown compassion in dealing with hard cases of termination of services of the employees

One Dr. Avtar Singh was working as a House Surgeon in Rajinder Hospital Patiala and his term was to expire on 31-12-1981. During the period he was serving in the said capacity, he was selected for the post of medical officer subject to the condition that his character and antecedents were satisfactory. He was permitted to join the post by 31-12-1981. While still working in the hospital, his name came to be associated with an agitation by the Nursing Staff of the Hospital and the conduct of Dr. Singh was considered as unbecoming of an employee because of the language used by him while replying to the show-cause notice served on him in that regard. His services were terminated as House Surgeon. Further, his selection for the post of Medical Office was also cancelled on the ground of his character and antecedents having not been certified as satisfactory. He sought relief in the matter before the Supreme Court which in its judgment dated 17-2-1983 observed as under:

> "We asked learned counsel appearing on behalf of the appellant whether the offence which the appellant is alleged to have been caused to the respondent can be retrieved by showing some sense of remorse by him though the "remorse" need not be expressed in any particular form which may permanently be held out against the budding doctor at the threshold of his career as a permanent stigma to be suffered by him throughout his life. Thereupon, the appellant unconditionally withdrew all the averments that he had made in reply to the show cause notice and added that if the language used by him had offended any one, it was never meant to hurt any one. At best it was an attempt of a young man at the threshold of his career to defend and save his character. The learned counsel unconditionally withdrew all the averments made in reply to the show cause notice. In our opinion, that is sufficient remorse and the chapter must end there."

[*Dr. Avtar Singh* v. *Medical Supdtt., Rajinder Hospital Patiala*, 1983 (2) SLJ 497]

An employee appointed on compassionate ground was found to have been irregularly employed after he had put in 16 years of service . His services were terminated without issuing any show cause notice. It was held that removing him from service at this stage will virtually relegate him to a life of penury and destitution. Order of termination was set aside with a direction to treat the petitioner as having been regularly appointed with all consequential benefits that flow from the order in terms of seniority, emoluments and promotion, etc.

[*Pritam Singh* v. *State of Haryana*, 1992 (5) SLR 503 (P&H)]

Where a person has rendered five years service in a department, he cannot be treated as temporary or for that matter removed on that basis. A temporary employee cannot be kept in suspended animation indefinitely. A person who is temporarily appointed but kept for 5 years acquires a mantle of permanence.

[*Laxman Mahadev Tuli* v. *Principal Shri Panchan Khemraj Mahavidyalaya Savantwadi (Bombay)*, 1988 (6) SLR 466 (DB)]

One Narendra Kumar Chandla was working as Sub-Station Attendant in Haryana State Electricity Board in the scale of Rs. 1400-2300. Due to cancer, his right arm was amputated. The doctor however certified that he was fit to resume his normal duties. Looking to his deformity, the respondents offered him a lower post of Carrier Attendant in the scale of Rs. 825-1300 with which he was not satisfied. He sought relief in this case from the High Court in the matter which, however, dismissed his writ petition. He then approached the Supreme Court which sought medical opinion in his case in the first instance and then after considering the same observed as under in their judgment dated 4-2-1994:

> "Article 21 protects the right to livelihood as an integral part to life. When an employee is afflicted with unfortunate disease due to which he is unable to perform the duties of the post he was holding, the employer must make every endeavour to adjust him in a post in which the employee would be suitable to discharge the duties. Asking the appellant to discharge the duties as Carrier Attendant is unjust........In view of the facts and circumstances of this case, we direct the respondent to appoint him to the post of L.D.C. and to relax the requirement of passing of typing test. Since he has been rehabilitated in the post of L.D.C., we direct the Respondents to protect his scale of pay of Rs. 1400-2300 and pay all arrears of salary.

[*Narendra Kumar Chandla* v. *State of Haryana*, 1994(2) SLJ 133 (SC)]

Sudhan Chandra Dey and others were employed as volunteers by Eastern Railways to help the staff to check ticket less travel. They were paid Rs. 8 each day. They worked for a long period without break. The scheme was abolished and the services of the volunteers were terminated. The effected employees sought relief and the Hon'ble Supreme Court in its decision dated 27-8-1998 regularised the services of the volunteers as casual employees with temporary status. This decision was taken not in recognition of their rights but with a view to solving human problem.

[*Sudhan Chandra Dey* v. *U.O.I.*, 1998 (4) RSJ SC 168]

A class IV employee's son was appointed on compassionate grounds on the condition that he would produce succession certificate within one month. He could not do so and his services were terminated. It was held that one month's time was woefully inadequate and the termination was held arbitrary.

[*Anwari Begum* v. *G.M.S.E. Railway*, 1988 (7) SLR 680 CAT (Cal)]

Orders terminating services of temporary employees were quashed on the ground of being "not *bona fide*" where they had worked for over a decade continuously in the department and the vacancies also existed and new entrants had been appointed.

[*Daya Kishan* v. *State of Haryana*, 1989 (1) SLR 432 (P&H)]

Article 21 of the Constitution of India lays down that no person shall be deprived of his life and personal liberty except according to procedure established by law. Article 311 of the Constitution compliments this Article in that it describes in detail the procedure which has to be followed before the penalty of dismissal, removal or reduction in rank is imposed on a civil servant. Thus Article 21 and Article 311 of the Constitution are inter-linked.

[*Board of Trustees, Port of Bombay* v. *Dilip Kumar*, AIR 1983 SC 109]

The Central Government employees went on one day's strike on 19-9-1968. A policy statement was issued by Government on the eve of the strike that all those who volunteer to work on that day will be considered for appointment to regular posts in relaxation of normal rules. One Nagaraju was working at that time as Extra Departmental Mail carrier and he did not join the strike. Later on, he staked his claim for appointment to the post of Postman on "regular basis" on the strength of the assurance held out in the policy statement. His representations to the departmental officers were rejected. He approached the Andhra Pradesh High Court for relief which in its judgment dated 28-12-1976 observed as under:

> "It has been pleaded by the petitioner that on that day, he had not only discharged his normal duties as an extra-departmental agent but had also performed extra duty at the Head Post Office on account of the fact that the employees working there had also gone on strike. According to him, therefore, in addition to his being an extra departmental agent he also qualified himself as a volunteer in as much as he had done extra duty resulting from the strike of the

Central Government employees on that day. It is undisputed that the petitioner had volunteered to do more work than he would have been otherwise required to do as an extra departmental agent. Since he did more work he qualified himself as a volunteer for appointment to a regular post in terms of the policy statement issued by the Central Government. He ought to have therefore been considered for the appointment to the post of postman. The departmental officers were in error in rejecting his application. In my opinion therefore the respondents should be directed to consider his application for his appointment to the post of a postman in terms of the policy statement issued by the Central Government in 1968 on the eve of the strike. I direct them accordingly. Nothing more can be done in this writ petition."

[*K. Nagaraju* v. *Post Master General, A.P. Circle,* 1977 SLJ 423 (AP)]

6.5 The courts do not give relief to persons who were appointed only as a stop-gap arrangement to meet emergent situations since they have no vested right to hold the posts

One Raj Rani and many others were appointed as Staff Nurses on contract basis for fixed tenures during the strike by regular staff nurses of Health Department of Haryana State during the year 1998. They were paid a salary of Rs. 200 per day. Their services were terminated when the strike was called off and the regular staff joined their duties. The petitioners pleaded that the action of the Government in terminating their services was arbitrary, irrational, unconstitutional and unjustified on the ground that they had been appointed on the basis of selection made by the competent authority. The stand of the Government was that the petitioners were appointed only as stop gap arrangement to cope with the situation created by the strike and that they have now become surplus due to the joining of duties by the regular staff. They have no vested right to hold the posts. This case came up before Punjab & Haryana High Court which in its judgment dated 22-9-1998 observed as under:

"We do not find any merit in the argument that the termination of the services of the petitioners is vitiated by

> arbitrariness or *mala fides*. Admittedly, the petitioners were engaged by the Government for a fixed tenure in order to meet out an contingency. While joining the service, the petitioners knew that their services can be terminated on the joining of regular staff. This is precisely what the Government has done. Therefore, there is no valid reason to hold that the respondents have acted in violation of the Articles 14 and 16 of Constitution.

We do not find any plausible or cogent reason to entertain the plea that a *mandamus* be issued to the respondents to frame a scheme for absorption of the petitioners against the vacant posts of Staff Nurses. We deem it proper to observe that in such policy matters the Court cannot issue a direction to the Government. Any such request must be addressed to the Government and not to the Court."

[*Raj Rani* v. *State of Haryana*, 1998 (4) RSJ 639]

Chapter 7

GIST OF THE LEADING JUDGMENTS RELATING TO TERMINATION OF SERVICES OF TEMPORARY EMPLOYEES

The Tribunals and the Courts have been delivering classic judgments from time to time on the subject of termination of services of temporary employees etc. which have enriched the literature on the subject, but unfortunately, these are scattered and reported in different journals. An attempt has been made hereunder to present the judgments at one place in a lucid language for proper understanding even by a layman. The readers will find that reference about some of these judgments have been made in the previous chapters in the book as well.

SYNOPSIS

7.1 It is necessary to go through the judgments in full in order to comprehend the import of the fine points of law discussed therein

It may appear on first hand after going through the gist of the judgments discussed below that there are certain apparent contradictions in the law on the subject as expounded by various Tribunals and Courts. This apprehension may or may not be correct. It is, therefore, necessary to go through the judgments in full in order to comprehend the true import of fine points of law discussed therein since facts and circumstances may be different in each case. In any case, the judgments of the Apex Court on the subject supplant any contradictory judgment delivered by subordinate courts.

7.2 Gist of judgments relating to termination of services of temporary employees

The services of a temporary Government servant can be terminated in accordance with the rules applicable to temporary Government servants. Where the order terminating the service on the face of it flows from a right to terminate service under the rules of service and it does not cast any stigma upon the employee, and is made on an overall assessment of service record and it is found that the employee is not fit to be confirmed, the provisions of Article 311 are not at all attracted.

[*State of Uttar Pradesh* v. *Tilak Singh*, 1975 SLJ 94: 1975 LIC 1021]

In relation to a temporary Government servant not holding a specified post, the termination of service is to be made by the authority which appointed him.

[*Om Parkash Gupta Swadheen* v. *Union of India*, AIR 1975 SC 1265]

Absence without leave constitutes misconduct and it is not open to the employer to terminate service without notice and inquiry or at any rate without complying with the minimum principle of natural justice.

[*L. Robert D'Souza* v. *Executive Engineer, Southern Railway*, 1982 (1) SLJ 319]

Termination of service of a temporary Government servant on an overall assessment of his service record when it is found that he is not fit to be retained in service, does not amount to punishment of dismissal or removal under Article 311.

[*State of Uttar Pradesh* v. *Tilak Singh*, 1975 SLJ 94]

Merely because the adverse remarks had been communicated and the adverse remarks related to indiscipline and quarrelsome nature of the petitioner, it cannot be contended that the termination was by way of punishment.

[*M. Rahtinavelu* v. *R.C. Khanna*, 1980 (2) SLR 38]

The Supreme Court in the case of *Jaishankar* v. *State of Rajasthan*, AIR 1966 SC 492, held that the removal of a Government servant from service for overstaying his leave without complying with the provisions of Article 311 of the Constitution is illegal even though it was sanctioned under the relevant service regulations. That ratio is equally applicable to temporary Government servants as well.

[*Ram Kishore Pandey* v. *Union of India*, 1982 Lab IC 281]

The respondent was appointed and confirmed by the Chairman of the Board of Control. The Board of Control abolished the post. Chairman, Board of Administration served the notice of termination on the respondent terminating his employment at the expiry of three months. Chairman of the Board of Administration was under the control of the Board of Control which is a superior authority. The notice of termination was vitiated because it was issued by an authority which was subordinate to the authority which appointed the respondent.

[*Union of India* v. *Vigian Bhushan Aggarwal*, 1983 (1) SLJ 77]

Under the rules made under the Punjab Agricultural Produce Market Act, it is the State Agricultural Marketing Board which is competent to terminate the services of its employees. Hence termination of services by the Secretary of the Board is not valid. A person whose services are illegally terminated is entitled to reinstatement and also to back wages.

[*Balwant Singh* v. *State of Haryana*,
(1983) 1 SLR 273 (P&H)]

Appellant, a temporary employee, was transferred. He did not immediately join duty at the new place and applied for leave instead. Even after expiry of leave, he did not join his duty but applied for further leave. Without proceeding to take disciplinary action, his service was terminated. Order held violative of Article 311(2).

[*N. Yellah Swamy* v. *Director of Industries*,
1971 (1) SLR 730 (AP)]

Chief Minister made statement in Legislative Assembly in answer to a question. "It is true that having put in 15 years of temporary service he is entitled to pension but on the other hand since his services were not satisfactory he can be removed on one month's notice. On re-consideration of the case the Government felt that he should be served a show cause notice. The Chief Minister's statement did cast stigma on his character. The order terminating his service and not allowing him pension was quashed."

[*Madan Mohan Prasad* v. *State of Bihar*,
AIR 1973 SC 1133]

Termination of services on mere involvement in a criminal case would be too hazardous and slander a consideration which can justify termination of services.

[*Pradyuman Sinh Indra Sinh* v. *State of Gujarat*,
1982 (2) SLR 650]

Where the impugned order while terminating the services of the petitioner had described him as 'at present under suspension', it can be inferred, on the face of it, that the order leaves a stigma on the petitioner. The fact that he is a suspended officer would make any future employer reasonably think that the petitioner must have been suspended in service on some serious allegations and may refuse employment to the petitioner on that ground alone. The impugned order, though passed under Rule 5(1) of the Temporary Service Rules, 1965, carries an indelible stigma and order was held violative of Article 311(2) of the Constitution.

[*N.B. Chakraborty* v. *Union of India*, AIR 1970 A&N 98]

It is open to an employer to terminate the services of the employee by mutual consent. For a termination of service by mutual consent, neither the provisions of Article 311 nor the principles of natural justice are attracted.

[*Mohd. Kutubuddin* v. *State of A.P.*,
(1969) II SCWR 856]

Government is entitled to terminate the services of temporary employee for not passing the prescribed examination.

[*State of Rajasthan* v. *Fateh Chand*, AIR 1970 SC 1099]

An order of termination of service in unexceptionable form preceded by an enquiry launched by the superior authorities only to ascertain whether the public servant should be retained in service, does not attract the operation of Article 311.

[*State of Punjab* v. *Sukh Raj Bahadur*, AIR 1968 SC 1089]

In a case, preliminary inquiry was held and the services of the temporary employee were terminated. No charge sheet was issued. It was held that the employee is not entitled to reasonable opportunity to show cause notice against the orders of termination within the meaning of Article 311 of the Constitution.

[*State of Uttar Pradesh* v. *Abdul Khaliq*, 1962 (1) SCWR 1086]

When preliminary enquiry is held against a temporary civil servant *ex parte* and his services are terminated without mention of any stigma, the order is simple order of discharge and Article 311(2) will not apply.

[*Champaklal Chiman Lal Shah* v. *Union of India*, AIR 1964 SC 1854]

Acceptance of resignation does not amount to termination of appointment for any misconduct or as a measure of penalty.

[*Raj Kumar* v. *Union of India*, (1968) II SCWR 914: AIR 1969 SC 180]

An official who has acquired experience but has not been successful at the selection is not to be replaced by a fresh recruit. While terminating the services of these not selected the principle of "last come first go" be applied to those who are similarly situated and the services of the junior must be terminated first.

[*Dr. S.C. Kaushik* v. *Union of India*, 1981 (1) SLR 214]

In a case a show cause notice was issued to the respondent under terms of appointment. The respondent admitted that his appointment was subject to the condition that his services were terminable without any notice. The impugned order of termination was not passed by way of any punishment. He cannot invoke the provisions of Article 311.

[*State of Nagaland* v. *G. Vasantha*, AIR 1970 SC 537]

If a Government servant is suspended and his services are terminated without holding any inquiry against him, such termination would amount to punishment which will attract the provisions of Article 311.

[*Union of India* v. *Gian Singh Kadian*, 1970 DLT 293]

In a case, the petitioner submitted his reply to charge sheet and thereafter his services were terminated. Order was quashed on the ground of infringement of provisions of Article 311.

[*Balraj Kumar Murria* v. *State of Punjab*, 1982 (1) SLR 355]

In a case, the charge sheet was withdrawn after about two years and on the same date a fresh charge sheet was served which was also withdrawn after more than five years and thereafter the services of the petitioner were terminated. It was held that from the sequence of events, one is reasonably entitled to draw the conclusion that the petitioner's service were terminated on the ground of misconduct although the charges had been formally withdrawn.

[*Dasarathi Lal Sharma* v. *Union of India*, 1977 (1) SLR 672]

In a case, an inquiry was held and the Enquiry Officer submitted his report. Government ordered withdrawal of enquiry report and terminated services of the employee. Order cannot be said to be by way of punishment.

[*State of Punjab* v. *Parsa Singh Teji*, AIR 1967 Punj 138]

If there be full scale departmental enquiry *i.e.* an enquiry officer is appointed, a charge sheet served, explanation called for and considered, any order of termination of service made thereafter will attract the operation of Article 311.

[*State of Punjab* v. *Sukh Raj Bahadur*, AIR 1968 SC 1089]

7.3 Criteria to judge as to whether the termination order is punitive or not

(a) Mere innocuous form of the order is non-conclusive;

(b) The court/judicial forum can look to the substance of the order to ascertain as to whether the order simplicitor terminating the services of a temporary employee is merely a cloak or camouflage;

(c) While determining the preceding point the Court can look into all the circumstances, the preceding, attendant and other relevant factors; and

(d) For determination of the questions 'as to whether the misconduct is a merely motive or is foundation of the order, question has to be decided after taking into account all the facts and circumstances of a given case.

[*Gopa Ram* v. *U.O.I.*, 1987 (1) SLJ 401 CAT]

(e) "The Courts can look into the discharge simplicitor of a probationer to find out as to whether the order is in the nature of penalty imposed for any misconduct without enquiry or a simple discharge order based on the formation of opinion that the probationer concerned is not suitable for the post in which he had been appointed on probation. If after considering all the facts and circumstances of the case, the Court finds that the order was based on an assessment of the suitability of the concerned probationer for the post, without reference to any misconduct, if any, alleged against him, the order has to be upheld, but if it is based on any alleged charges, it has to be set aside notwithstanding its form."

[*K.S. Raghuramaiah* v. *Dy. General Manager and Divisional Controller, Karnataka State Road Transport Corporation*, 1980 SLJ 353]

(f) "A temporary hand has no right to the post. It is also not denied that both under the contract of service and the service rules governing the respondent, the State has a right to terminate his services by giving him one month's notice. The order to which exception is taken is *ex facie* an order of termination of service simpliciter. It does not cast any stigma on the respondent nor does it visit him with evil consequences, nor is it founded on misconduct. In the circumstances, the respondent could not invite the Court to go into the motive behind the order and claim the protection of Article 311 (2) of the Constitution."

[*State of Uttar Pradesh* v. *Ramachandra Trivedi*, 1976 SLJ 583 SC]

Termination of services on certain vague unconfirmed confidential police reports is illegal and void.

[*Hardit Singh* v. *State of Punjab*, 1977 (2) SLR 749 (P&H)]

The appointment of the respondent was "subject to verification of his character and antecedents by police." The report of police verification merely stated that the respondent was unsuitable for employment under the Government. The respondent protested that there was no basis for such report. It was held in the facts and circumstances of the case that no prejudice would be caused to the State authorities if the gist or the extract of the report so far as the same is against the respondent is made known to him and he is given an opportunity to make representation against such report.

[*State of West Bengal* v. *Madan Mohan Beg*, 1977 SLJ 677]

In a case, a notice terminating service was sent to officer by registered post at the leave address but its service was deliberately avoided. It may be treated effective service.

[*Nilendu Bhushan Chakravarty* v. *Union of India*, 1975 (1) SLR 149]

A civil servant was put off duty on the ground that allegations of misconduct against him were under inquiry. After about six weeks, his services were terminated. The order of termination did not specify the ground upon which the order was based and *prima facie* it was innocuous one. It was held that the impugned order of termination virtually amounted to dismissal and could not have been passed in absence of holding inquiry in accordance with provisions of Article 311(2) of the Constitution.

[*Ananta Charan Mahapatra* v. *Inspector of Post Offices*, AIR 1980 Ori 165 (FB)]

Respondent was appointed under an agreement and was to be allowed to remain in service upto the age of 55 years. The agreement provided that his services are liable to be terminated on six months' notice on either side. Held, the respondent was holding a civil post within the meaning of Article 311(1). Termination of service on six months' notice would not only amount to merely termination of service but also his removal from service within the meaning of Article 311(1). Notice of termination without complying with the provisions of Article 311(2) was void.

[*Union of India* v. *M.A. Chaudhary*, 1975 SLJ 1]

Where a person is appointed in temporary or officiating capacity for fixed term under the terms of employment and there is nothing in the said order permitting premature termination of his appointment before the expiry of the period fixed in that order, he acquires a right to hold the post till the expiry of that period, and his services cannot be terminated before the expiry of that period unless he has been guilty of some misconduct, negligence, inefficiency or other disqualifications and appropriate proceedings are taken under the rules read with Article 311(2) of the Constitution..

[*Prasanta Mohpatra* v. *State of Orissa*, AIR 1969 Ori 61]

Employment can be terminated before the employee completes full period of his appointment. The relation between person appointed and the employer being contractual, termination of relationship will not entitle the servant to a declaration that his employment had not been validly determined.

[*Dr. Bool Chand* v. *Chancellor, Kurukshetra University*, (1968) 2 SCJ 171]

The provisions of Article 311 of Constitution do not apply to employees of a company or corporation, in as much as they do not hold civil posts under the Government. The employee cannot make any grievance by challenging the termination order on the ground that since it was a penalty, he was entitled to an opportunity. The administrative control vests in the Company and it is the Company which has the power to frame Rules and Regulations regarding the employment of its employees. Articles of a Company are the internal regulations of the Company. They cannot be enforced by means of a writ under Article 226 of the Constitution.

[*Raja Harendra Singh* v. *Union of India*, 1982 LIC 1733].

The Constitution guarantees special concession to the members of the Scheduled Castes and Tribes in the matter of recruitment but no constitutional provisional or any other law appears to provide special protection regarding termination of services of Government servants belonging to Scheduled Castes and Scheduled Tribes.

[*Rama Nand Ramnarayan Raidas* v. *State of M.P.*, 1979 (3) SLR 671]

The services of women khalasis were terminated on the ground that women are intrinsically incapable of heavy physical work. It is discriminatory and unconstitutional. The criterion of strength based exclusively on gender bias is anathema to the principle of equality. There can be stronger females than male physically, spiritually, biologically, mentally and morally.

[*Achinna Ammini* v. *U.O.I.*, 1990 (12) ATC 128 (Ernakulam)]

7.4 Detailed gist of the leading judgments delivered by the Courts/Tribunals on the subject of termination of services of temporary employees

The leading judgments on the subject of termination of services of temporary employees have been dealt with under appropriate heads in the preceding pages. There are generally, more than one point of law on which the Courts would have shed light in a judgment. It is, therefore, considered necessary to refer to such judgments in greater details:

The judgment in this case decided by the Supreme Court has already been discussed in Chapter 5 and may be referred to. Other points of law dealt with in that judgment are mentioned below:

(a) The termination of services of an officer cannot be ordered on the vague allegation that he has a "notoriety" for corruption. The "notoriety" must be based on some thing more than a mere allegation. Any statutory employer must take care when terminating the career on the ground of unsuitability, to ensure that its order is founded on definable material 'objectively assessed' and relevant to the ground of termination.

(b) Where allegations of misconduct are levelled against a Government servant and it is a case where the provisions of Article 311(2) of the Constitution should be applied, it is not open to the competent authority to take a view that holding the enquiry contemplated by that clause would be a bother or a nuisance and that, therefore, it is entitled to avoid the mandate of that provision and resort to the guise of an *ex facie* innocuous termination order.

(c) An order terminating the services of even an *ad hoc* employee, if really based on misconduct, is by way of punishment and attracts Article 311 of the Constitution.

[*Nepal Singh* v. *State of Uttar Pradesh*, 1984 (3) SLR 126 SC]

The classic judgment of Justice R.S. Pathak in this case is worth quoting:

"The law, it seems to me, is that where the services of a temporary Government servant or of a probationer Government servant are terminated by an order which does not *ex facie* disclose any stigma or penal consequences against the Government servant is merely a termination order simplicter there is no case ordinarily for assuming that it is anything but what is purports to be. Where, however, the order discloses on the face of it that a stigma is cast on the Government servant or that it visits him with penal consequences, then plainly the case is one of the punishment. There may still be another kind of case where although the termination of services is intended by way of punishment, the order is framed as a termination simpliciter. In such a case, if the Government servant is able to establish by material on the record that the order is in fact passed by way of punishment, the innocence of the language in which the order is framed will not protect it if the procedural safeguards contemplated by Article 311(2) of the Constitution have not been satisfied. In a given case, the Government servant may succeed in making out a *prima facie* case that the order was by way of punishment but an attempt to rebut the case by the authorities may necessitate for the official records for the purpose of determining the truth. It is in such a case generally that the official records may be called for by the court. It is not open to the court to send for the official records on a mere allegation by the Government servant that the order is by way of punishment. For unless there is material on the record before the Court in support of that allegation, an attempt by the Court to find out from the record whether the termination of service is based on the unsuitability of the Government servant in relation to the post held by him or is in reality an order by way of punishment will in effect be an unwarranted attempt to delve into the official records for the purpose of determining the nature of the order on the basis of a mere allegation of the Government servant. On a sufficient case being made out on the merits before the Court by the Government servant it is open to the Court to resort to scrutiny of the official records for the purpose of verifying the truth. I am unable to see why the Court should decline to peruse the official records in an appropriate case and why, where considerations of privilege and confidentiality do not suffer, the information set forth in the records should not be made available to the Government servant. The mere possibility that the official records could confirm what the Government servant had set out to prove and *prima facie* had, indeed, proved should not shut out disclosure of the information."

[*State of Maharashtra* v. *V.R. Saboji*, 1979 SLJ 621 (SC)]

In this case, the petitioner stated that action initiated by calling his explanation read along with contentions in the counter would show that sufficient material is on record to establish that his services were terminated only by way of punishment on the ground of negligence involving loss of Rs. 493 to Government apart from his not being punctual, going on leave frequently without prior permission and in making false representations that certain categories of seeds had been sent on the oral instructions of the Director. It is contended that these facts in the counter establish that applicant's termination is due to acts of misconduct and it is open to the Court to resort to scrutiny of the official records for the purpose of verifying the truth *i.e.* whether the applicant's termination by an innocuous order is due to his functioning. Reliance was also placed upon the decision in *Jarnail Singh* v. *State of Punjab*, AIR 1986 SC 1626 which was a case wherein services of certain *ad hoc* employees were terminated by an innocuous order of termination. The Supreme Court held in that case that the mere form of the order is not sufficient to hold that the order of termination was innocuous and that the circumstances of the order as well as the basis of the order have to be taken into consideration. The Supreme Court further held as follows:

> "In other words when an allegation is made by the employee assailing the order of termination as one based on misconduct, though couched in innocuous terms, it is incumbent on the Court to lift the veil and to see the real circumstances as well as the basis and foundation of the order complained of. In other words, the Court, in such case, will lift the veil and will see whether the order was made on the ground of misconduct, efficiency or not."

The Supreme Court on the facts of the case had found in that case that in view of allegations of serious misconduct and also adverse entries in the service record, reasonable opportunity ought to have been given to him in accordance with the Article 311(2) of the Constitution. It was further held that though the authorities terminated the services of the applicant on the ground that "these posts are no longer required" they have retained and regularized the services of *ad hoc* employees who were junior to the prejudice of the rights of the petitioners thereby violating the statutory principle of equality and non-arbitrariness and want of discrimination enshrined in Articles 14 and 16 of the Constitution. From the decision in *State of Maharashtra* v. *V.R. Saboji case*, 1979 SLJ 621 SC, it is clear that "if a Government servant is able to establish by material on the record that the order is in fact passed by way of punishment, the innocence of the language in which the order is framed will not protect it if the procedural safeguards contemplated by Article 311(2) of the Constitution have not been satisfied. Since the applicant has alleged that termination of his services was due to high handed action on the part of the employer, it is incumbent on the Hon'ble Court to lift the veil and to see for itself the circumstances as well as the basis and foundation of the order complained of."

[*A.S. Jeevarathnam* v. *Director Sh. K.N. Arora*, 1990 (1) SLJ 129 CAT (Hyd Bench)]

It was held by the Supreme Court that:

> "If the services of a temporary Government servant are terminated in accordance with the conditions of his service on

the ground of his unsatisfactory conduct or on his unsuitability for the job and or for his work being unsatisfactory, or for a like reason which marks him off in a class apart from other temporary servants who have been retained in service, there is no question of the applicability of Article 16.

Conversely, if the services of a temporary Government servant are terminated, arbitrarily, and not on the ground of his unsuitability, unsatisfactory conduct or the like which would put him in a class apart from his juniors in the same service, a question of unfair discrimination may arise notwithstanding the fact that in terminating his service the appointing authority was purporting to act in accordance with the terms of the employment. Where a charge of unfair discrimination is levelled with specificity, or improper motives are imputed to the authority making the impugned order of termination of the service, it is the duty of the authority to dispel that charge by disclosing to the Court the reason or motive which impelled it to take the impugned action. Excepting, perhaps, in cases analogous to those covered by Article 311(2), Proviso (c), the authority cannot withhold such information from the Court on the lame excuse that impugned order is purely administrative and not judicial, having been passed in exercise of its administrative discretion under the rules governing the conditions of the services."

[*Manager Government Branch Press* v. *D.B. Belliappa*, 1979 SLJ 233]

In this case, the services of one Dr. Md. Iskander Ali who was a probationer were terminated by order simplicitor although there were allegations of negligence on his part for not attending to a baby who had died due to his negligence. The appointing authority did not consider it necessary to continue with the enquiry but decided to terminate the service of the respondent as he was not found suitable for the job. It is well settled by a long course decisions of Supreme Court that in the case of a probationer or of a temporary employee, who has no right to the post, such a termination of his service is valid and does not attract the provisions of Article 311 of the Constitution. In the case of *Shamsher Singh* v. *State of Punjab,* (1975) 1 SCR 828, a similar case was considered in all its aspects by a Constitution Bench of the Supreme Court comprising seven judges and the Court adumbrated the following proposition of law:

> "Before a probationer is confirmed the authority concerned is under an obligation to consider whether the work of the probationer is satisfactory or whether he is suitable for the post. In the absence of any Rules governing a probationer in this respect the authority may come to the conclusion that on account of inadequacy for the job or for any temperamental or other object not involving moral turpitude the probationer is unsuitable for the job and hence must be discharged. No punishment is involved in this... The fact of holding inquiry is not always conclusive. What is decisive is whether the order is really by way of punishment. A probationer whose terms of service provided that it could be terminated without any notice and without any cause being assigned could not claim the protection of the Article 311(2)......... An order terminating the services of a temporary servant or probationer under the Rules of Employment and without anything more will not attract Article 311. When a departmental enquiry is contemplated and if an enquiry is not in fact proceeded with, Article 311 will not be attracted unless it can be shown that the order though unexceptionable in form, is made following a report based on misconduct."
>
> [*Oil and Natural Gas Commission* v. *Dr. Md. Iskander Ali,* 1980 SLJ 591 SC]

> "Shortly put, the principle is that when a servant has right to a post or to a rank either under the terms of the contract of employment express or implied, or under the rules governing the conditions of his service, the termination of the service of such a servant or his reduction to a lower post is by itself and *prima facie* a punishment, for it operates as a forfeiture of his right to hold that post or that rank and to get the emoluments and other benefits attached thereto. But if the servant has no right to the post, or where he is appointed to a post, permanent or temporary either on probation or on an officiating basis and whose temporary service has not ripened into a quasi permanent service as defined in the

Temporary Service Rules, the termination of his employment does not deprive him of any right and cannot, therefore, by itself be a punishment. One test for determining whether the termination of the service of a Government servant is by way of punishment is to ascertain whether the servant but for such termination had the right to hold the post. If he had a right to the post as in the cases hereinbefore mentioned, the termination of his service will by itself be a punishment and he will be entitled to the protection of Article 311. In other words and broadly speaking, Article 311(2) will apply to those cases where the Government servant, had he been employed by a private employer will be entitled to maintain an action for wrongful dismissal, removal or reduction in rank. To put it in another way, if the Government has, by contract express or implied, or, under the rules, the right to terminate the employment at any time, then such termination in the manner provided by the contract or the rules, is *prima facie* and *per se*, not a punishment and does not attract the provisions of Article 311."

[*Parshotam Lal Dhingra* v. *Union of India*, 1958 SCR 828]

The question as to whether it is necessary to disclose the reasons in the orders for termination of services issued under Rule 6 of Extra-Departmental Agents (Conduct & Service) Rules, 1964 came up for consideration before Kerala High Court in the following cases:

(i) *A.K. Sethi* v. *Senior Supdt. of Post Offices*, 1973 KLJ 501;

(ii) *Thankappan* v. *S.P. Officers Telegraphs*, 1977 KLT 362;

(iii) *Madhavankutty* v. *Post Master, Quilon*, 1978 KLT 605.

This point became an issue for consideration before the same High Court in *E. Kunhiraman Nair* v. *Supdtt. of Post Offices, Cannanore Division*, 1984 (1) SLJ 157. In that case, the services of the applicant who was functioning as an Extra Departmental Branch Post Master were terminated on "administrative grounds" under Rule 6 of EDA (CR) Rules, 1964. The main challenge to the order was that "administrative grounds" without indicating precisely the reasons for termination is not in accordance with the provisions of Rule 6 . The Court took upon itself the task of comparing and contrasting the provisions of

Rule 5 of CCS (TS) Rules, 1965 and Rule 6 of EDA (C&S) Rules, 1964 as under:

Rule 5 of CCS (TS) Rules, 1965 & Rule 6 of E.D.A. (C&S) Rules, 1964 read as under:

Rule 5 of CCS (TS) Rules, 1965:

> "5(1)(a) The services of a temporary *Government servant* shall be liable to termination at any time by notice in writing given either by the Government servant to the appointing authority or by the appointing authority to the Government servant;
>
> (b) The period of such notice shall be one month."

Rule 6 of E.D.A. (C&S) Rules, 1964:

> "6. *Termination of Services.*—The services of an employee shall be liable to termination by the appointing authority at any time without notice for generally unsatisfactory work within 3 years from the date of appointment or on any administrative ground unconnected with his conduct,"

It was observed by the Court that the services of a Government servant governed by Rule 5 of CCS (TS) Rules, 1965 are liable to termination at any time by notice in writing either by Government servant to the appointing authority or by the appointing authority to the Government servant. The period of such notice is to be one month. Unlike Rule 6 of the Extra Departmental Agents (Conduct and Services) Rules, 1964, Rule 5 of the Central Civil Services (Temporary Services) Rules, 1965 enables termination without recording any reason. Under Rule 6, however, recording of reasons for termination is necessary. The provisions of Rule 6 appear to be inconformity with the views expressed by the Supreme Court in *Government Branch Press* v. *D.B. Belliappa,* AIR 1979 SC 129 which are reproduced below:

> "Where a charge of unfair discrimination is levelled with specificity, or improper motives are imputed to the authority making the impugned order of termination of the service, it is the duty of the authority to dispel that charge by disclosing to the Court the reason or motive which impelled it to take the impugned action. Excepting, perhaps, in cases analogous to those covered by Article 311(2), Proviso (c), the authority

cannot withhold such information from the Court on the lame excuse that impugned order is purely administrative and not judicial, having been passed in exercise of its administrative discretion under the rules governing the conditions of the services. "The giving of reasons", as Lord Denning put in *Breen* v. *Amalgamated Engineering Union,* (1971) 1 All FR 1148 "is one of the fundamentals of good administration" and, to recall the words of this court in *Khudi Ram* v. *State of West Bengal,* 1975 (2) SCR 932: AIR 1975 SC 550, in a Government Laws. "There is nothing like unfettered discretion immune from judicial reviewability." The executive, no less than the judiciary, is under a general duty to act fairly. Indeed, fairness founded on reason is the essence of the guarantee epitomized in Articles 14 and 16(1)."

[*E. Kunhiraman Nair* v. *Supdtt. of Post Offices, Cannanore Division,* 1984 (1) SLJ 157]

Chapter 8

TERMINATION OF SERVICES OF A PROBATIONER

"No abstract propositions can be laid down that where the services of a probationer are terminated without saying any thing more in the order of termination that the services are terminated, it can never amount to a punishment in the facts and circumstances of a case. If, however, the probationer is discharged on the ground of misconduct, inefficiency or for similar reasons without a proper inquiry and without getting a reasonable opportunity of showing cause against his discharge, it may, in a given case amount to his removal from service within the meaning of Article 311 (2) of the Constitution.

(Supreme Court)"

SYNOPSIS

8.1 Who is a Probationer?

8.2 Difference between a Temporary Employee and a Probationer

8.3 Difference between an "Apprentice" and a "Probationer"

8.4 Applicability of CCS (TS) Rules, 1965 to probationers

8.5 Government of India instructions regarding assessment of the work of probationers, their confirmation and discharge

8.6 There is no concept of "Deemed confirmation" of a Probationer

8.7 The time specified in the Rules for notifying to the Probationer about the termination/extension of his probationary period is not mandatory but only directory in nature

8.8 Observation of the Courts about the automatic confirmation of the Probationers

8.9 Unless the rules specifically provide, there is no concept of 'deemed confirmation" in service law jurisprudence

8.10 There can be no automatic confirmation of a Probationer on the very first day of the expiry of the specified period of probation mentioned in appointment letter of an employee

8.11 Unless the rules provide for a maximum period of probation, this period cannot be over unless some specific order in that regard is passed

8.12 Where the Rules/Regulations provide that the total period of probation including extension, if any, shall not exceed beyond a prescribed period, the employee concerned is deemed to have been confirmed in the said post

8.13 Where the service Regulations provide that as express order of confirmation is required to be issued even after completion of the prescribed maximum period of probation, such an employee continues to remain as Probationer till that order is issued

8.14 Propositions of law laid down by Supreme Court in *State of Bihar* v. *Gopi Krishna Prasad,* AIR 1960 SC 689 regarding termination of the services of a Probationer

8.15 Principles of law laid by Supreme Court in (i) *State of Punjab* v. *Sukh Raj Bahadur,* AIR 1968 SC 1089 and (ii) *Shamsher Singh* v *State of Punjab,* 1974(2) SCC 861 regarding termination of the services of the temporary employees/Probationers

8.16 The order of termination of the services of a Probationer is liable to be quashed if the foundation of that order is based on criminal/departmental proceedings initiated against him

8.17 The services of a Probationer can be terminated if he is found unsuitable for the post despite the fact that some sort of inquiry was initiated which was not completed

8.18 A probationer cannot be merely discharged without following the procedure laid down in Article 311(2) of the Constitution when the basis of termination is some alleged misconduct

8.19 The order of discharge of a Probationer is liable to be quashed if the language used therein implies some sort of stigma attaching on him

8.20 The services of a probationer who has completed long years of service after successfully completing the probationary period cannot be terminated without assigning any reason

8.21 The Court has the power to go behind the innocuous order of discharge of a Probationer to ascertain the true character of the order

8.22 The services of a Probationer can be terminated by the competent authority on ground of his unsuitability for the post he is holding - criteria for deciding "unsuitability" of the probationer

8.23 Terminating the services of a probationer on the ground of unsatisfactory performance without adequate basis is sure to invoke the wrath of the judicial authorities with penal

8.1 Who is a Probationer?

A probationer is a person who has been appointed on probation against a substantive vacancy in the cadre of a department. The terms of his probation generally lay down the conditions about the period of his probation, his discharge and also whether he would be automatically confirmed after completing successfully the period of his probation, etc. A probationer may be a fresh entrant in service or an employee who is already in service and who has been promoted to a higher post. Both types of probationers are on "trial". The first being on "trial" as to whether he is, at all suitable for the post for which he has been recruited while the latter is also on "trial" to see as to whether he is fit to shoulder higher responsibilities of the post to which he has been promoted.

8.2 Difference between a Temporary Employee and a Probationer

A temporary employee is a person who has no vested right to continue on the post to which he has been appointed temporarily and his services can be dispensed with as per conditions of his appointment. A Probationer, on the other hand, is a person who has been appointed on probation against a substantive vacancy in the cadre of a department. The terms of his probation generally lay down the conditions about the period of his probation, his discharge and also whether he would be automatically confirmed after completing successfully the period of his probation, etc. In the case of a temporary employee, there are generally no such terms and conditions.

The tenure of both the temporary employees and of Probationers is thus of a precarious character. The services of a temporary employee can be "terminated" under Rule 5 of CCS (TS) Rules or other similar Rules applicable to him. Probationers can be "discharged" under the terms of their contract, which may expressly provide for such termination.

8.3 Difference between an "Apprentice" and a "Probationer"

An Apprentice is a person who is deputed for training in a trade or business with a view to get employment. He draws stipend at a monthly rate during the period of his training but is not employed in or against any substantive post in the cadre of the department. It is only on the successful completion of the training that he can be considered for appointment on "Probation" for the prescribed period. Thus, an apprentice is a 'Probationer' in-waiting.

8.4 Applicability of CCS (TS) Rules, 1965 to probationers

Rule 1 (4) of CCS (TS) Rules 1965 specifies categories of staff to whom, these Rules are not applicable. The question as to whether the said Rules are applicable to Probationers came up for consideration before Bombay High Court in *Ishwar Lal J. Naik* v. *S.C. Arya, Principal, Government Arts & Science College, Daman*, 1984 (1) SLJ 1 which in its judgment dated 8-8-1983 observed as under:

> "Sub-rule (4) of rule 1 of the Temporary Service Rules specifies categories of Government servants to whom these Rules do not apply. A Government servant on probation has not been included in this sub-rule and has therefore not been excluded from the purview of the Temporary Service Rules. Rule 5 of the Rules applies to a temporary Government servant and excludes a Government servant who is in permanent service. Sub-rule (3) of rule 1 provides that the Temporary Service Rules shall apply subject to what has been said in sub-rule (4) to all persons who hold a civil post, but do not hold a lien or a suspended lien on any post under Government of India or in State Government. In other words, the Rules will apply to all persons who hold a civil post

under a Government except those who hold a lien or a suspended lien on any post. In other words, the Rules would apply to all Government servants who are not permanent."

Thus applicability of CCS (TS) Rules, 1965 is not excluded to Probationers.

8.5 Government of India instructions regarding assessment of the work of probationers, their confirmation and discharge

Government of India have been issuing instructions on the subject from time to time, a gist of which is given below:

"(a) General Principles

(i) Instead of treating probation as a formality, the existing powers to discharge probationers should be systematically and vigorously used so that the necessity of dispensing with the services of employees at later stages may arise only rarely.

(ii) Concentration of attention on the probationer's ability to pass the probationary, or the departmental examination tends to obscure the wider object of probation. In judging the fitness for confirmation of employees selected on the result of a rigorous written examination, passing the probationary or a departmental examination should be an essential, but not the most important part of the qualification for confirmation. There should be a very careful assessment of the outlook, character and aptitude for the kind of work that has to be done in the service before a probationer is confirmed, and only those persons who possess qualities of mind and character needed in the particular service, and the constructive outlook and human sympathy needed in the public service generally should be confirmed.

(iii) A probationer should be given an opportunity to work under more than one officer during the period of his probation and reports of his work obtained from each one of those officers. The reports for the whole period may then be considered by a Board of senior officials for determining whether the probationer concerned is fit to be confirmed in service. For this purpose, separate forms of report on the probationers, which should be distinct from usual confidential report forms may be devised for each of the services in consultation with the O & M Division of the Cabinet Secretariat (Department of Personnel).

(iv) It would be desirable to have uniformity as regards the period of probation in different services and it is therefore recommended that the period of probation should normally be two years, but where there are any special reasons for prescribing a longer or shorter period, a suitable period may be fixed in consultation with the Cabinet Secretariat (Deptt. of Personnel)

(v) In some services, those appointed thereto by promotion are not kept on probation. Since performance in a lower service can only indicate an employee's potentialities for a higher post, it is necessary that his suitability should be judged before he is confirmed in the higher post. It is, therefore, recommended that those promoted as well as the fresh entrants to a service should be kept on probation for a period of two years. The controlling authority may, however, have the discretion to count the period of successful officiation in the service as probationary period.

(vi) While the normal probation may certainly be extended in suitable cases, it is not desirable that an employee should be kept on probation for years as happened occasionally at present. It is, therefore, suggested that, save for exceptional reasons, probation should not be extended for more than a year and no employee should be kept on probation for more than double the normal period.

(vii) The decision whether an employee should be confirmed or his probation extended should be taken soon after the expiry of the initial probationary period, that is ordinarily within six to eight weeks and communicated to the employee together with the reasons in case of extension. A probationary who is not making satisfactory progress or who shows himself to be inadequate for the service in any way should be informed of his shortcomings well before the expiry of the original probationary period so that he can make special efforts at self improvement.

(viii) In case of temporary Government servants who are retained or are likely to be retained in service for more than two years, there should be screening process analogous to that of persons appointed substantively. The object of this screening would be to terminate the appointments of those who appear to be inadequate for the service, but a person who satisfies the test would not acquire any special status, and would continue to be liable to discharge, etc. in accordance with the original conditions of his employment.

[G.I., M.H.A. O.M. No. 44/1/59-Estts (A) dated the 15th April, 1959]

(b) Period of probation in various Central Services

"1. Para 1 (v) of Ministry of Home Affairs, O.M. No. 44/1/59-Estt. (A) dated the 15th April, 1959 (reproduced above) stipulates that the fresh entrants as well as those promoted should be kept on probation for a period of two years to judge the potentialities of an officer for a higher cadre. On review, it has now been decided that –

(i) Save as provided in Clause (ii) below, direct recruits to a post/service shall be on probation for a period of two years.

(ii) Direct recruits to posts carrying a pay scale, the minimum of which is Rs. 2,000 (Fourth Pay Commission) or above or to posts for which the maximum age limit for recruitment is 35 years or above and where no training is involved, shall be on probation for a period one year only.

(iii) Persons who are inducted into a new service through promotion shall also be placed on probation for two years; but there will be no probation for a person promoted from one grade to another within the same service, except where the promotion involves a change in the Group of posts in the same service e.g. promotion from Group "B" to Group 'A' in which case the probation shall be for two years.

(iv) Wherever probation includes 'on the job' or 'institutional training' combined with actual performance on the job, probation for a period of two years should be prescribed in the Recruitment Rules.

(v) In the case of those who are re-employed before the age of superannuation, *e.g.*, Ex-Military personnel, there will be a problem of two years on their appointments/re-employment to civil posts except in respect of cases covered by Clause (ii) above.

(vi) There will be no probation in the case of officers appointed to various posts on—

(a) contract basis;

(b) deputation;

(c) tenure basis;

(d) re-employment after superannuation; and

(e) permanent transfer.

2. On the expiry of the period of probation, steps should be taken to obtain the assessment reports on the probationer and to—

(i) Confirm the probationer/issue orders regarding confirmation, as the case may be, if the probation has been completed to the satisfaction of the competent authority:

(ii) Extend the period of probation [in terms of Para 1 (vii) of the O.M. dated the 15th April, 1959] or discharge the probationer or terminate the services of the probationer, as the case may be, in accordance with the relevant rules and orders, if the probationer has not shown satisfactory performance during the period of probation.

3. The date from which confirmation should be given effect to is the date following the date of satisfactory completion of the prescribed period of probation or the extended period of probation, as the case may be. The decision to confirm the probationer or to extend the period of probation, as the case may be should be communicated to the probationer normally within 6 to 8 weeks. Confirmation of the probationer after completion

of the period of probation is not automatic but is to be followed by formal orders. As long as no specific orders of confirmation or satisfactory completion of probation are issued to a probationer, such probationer shall be deemed to be continuing on probation.

[G.I., M.H.A. (D.P. & A.R.) O.M. No. 21011/2/80-Estt. (C), dated the 19th May, 1983; O.M. No. 21011/3/83-Estts. (C) dated the 24th Februry, 1984 and 5th December, 1984 and O.M. No. 21011/2/89-Estt. (C) dated the 26th April, 1989]

(c) Decision to confirm or to extend the period of probation should be communicated to the probationer within 2 months—

"2. Inspite of the simplification of the procedure as indicated in the preceding para and reiteration of the existing instructions, delay in complying with procedural requirements of completion of probation/ confirmation continue to occur. The Fifth Central Pay Commission, while taking a serious view of the existing situation have *inter alia* recommended in para 124.50 of their report that provisions should be made for holding concerned officers responsible in cases of delay in confirmation.

3. The Union Public Service Commission in their 47th Annual Report for the year 1996-97 have observed that:

"During 1996-97, cases of 665 officers were referred to the Departmental Promotion Committee for confirmation after delays of more than two years."

4. In view of the above, it is once again reiterated that decision to confirm a probationer or to extend the period of probation, as the case may be, should be communicated to the probationer normally within six to eight weeks. In order to ensure that delays do not occur in confirmation, timely action must be initiated in advance so that time limit is adhered to.

[G.I., Deptt. of Per. & Trg., O.M. No. 18011/2/98-Estt. (C) dated the 28th August, 1998)

(d) Uniform probation period should be prescribed for both promotees and direct recruits—

In terms of these instructions in the case of promotions involving a change of Group, for example from Group 'B' to Group 'A', the period of probation to be prescribed is two years. Further, for direct recruits to posts which carry a pay scale the minimum of which is Rs. 5,000 (Fourth Pay Commission) and above or to posts for which the maximum age limit is 35 years or above, the period of probation is one year where no training is involved and two years where probation includes institutional/on the job training.

[G.I., Deptt. of Per. & Trg., O.M. No. 21011/1/94-Estt. (C) dated the 20th April, 1995]

8.6 There is no concept of "Deemed confirmation" of a Probationer

As stated in the preceding sub-paras, the relevant service rules generally include a clause about the period of probation which a new entrant or a promotee will have to undergo before he is confirmed in the said post. The period of probation is normally one to two years depending upon the requirements of a particular job. In such cases, the services of a probationer do not get automatically confirmed after the prescribed period of probation is over. A specific order in this regard needs to be issued. Till then, the probationer continues to be a probationer till even after the probation period is over. There are, however, certain special cases, where the service Rules prescribe a certain period of time beyond which probationary period cannot be extended. In such cases, if the concerned employee is allowed to continue beyond that maximum period of probation admissible, then, by implication, the employee stands confirmed automatically.

In service matters, the significance of a probationer getting confirmed is of vital compliance. The moment he is confirmed, he sheds off the rules applicable to temporary employees and gets protection of Article 311(2) of the Constitution in matters relating to security of his employment.

The Supreme Court in *State of Punjab* v. *Dharam Singh,* AIR 1968 SC 1210 dealing with the case of confirmation of a probationer observed as under:

"This court has consistently held that when a first appointment or promotion is made on probation for a specific period and the employee is allowed to continue in the post after the expiry of the probationary period without any specific order of confirmation, he should be deemed to continue in his post as a probationer only. In the absence of any indication to the contrary in the original order of appointment or of promotion, an express order of confirmation is necessary to give the employee a substantive right to the post, and the mere fact that he is allowed to continue in the post after the expiry of the specified period of probation, it is not possible to hold that he should be deemed to have been confirmed."

The reason for this conclusion is that where on the completion of the specified period of probation the employee is allowed to continue in the post without an order of confirmation, the only possible view to take in the absence of anything to the contrary in the original order of appointment or promotion, is that the initial period of probation has been extended by necessary implication.

In the case of a probationer, Rule 15 of Service and Conduct Rules which were applicable to him provided as under:

"Every employee appointed substantively to a post shall be placed on probation for one year. However, in an individual case, the period of probation may be extended but in no case, the total period of probation shall exceed two years. On satisfactory completion of the period of probation of an employee, the appointing authority shall confirm such employee in the appointment. It further provided "If, however, the probation period of an employee is not extended during the period of such a probation, the same shall be deemed to have been completed satisfactorily from the due date and the employee confirmed accordingly."

Since the probation period of one year was never extended, the petitioner deemed himself to have been confirmed according to Rule 15 quoted above. His services were however terminated *vide* letter dated 1-9-1983 which reads as under:-

"Since your services are no longer required, your appointment as Assistant Director, Physical Education, is hereby terminated w.e.f. 31st of August, 1983 (after noon) as already noted by you."

The order of termination was challenged by the petitioner in Punjab and Haryana High Court *Ramesh Kumar* v. *Maharishi Dayanand University, Rohtak,* 1990 (1) SLJ 3 primarily on the ground that since the probationary period of one year was never extended, the petitioner will be deemed to have been confirmed in view of the said Rule 15. The Hon'ble High Court in its judgment dated 11-4-1989 observed as under:

"After hearing the learned counsel for the parties and after going through case law cited at the bar. I am of the considered view that the impugned order was wholly wrong and illegal. It is rule 15 which governs the case of the petitioner. According to the said rule, if the probation period of an employee is not extended during the pendency of such probation, the same shall be deemed to be completed satisfactorily from the due date and the employee confirmed accordingly. The rule is thus specific in that there was no extension of the probation period, then according to the said rule, the probation period will be deemed to have been completed satisfactorily from the due date and on that basis the employee will be presumed to have been confirmed accordingly."

8.7 The time specified in the Rules for notifying to the Probationer about the termination/extension of his probationary period is not mandatory but only directory in nature

It goes without saying that the entire period of probation including the last day of the probationary period has to be assessed by the competent authority who would have to pass an order whether or not his performance has been satisfactory and whether he deserves to be admitted as a full member of the service and confirm him as such. In the absence of any rule declaring that unless the probation is extended, the probationer would be deemed to have completed his probation or to have become a full member of the service or deemed to have been confirmed upon mere completion of the period of probation, no probationer can claim that he has been confirmed in service or has become a full or permanent member of the service. There is bound to be a time lag between the last date of the prescribed probationary period and the date on which his probationary period is extended or terminated. But the time lag has to be reasonable. What is reasonable time? The Hon'ble Supreme Court in *Kedar Nath Bahi* v. *State of Punjab,* 1972 SLR 320 observed as under:

"Before parting with this judgement, it deserves highlighting that in the case of *Hari Singh Mann* v. *State of Punjab,* 1974 (2) SLR 696 (SC), even a period of two months and ten days after the expiry of the period of probation for passing an order dispensing with the service of the probationer was held to be "reasonable". In sharp contrast thereto herein the order of extension of probation by the principal of the college was passed within a week of the expiry of the specified period of one year's probation. This period of a week, therefore, cannot possibly be deemed unreasonable in the peculiar circumstances of the case. The net result, therefore, is that the appellant would continue to be a probationer till his services were finally terminated after the expiry of the extended period of probation."

8.8 Observation of the Courts about the automatic confirmation of the Probationers

The gist of some of the leading cases on the subject are given below:

(i) *Guru Nanak University* v. *Dr (Mrs.) Iqbal Sandu,* AIR 1976 P&H 69

"In the recent judgment of their Lordships of the Supreme Court in *Hari Singh Mann* v. *State of Punjab,* 1975 SLJ 14 it has been reiterated that the power and the right of the employer to judge about the fitness for work or suitability for the post is inherent and he cannot be robbed thereof. Therefore, a construction which tends to rob the employer of his basic right to assess the work and conduct of the probationer by all means and if not satisfied therewith then to refuse to confirm him in the post has to be avoided because it would manifestly defeat the very purpose and object of the rules."

(ii) *Shri Kedar Nath* v. *State of Punjab*, AIR 1972 SC 873

"... The appellant contends that these orders extending the period of probation were irregular and illegal. Either he should have been discharged within the first six months of probation or, if he not so discharged he was entitled to automatic confirmation. We do not think that this contention is correct. The law on the point is now well settled. Where a person is appointed as a probationer in any post and a period of probation is specified, it does not follow that at the end of the said specified period of probation, he obtains confirmation automatically even if no order is passed in that behalf. Unless the terms of appointment clearly indicate that confirmation would automatically follow at the end of the specified period, or there is a specific service rule to that effect, the expiration of the probationary period does not necessarily lead to confirmation. At the end of the period of probation an order confirming the officer is required to be passed and if no such order is passed and he is not reverted to his substantive post, the result merely is that he continues in this post as a probationer".

(iii) *Hari Singh Mann* v. *State of Punjab*, 1974 (2) SLR 696 SC]

"....On principle also, we are inclined to the view that some reasonable time must be permitted to the dismissing authority to pass the necessary order either terminating the services of the probationer or confirming him. It will depend on the facts and circumstances of each case as to what is the reasonable time."

8.9 Unless the rules specifically provide, there is no concept of 'deemed confirmation' in service law jurisprudence

One Veerappa R. Saboji was appointed as a Civil Judge and was put on a probation for 2 years. He successfully completed the period of probation but no orders were issued regarding his confirmation. His services were terminated without assigning any reason after about 11 years. This case came up before the Hon'ble Supreme Court in *State of Maharashtra* v. *Veerappa R. Saboji*, 1979 SLJ 621, it was pleaded on behalf of Saboji that he was a confirmed employee in accordance with the provisions contained in Bombay Judicial Rules, 1956 and that his termination of services was bad. The Court observed as under:

> "There is no provision in Rule 4(2)(iv) of Bombay Judicial Services Rules, 1956 relating to "Deemed confirmation". In the absence of the order of confirmation, termination of services by order simplicitor even after 11 years of service cannot be challenged. In this case probation would be deemed to have been extended. Violation of Article 14 or 16 of the Constitution does not arise."

8.10 There can be no automatic confirmation of a Probationer on the very first day of the expiry of the specified period of probation mentioned in appointment letter of an employee

One Kartar Singh was appointed as a lecturer in a college on probation on 16-7-1973 for one year. The petitioner was also governed by Rule 3 of Punjab University Calender which reads as follows:

> "The employee appointed on one year's probation would be confirmed if his work is found satisfactory. The employer shall notify to the teacher in writing before the expiry of one year's probationary period, if his period of probation is to be extended and in the absence of such a notice the teacher would be deemed to have been confirmed. The probationary period shall in no case be extended beyond two years from the date of appointment...."

Before the expiry of the said period of one year which was on 15-7-1974, no notice was issued to the teacher. However, on 11-8-1974, he was informed that his probationary period has been extended for a further period of one year. Eventually, his services were terminated on 15-7-1975 which he challenged in Punjab and Haryana High Court in *Kartar Singh* v. *Director Public Instruction Punjab*, 1982 (2) SLJ 242. His main contention was that since he was not notified about the extension of the period of his probation before the expiry of one year, he stands automatically confirmed. The Court in its judgment dated 19-8-1980 observed as under:

> "..... Rule 3 is in no way a stipulation for automatic confirmation of a probationer on the very first day of the expiry of the stipulated period of probation. The point of time

specified in the Rule for notifying the probationer about the extension of the period of his probation is not mandatory but discretionary. It cannot be said that the period of about 2 months 10 days which had elapsed is an unreasonable period........ The appeal filed by the petitioner is rejected and the order of his termination of his service is upheld."

8.11 Unless the rules provide for a maximum period of probation, this period cannot be over unless some specific order in that regard is passed

One A.S. Jeevarathnam was appointed as a store keeper on *ad hoc* basis on 20-4-1981 in Deptt. Of Agriculture, Hyderabad initially for a period of 3 months which was extended from time to time. Subsequently he was put under probation for a period of 2 years w.e.f. 20-10-1981 on the following terms and conditions:

"2. Xxxxx

He will be on probation for a period of two years w.e.f. the forenoon of 20-10-1981, if no action is taken by the competent authority within the period of 2 years in respect of the probationary period, the same shall be deemed to have been extended until further orders.

3. The appointment is liable to be terminated at any time without notice and without assigning any reason during the period of probation and thereafter on one month's notice given by either side viz. The appointing authority or the appointee. The appointing authority however, reserves the right to terminate the services of the appointee before expiry of stipulated period on payment of a sum equivalent to the pay and allowances for the period of notice or the unexpired portion thereof, respectively."

His services were terminated on 18-6-1984 against which the petitioner approached CAT (Hyderabad Bench) [on *A.S. Jeevarathnam* v. *Director, Shri K.N. Arora, Regional Station for Forge and Demonstration Manidipally,* SLJ 1990 (1) CAT 129 on the grounds that he is deemed to be a confirmed employee and that his order of termination is, in fact, an order of punishment. The Tribunal in its judgment dated 25-11-1988 with regard to the first point observed as under:

"By the impugned order dated 18th June, 1984, a sum of Rs. 1497.90 which constitutes a sum equivalent to the amount of pay and allowance for one month's notice in lieu of notice was tendered to the applicant in terms of para 3 of the appointment order. Hence, the Department has proceeded on the basis that the applicant's probation was extended and during the said period of probation he was liable to be terminated on payment of one month's notice. It was contended by the petitioner that since no orders of extension of probation were issued he is deemed to have been confirmed. Reliance in this regard was placed by him in *Om Prakash* v. *U.P. Co. Op. SFF Lucknow,* AIR 1986 SC 1844 and *M.K. Aggarwal* v. *Gurgaon Gramin Bank,* AIR 1988 SC 286; it was held in the former case that an employee continuing in a post after completing the maximum period of probation under the rules stands confirmed by implication. The facts of later case are that the appellant M.K. Aggarwal was appointed as Manager of Rural Bank on probation for a period of one year which was extendable by 6 months. It was further stipulated that 18 months was the maximum period of probation. The employer had neither confirmed nor discharged the employee. There was no controversy over salutary consideration. In the circumstances, the petitioner was confirmed.

These two cases clearly establish the position that where the regulations or the service rules provide for a maximum period of probation and the employee has continued beyond that period, then it must be deemed that he has completed the period of probation. In the present case, however, no statutory rules have been cited by either of the parties to establish that a maximum period of probation had been prescribed and that applicant continued beyond such maximum period. All that we have before us is the appointment order which categorically states that if no action is taken by the competent authority within the period of 2 years of probation, the same shall be deemed to have been extended until further orders. This case is covered by the decision of the Supreme Court in *State of Mahrashtra* v. *V.R. Saboji,* 1979 SLJ 621 (SC) wherein it was held that " in a case where there is no automatic confirmation on the expiry of the probation, the ordinary and normal rule is that without an express order of confirmation the Government servant will not be taken to have been confirmed in the post to which he was appointed temporarily and/or on probation." As the order of appointment is to the effect that unless ordered otherwise, the applicant is deemed to continue on probation and as no statutory rule is placed before to the contra, the decision cited by the learned counsel for applicant viz. *M.K. Aggarwal* v. *Gramin Bank,* AIR 1988 SC 286 and *Om Parkash Maurya* v. *Co-operative Sugar Federation, Gurgaon,* AIR 1986 SC 1844 would not apply. It would follow that the applicant has been continuing on probation when the termination order was passed and therefore it was open to the employer to terminate his services by giving prescribed notice or salary in lieu thereof".

8.12 Where the Rules/Regulations provide that the total period of probation including extension, if any, shall not exceed beyond a prescribed period, the employee concerned is deemed to have been confirmed in the said post

In the case of *State of Punjab* v. *Dharam Singh,* 1968 SLR 247 the maximum period for probation in Punjab Education (Provincialised Cadre)-III Rules, 1961, was three years. In that case the services of Dharam Singh, who was a teacher governed by the above mentioned Rules, were terminated long after the expiry of probationary period of three years. The order of termination was quashed and it was held by the Supreme Court:

(i) Though appointing authority did not pass formal orders of confirmation in writing, it should be presumed to have passed orders of confirmation by allowing them to continue service after three years;

(ii) After such confirmation the authority has no power to dispense with his services on the ground that his work or conduct during the period of probation was unsatisfactory.

It was further observed by the Court that the rules forbid extension of the period of probation beyond three years. Where the Service Rules fix a certain period of time beyond which the probationary period cannot be extended, and an employee appointed or promoted to a post on probation is allowed to continue in that post after completion of the maximum period of probation without an express order of confirmation, he cannot be deemed to continue in that post as a probationer by implication. The reason is that such an implication is negatived by the service rule forbidding the extension of the probationary period beyond the maximum period fixed by it. In such a case, it is permissible to draw the inference that the employee allowed to continue in the post on completion of the maximum period of probation has been confirmed in the post by implication.

The view enunciated in *Dharam Singh's case* was followed and reiterated by the Court in *Paramjit Singh Sandhu* v. *Ram Rakha*, 1979 (2) SLR 88, in the following terms:

> "Rule 8 of the Service Rules prescribes the period of probation of two years and the proviso confers power to extend the period of probation by not beyond one year meaning thereby that in any case the Government would not have the power to extend the period of probation beyond a period of three years. In this situation, the ratio in *Dharam Singh's case* would *mutatis mutandis* apply and it would have to be held that the direct recruit who had completed the period of probation of two years and in the absence of extension of probationary period, would be deemed to be confirmed by necessary implication."

8.13 Where the service Regulations provide that as express order of confirmation is required to be issued even after completion of the prescribed maximum period of probation, such an employee continues to remain as Probationer till that order is issued

Before a probationer is confirmed, the authority concerned is under an obligation to consider whether the work of the probationer is satisfactory or whether he is suitable for the post. In the absence of any rules governing a probationer in this respect, the authority may come to the conclusion that on account of inadequacy for the job or for any other reason not involving moral turpitude the probationer is unsuitable for the job, he can be discharged. No punishment is involved in this. The authority may in some cases be of the view that the conduct of the probationer may result in dismissal or removal on an inquiry. But in those cases the authority may not hold an inquiry and may simply discharge the probationer with a view to giving him a chance to make good in other walks of life without a stigma at the time of termination of probation. If, on the other hand, the probationer is faced with an enquiry on charges of misconduct or inefficiency or corruption, and if his services are terminated without following the provisions of Article 311 (2) he can claim protection. In *Gopi Krishna Prasad* v. *Union of India*, AIR 1960 SC 689, it was held that if the Government proceeded against the probationer in the direct way without casting any aspersion on his honesty or competence, his discharge would not have the effect of removal by way of punishment. Instead of taking the easy course, the Government may choose the more difficult one of starting proceedings against him and branding him as a dishonest and incompetent officer.

The ratio laid down in *Dharam Singh's case*, 1968 SLR 247 was whittled down by a larger Bench of the Supreme Court in *Shamsher Singh case*, 1974 (2) SCC 861 where the order of termination of the services of a probationer long after the completion of the maximum period of probation was held legal. In the said case, there was a provision in the Regulations applicable to the applicant that the completion of maximum period of three years probation would not confer on the probationer the right to be confirmed till there was a permanent vacancy in the Cadre. It further said that an express order of confirmation was necessary. So their Lordship observed that the provision in the regulations was in the negative form and the completion of maximum period of probation of three years would not confer a right of confirmation till there was a permanent vacancy in the Cadre.

8.14 Propositions of law laid down by Supreme Court in *State of Bihar* v. *Gopi Krishna Prasad*, AIR 1960 SC 689 regarding termination of the services of a Probationer

"(a) Appointment to a post on probation gives to the person so appointed no right to the post and his service may be terminated without taking recourse to the proceedings laid down in the relevant rules for dismissing a public servant or removing him from service.

(b) The termination of employment of person holding a post on probation without any enquiry whatsoever cannot be said to deprive him of any right to a post and is therefore no punishment.

(c) But instead of terminating such a person's service without any enquiry if the employer chooses to hold an enquiry into his alleged misconduct or inefficiency or for some similar reason, the termination of service is by way of punishment because it puts a stigma on his competence and thus effects his future career. In such a case he is entitled to the protection of Article 311 (2) of the Constitution.

(d) In the last mentioned case if the probationer is discharged on any one of these grounds without a proper enquiry and without his getting a reasonable opportunity of showing cause against his discharge it will amount to a removal from service within the meaning of Article 311(2) of the Constitution and will therefore be liable to be struck down.

(e) But if the employer simply terminates the service of a probationer without holding an enquiry and without giving him reasonable chance of showing cause against his removal from service the probationary civil servant can have no cause of action even though the real motive behind the removal from service may have been that his employer thought him to be unsuitable for the post he was temporarily holding on account of his misconduct or inefficiency or some such cause."

8.15 Principles of law laid by Supreme Court in (i) *State of Punjab* v. *Sukh Raj Bahadur*, AIR 1968 SC 1089 and (ii) *Shamsher Singh* v. *State of Punjab*, 1974 (2) SCC 861 regarding termination of the services of the temporary employees/probationers

(i) *State of Punjab* v. *Sukh Raj Bahadur*, AIR 1968 SC 1089

1. The service of a temporary servant or a probationer can be terminated under the rules of his employment and such termination without anything more would not attract the operation of Article 311 of the Constitution.

2. The circumstances preceding or attendant on the order of termination service have to be examined in each case, the motive behind it being immaterial.

3. If the order visits the public servant with any evil consequences or casts an aspersion against his character or integrity, it must be considered to be one by way of punishment, no matter whether he was a mere probationer or a temporary servant.

4. An order of termination of service in unexceptionable form preceded by an enquiry launched by the superior authorities only to ascertain whether the public servant should be retained in service does not attract the operation of Article 311 of the Constitution.

5. If there be a full scale departmental enquiry envisaged by Article 311 *i.e.* an Enquiry Officer is appointed, a charge sheet submitted, explanation called for and considered, any order of termination of service made thereafter will attract the operation of the said Article."

(ii) *Shamsher Singh* v. *State of Punjab*, 1974 (2) SCC 861

> "No abstract proposition can be laid down that where the services of a probationer are terminated without saying anything more in the order of termination that the services are terminated it can never amount to a punishment in the facts and circumstances of the case. If a probationer is discharged on the ground of misconduct, or inefficiency or for similar reason without a proper inquiry and without his getting a reasonable opportunity of showing cause against his discharge it may in a given case amount to his removal from service within the meaning of Article 311(2) of the Constitution."

8.16 The order of termination of the services of a Probationer is liable to be quashed if the foundation of that order is based on criminal/departmental proceedings initiated against him

One Balbir Singh was appointed to Grade II of DANI Police Service on 29-6-1982. He was placed under probation for a period of 2 years which could be extended under Rule 21 of 1971 Rules applicable to him at the discretion of the Central Government. The period of probation of 2 years expired on 28-6-1984. There was no communication of any adverse remarks to him. However, he was involved in a criminal/departmental case and was placed under suspension on 9-9-1983. His period of probation was extended on 21-4-1988. His services were terminated on 12-12-1988 which he challenged before CAT (New Delhi Bench) in the case of *Balbir Singh* v. *U.O.I.*, 1989 (4) SLJ 292 CAT, which observed as under:

"The question arises as to whether the termination of the services of the applicant was based on his general unsuitability or that his foundation was the alleged acts of misconduct for which criminal proceeding/departmental action had been initiated against him. Admittedly, no adverse remarks were communicated to the applicant during the period of probation. According to the office memorandum issued by the Ministry of Home Affairs on 15-4-1989, the decision whether an employee should be confirmed or that his probation should be extended should be taken soon after the expiry of the initial probationary period, *i.e.* ordinarily within 6 to 8 weeks and communicated to the employee together with the reasons therefor in case of extension. A probationer who is not making satisfactory progress or who shows himself to be inadequate for the service in any way should be informed of his short comings well before the expiry of the original probationary period so that he can make special efforts at self improvement."

It is well settled legal position that even if the termination order is innocuous and does not show any element of stigma, the court has jurisdiction to find out what actually is the foundation of the order. The apparent innocuous order would be linked with the stigma as the link is not far to seek as respondent himself has disclosed what actually were the grounds for making the order. If the innocuous order is grounded upon features with stigma against the effected officer, he is entitled to defend himself in a proceeding provided under the rules applicable to him.

8.17 The services of a Probationer can be terminated if he is found unsuitable for the post despite the fact that some sort of inquiry was initiated which was not completed

One Dr. Iskandar Ali was appointed on a purely temporary basis as Medical Officer in O.N.G.C. and was put on a probation for a period of one year. The conditions of his appointment stipulated that the said period of probation was extendable at the discretion of the appointing authority, if necessary. It was, in fact, extended for a further period of six months. While on extended period of probation, his services were terminated on 28-12-1967 without assigning any reason. It was contended by the petitioner that the appointing authority chose to institute a departmental inquiry against him for dereliction of duty and negligence in not attending to a baby who died due to his alleged carelessness. The enquiry should have been carried to its logical end and charge sheet having been issued, the provisions of Article 311 of the Constitution were clearly attracted and therefore it was not open to the department to have terminated the services by giving the order a cover of termination simplicitor. In other words, the contention was that the real motive behind termination of the service of the respondent was to inflict a punishment on him and as the department did not comply with the requirement of Article 311 of the Constitution, the order impugned was illegal. The department, however, took the stand that although an enquiry was held yet it was not continued and no punishment was imposed on the petitioner. Further, petitioner was a mere probationer and the order terminating his services was an order of termination simplicitor without involving any stigma or penalty. As the petitioner was a temporary employee on probation, it was open to the employer to terminate his services at any time before he was confirmed, if the employer was satisfied that he was not suitable for being continued in service.

This case came up before the Hon'ble Supreme Court in *Oil and Natural Gas Commission* v. *Dr. Md. S. Iskandar Ali*, 1980 SLJ 591 which in its judgment dated 14-4-1980 observed as under:

> "From the facts of the case, it is manifest that even if misconduct, negligence, inefficiency may be the motive or the inducing factor which influences the employer to terminate the services of the employee on probation, such termination cannot be termed as penalty or punishment. The short history of the service of the respondent clearly shows that his work had never been satisfactory and he was not found suitable for being retained in service and that is why even though some sort of an enquiry was started, it was not proceeded with and no punishment was inflicted on him. In these circumstances, therefore, if the appointing authority considered it expedient to terminate the services of the respondent, a probationer, it cannot be said that the order of termination attracted the provisions of Article 311 of the Constitution. Thus, if the appellant found that the respondent was not suitable for being retained in service that will not vitiate the order impugned. For these reasons, therefore, we are satisfied that

the order terminating the services of the respondent was valid and did not involved any stigma and was fully justified in the facts and circumstances of the present case."

8.18 A Probationer cannot be merely discharged without following the procedure laid down in Article 311(2) of the Constitution when the basis of termination is some alleged misconduct

One Gadekar was working as a conductor in Karnataka State Road Transport Corporation. He was appointed on probation for a period of six months on 12-5-1978 which was extended by a further period of six months on 12-11-1978. There was a written complaint dated 5-2-1979 against him regarding alleged misappropriation of an amount of Rs. 3.85 by him on the basis of which the competent authority made an order on 19-2-1979 on the body of complaint itself which reads as under:

> "We are repeatedly cautioning the conductor to show improvement in his work. Again and he is pilfering the Karnataka State Road Transport's revenue. This clearly shows that he is not in a position to show any improvement in his work inspite of cautioning him. He is discharged from service as per rules."

Pursuant to the said order dated 19-2-1979, he was "discharged" from service which reds as under:

> "xxxx You were cautioned and given chance to show improvement in your work but as you have not been able to show adequate improvement I am sorry to inform you that I have found you not suitable for the job for which you were appointed.
>
> You may be suitable for some other job but you have not been found suitable for the above post to which you were employed on probation.
>
> Hence you are hereby discharged from service with immediate effect."

He challenged his order of 'discharge' before Karnataka High Court in *N.S. Gadekar* v. *Karnataka State Road Transport Corporation*, 1981 (2) SLJ 685 pleading that the order of discharge was, in fact, in the nature of imposition of a penalty for misconduct and attracts provisions of Article 311(2). This was contested by the respondents asserting that the impugned order was not liable to be set aside as the contents of the order communicated to the petitioner did not attach any stigma to the character and conduct of the petitioner and it is not open for the Court to delve into the files of the K.S.R.T.C. to come to the conclusion as to whether an order which on the face of it appears to be an order of discharge, was in reality an order in the nature of imposition of penalty. The respondents relied on the judgment of the Supreme Court in *Saboji case,* 1979 SLJ 621 in their support which reads as under:

> "Ordinarily and generally the rule laid down in most of the cases by this Court is that you have to look to the order on the face of it and find whether it casts any stigma on the Government servant. In such a case there is no presumption that the order is arbitrary or *mala fide* unless a very strong case is made out and proved by the Government servant who challenges such an order."

The Hon'ble High Court in its judgment dated 24-6-81 observed as under:

> "xxx Coming to the facts of the present case, a mere reading of the order communicated and its original on the file indicates that their contents are at variance. While the order communicated makes no reference to any misconduct, the original order does, and this leaves a permanent bad record about the antecedents of the petitioner. Usually the antecedents of a person once discharged from service are ascertained by any employer, before deciding his suitability for employment. Therefore when a person discharged from service pleads that the discharge is in truth a penalty imposed for any alleged misconduct, which was neither admitted nor proved at any time during the period of probation, it is competent for this Court to look into the original order made on the file and the looking into it, as indicated by me earlier, does not amount to delving *i.e.* digging deep into the records. It is no doubt true that if in the office order passed on the file also the competent authority has made no reference to the charge of pilferage alleged against the petitioner, but has referred only to his record of service on which it formed the opinion that the petitioner was not suitable for the post there would have been no record to the effect that any misconduct

(not admitted or proved) during the period of probation constituted the basis for discharge and in that event this Court would not interfere with the order of discharge by making a probe into the records, even if the petitioner were to contest that some allegation made against him immediately prior to the passing of the order of discharge was the basis for the passing of the discharge order. An inquiry of that type by the Court would amount to the examining of the motive of the authority in passing the order and such an investigation cannot be undertaken by the Court. This is obviously for the reason that an allegation of misconduct made against a probationer does not have effect of depriving the competent authority of its power to discharge the probationer, if on the basis of his record of service he is found unsuitable for confirmation. In the present case, it cannot be said that the charge of pilferage constituted a "motive" and not the "basis" as it is specifically adverted to the order passed by the competent authority. After seeing the contents of the original order which expressly refers to a misconduct as a basis for the discharge order, I think that it is impermissible for me to say and I would not be right in saying that the order is not based on the misconduct just because it is not correctly communicated. Therefore I find no substance in the contention urged for the Corporation."

8.19 The order of discharge of a Probationer is liable to be quashed if the language used therein implies some sort of stigma attaching on him

One R.K. Jain, was selected in I.P.S. and was put on probation for a period of 2 years. His probationary period was extended for one year on 24-4-1984. While under extended probation period, he was 'discharged ' under clause (bb) of Rule 12 of I.P.S. Probation Rules, 1954 by an order dated 24-1-1985 which reads as under:

"Whereas the Central Government is satisfied that Shri R.K. Jain, appointed to the Indian Police Service on probation on the result of the Civil Service Examination held in the year 1980 has been found lacking in qualities of mind and character needed for the Service, he is hereby discharged under Clause (bb) of Rule 12 of the Indian Police Service (Probation) Rules, 1954."

It transpired that while he was on probation, there was an allegation against him that he made some immoral suggestion to a lady probationer and an opinion had been formed that he was lacking in qualities of mind and character. A warning was issued to him on 5-8-1982 stating that he had behaved improperly with Mrs. Meeran who was his co-probationer and that he should conduct himself properly and that if any further lapse is reported against him, it will be seriously viewed. A copy of the same was kept in his C.R. folder. To this Memo, Shri Jain filed a representation which was rejected by Director, Hyderabad Police Academy on 28-8-1984 stating that the warning issued was proper and justified. No formal inquiry was, however, made under the relevant disciplinary rules applicable to the officer. The Probationer challenged the order of his discharge before CAT (Ahmedabad Bench) in the case *R.K. Jain* v. *U.O.I.*, 1989 (4) SLJ CAT 995 and the Tribunal in its judgment dated 12-9-1988 observed as under:

> "There is ample evidence on record to show that there is a nexus between the incident in which the petitioner allegedly made immoral suggestion to a fellow lady probationer who was also a married woman and for this, a preliminary enquiry was made but not under D & A Rules governing the petitioner..... In the facts and circumstances of this case, we have no doubt that the order of discharge carries a stigma and has the effect of punishment..... We set aside the impugned order...."

8.20 The services of a probationer who has completed long years of service after successfully completing the probationary period cannot be terminated without assigning any reason

One Labh Singh and certain other employees of F.C.I. had completed 14 years of service. They had successfully completed the prescribed period of probation of 2 years. There was no provision in the Rules for extension of the said period of 2 years. However, the confirmation orders of the employee had not been issued in all cases. Their services were terminated under Rule 19(1) of the Regulations applicable to them without assigning any reason. This case came up for consideration before Punjab and Haryana High Court in *Sr. Regional Manager F.C.I.* v. *Labh*

Singh, 1987(1) SLJ 109 and the Hon'ble Court in its judgment dated 17-7-1986 observed as under:

> "Regulation 19 of FCI (Staff) Regulation, 1971 provide that services of regularly employed persons can be terminated without assigning any reasons or holding any inquiry. Since Regulation 19(1) invests the employer with arbitrary, uncanalised and drastic powers enabling him to dismiss or dispense with the services of a permanent employee, it offends Article 14 of the Constitution. Though the order of termination of services is couched in innocuous terms, the attending circumstances and the basis of the orders as revealed in the written statement, but it clearly establish that the orders have been passed on the basis of alleged misconduct or inefficiency of the respondents. The order of termination of services of the employees is set aside......."

8.21 The Court has the power to go behind the innocuous order of discharge of a Probationer to ascertain the true character of the order

One Anoop Jaiswal was an I.P.S. Probationer. In an incident, there was charge against him for reporting late for parade. According to the authorities, he was considered to be one of the ring leaders who was responsible for the delay for which explanation was called for from all the probationers. In that explanation, he sincerely regretted the lapse while denying the charge of instigating others in reporting late. On the basis of the explanation and interview but without holding any proper enquiry the Director recommended to the Government of India that the appellant should be discharged from the service. The Government accordingly passed an order of discharge of the appellant on the ground of unsuitability for being a member of the IPS. under Rule 12(b) of I.P.S. Probation Rules. He challenged the order of his discharge in the Supreme Court in [AIR 1984 SC 605].

Dealing with his case, the Supreme Court invited reference to the case of *Shamsher Singh* v. *State of Punjab,* AIR 1974 SC 2192 wherein Chief Justice had observed that the order of termination of the service of one of the two judicial officers of Punjab Judicial service concerned in that case, was clearly by way of punishment in the facts and circumstances of that case. It was held in that case:

"Even an innocuously worded order terminating the service may in the facts and circumstances of the case, establish that some sort of enquiry into the allegations of serious and grave character of misconduct involving stigma had been made in infraction of the provision of Article 311. In such a case the simplicity of the form of the order will not give any sanctity. That is exactly what had happened in the case of *Ishwar Chand Agarwal*. The order of termination is illegal and must be set aside."

While analyzing the background of that case, the Apex Court observed:

"It is now well settled that where the form of the order is merely a camouflage for an order of dismissal for misconduct, it is always open to the court before which the order is challenged, to go behind the form and ascertain the true character of the order. If the court holds that the order though in the form is merely a termination of employment is in reality a cloak for an order of punishment, the court would not be debarred, merely because of the form of the order, in giving effect to the rights conferred by law upon the employee."

x x x x x

Coming to the facts of the present case, the Apex Court observed:

"Even though the order of discharge may be non-committal, it cannot stand alone. Where the report/ recommendation of the service authorities is the basis or foundation for the order, that should be read along with the order for the purpose of determining its character. If on reading the two together the court reaches the conclusion that the alleged act of misconduct was the cause of the order and that but for that incident it would not have been passed then it is inevitable that the order of discharge should fall on the ground where the aggrieved officer is not afforded a reasonable opportunity to defend himself as provided in Article 311 (2). It is not open to the competent authority to take the view that inquiry would be a nuisance and to resort to an *ex facie* innocuous order. It is wrong to assume that it is only when there is a full scale departmental inquiry any termination made thereafter will attract the operation of Article 311(2)."

8.22 The services of a probationer can be terminated by the competent authority on ground of his unsuitability for the post he is holding - criteria for deciding "unsuitability" of the probationer

There is no dispute regarding the legal position that in the case of terminating services of a probationer on account of unsatisfactory work in accordance with the conditions of service the order would not amount to punishment . It is only if an order is passed for other reasons not relating to satisfactory work that may amount to imposing punishment in the garb of passing a simple order of terminating the services during the probationary period. The Supreme Court laid down the following criteria in respect of the above proposition in *Purshottam Lal Dhingra* v. *Union of India,* AIR 1958 SC 36:

> "The protection of Article 311 of the Constitution applies to temporary Government servants also where dismissal, removal or reduction in rank is sought to be inflicted by way of punishment. But it is equally well settled that where the services of temporary Government servants are terminated not by way of punishment, Article 311 will not apply and the services of such a servant can be terminated under the terms of the contract or by giving him the usual one month's notice."

Aforesaid observations were noticed in *Ranendra Chandra Banerjee* v. *Union of India,* AIR 1963 SC 1552. In *Dr. T.C.M. Pillai* v. *Indian Institute of Technology,* AIR 1971 SC 1811, it was laid down by Supreme Court as under:

> "It is well settled that a probationer or a temporary servant can be discharged if it is found that he is not suitable for the post which he is holding. This can be done without complying with the provisions of Article 311(2) unless the services are terminated by way of punishment. Suitability does not depend merely on the excellence or proficiency in work. There are many factors which enter into consideration for confirming a person who is on probation. A particular attitude or tendency displayed by an employee can well influence the decision of the confirming authority while judging his suitability or fitness for confirmation."

Hari Singh Mann v. *State of Punjab,* AIR 1974 SC 2263 was a case where the services of an employee were terminated on the ground of unfitness. It was held that it left a stigma attracting rule 9 of the Punjab Civil Services (Punishment and Appeal) Rules. In *Manager, Government Branch Press* v. *D.B. Veerappa,* proposition of law was laid down as under:

> "If the services of a temporary Government servant are terminated in accordance with the conditions of his service on the ground of unsatisfactory conduct or his unsuitability for the job and/or for his work being unsatisfactory, or for a like reason which marks him a class apart from other temporary servants who have been retained in service, there is no question of the applicability of Article 16. Conversely, if the services of a temporary Government servant are terminated arbitrarily and not on the ground of his unsuitable, unsatisfactory conduct or the like which would put him in a class apart from his juniors in the same service, a question of unfair discrimination may arise, notwithstanding the fact that in terminating his service, the appointing authority was purporting to act in accordance with the terms of his employment."

In *Jarnail Singh* v. *State of Punjab,* 1986 (2) SLR 278 it was held that in the case of *ad hoc* employee whose services were terminated by way of punishment without giving him any opportunity while persons junior to him were retained in service, the order of termination violated Articles 14 and 16 of the Constitution. Ratio of the decision in *Parshotam Lal Dhingra's case* was noticed. In *Hardeep Singh* v. *State of Haryana,* 1987 (4) SLR 576, the Supreme Court dealt the case of Probationer whose services were terminated on the ground of taking part in "non-taking of food campaign". The order on the face of it appears to be simple in nature but it was held that it was passed by way of punishment which violated the provisions of Article 311(2) of the Constitution and Rule 16.24 of the Punjab Police Rules.

From the ratio of the decisions noticed above, it is clear that in case of temporary employees appointed on probation, their services can be terminated according to the conditions of appointment order during the period of probation on account of unsatisfactory work or unsuitability and in that case the provisions of Articles 311(2) of the Constitution or other service rules relating to punishment would not be attracted. On the other hand, if, in fact the order relating to misconduct of the employee is passed which would leave a stigma, though order may have been so worded to indicate that the same was passed in accordance with the conditions of appointment letter, the same would amount to imposing punishment and such a termination would amount to removal from service attracting the provisions of Article 311(2) of the Constitution and other service rules relating to punishment.

8.23 Terminating the services of a probationer on the ground of unsatisfactory performance without adequate basis is sure to invoke the wrath of the judicial authorities with penal consequences for humiliating and harassment suffered by the petitioner

One Neeta Mehta was appointed as Medical Officer on the recommendation of the Haryana Public Service Commission on probation for a period 2 years on 16-5-1994. The order of appointment mentioned that the probationary period could be extended by one year which was done in her case on 25-5-1996. The extended period of probation ended on 14-5-1997. Her services were terminated on 8-1-1998 *i.e.* after 8 months after the extended period of probation was over. She challenged her order of termination before P&H High Court on the ground that it was wholly arbitrary and unconstitutional. The stand of the department was that her work and conduct was not satisfactory during the period of probation and she had been communicated adverse remarks from her C.R. during the period. The Hon'ble court in its judgment dated 6-5-98 observed as under:

> "A careful scrutiny of the office nothings and the order passed by the Financial Commissioner depicts total non-application of mind by the concerned officers/officials. The office note suggesting that the petitioner's period of probation be extended because her two reports were not good is *ex facie* erroneous. That apart, the manner in which the learned Financial Commissioner dealt with the case of the petitioner leaves much to be desired. To us, it appears that the concerned officer did not bother to go through the records before she decided to dispense with the service of the petitioner. In our view, on the basis of the entries made in the

Annual Confidential Reports of the petitioner, no reasonable person could form an opinion that her work and conduct was unsatisfactory warranting termination of her service. If the competent authority had taken trouble to go through the record of the petitioner, it could not have been possible for her to direct the termination of petitioner's service. We, therefore, hold that the order terminating the service of the petitioner has been passed in a casual and arbitrary manner and, therefore, it is not only violative of Article 14 of the Constitution but suffers from malice in law.

For the reasons mentioned above, the writ petition is allowed. Order dated 8.1.1998 is quashed. For the harassment and humiliation suffered by her on account of the termination of service, the petitioner shall get costs of Rs. 10,000/- from the respondents. The Government shall be free to recover the same from the officer who may be found responsible for having passed wholly arbitrary order terminating the petitioner's service."

[*Dr. (Mrs.) Neeta Mehta* v. *State of Haryana*, 1998 (4) RSJ 4]

8.24 Can a probationer be discharged during the period of probation on the ground of unauthorized absence from duty?

One Madan Lal was appointed as a constable in J&K Police on 8-3-1974 and was put on probation for a period of 3 years. He was discharged from service on 2-12-1974 with immediate effect on the following two grounds:

(i) That the petitioner was a probationer and

(ii) That he was a habitual absentee.

The petitioner challenged the order of his discharge on various grounds before J&K High Court which in its judgment dated 8-4-1977 observed as under:

"The petitioner does not dispute that he was a temporary employee and could have been discharged from service without assigning any reason. His attack is however two fold. Firstly, he contends that even as a probationer, the petitioner had a right to remain in service for not less than three years, and secondly, the other ground of termination of service, namely 'habitual absentee' tantamounts to a stigma. The respondent on the other hand contended that the remark "habitual absentee" is not a stigma as it does not involve the moral turpitude of the petitioner. They made reference to decision of the Supreme Court in *Shamsher Singh* v. *State of Punjab*, 1975 SLJ 1 (SC), in support of their contention. In the peculiar circumstances of the instant case, it is not necessary for me to hold whether or not the aforesaid words constitute a stigma as in my opinion the impugned order even otherwise tantamounts to a punishment. The petitioner was to continue in service for a period of not less than three years. He has been deprived of more than two years service as a consequence of the impugned order which *per se* is a punishment because it operates as a forfeiture of the petitioners rights to salary etc. by bringing about the premature termination of his employment. The respondent has not been able to point out any rule under which the temporary service of the petitioner as a probationer could be terminated on the ground that that he was a habitual absentee. In these circumstances therefore I have no alternative but to hold that the impugned order was passed by way of punishment and is liable to be quashed."

[*Madan Lal* v. *Principal J & K Police Training School, Udhampur*, 1977 SLJ 706]

8.25 There is no bar to the termination of the services of probationer even during the stipulated period of probationary period itself if the circumstances so warrant

One K.M. Nair was selected for the post of A.S.I. Railway Protection Force and was put on probation for a period of four years commencing from 5-8-1974. On 30-10-1975, his probation was terminated and he was reverted. The case of the petitioner was that termination of his probation within the stipulated period of 4 years was by way of punishment and as such void. This case came up before Kerala High Court which in its judgment dated 31-3-1982 observed as under:

"The probation can be terminated even while the probation continues. If the probation had run out the specified period, there is no question of termination. In that event the probation has either to be declared to have been satisfactorily completed or the authority may refuse to make such declaration. Alternatively the probation can be extended. But in such cases the question of termination does not arise.

I am of the view that the authority which terminated the petitioner's probation had the competence to do so. Whether the discretion vested in the authority to terminate the probation had been validly exercised is a matter which is not open to question unless there is evidence to show that the order is vitiated by reason of *mala fide* or the like. I am not satisfied that the impugned orders suffer from any such defect."

[*K.M. Bhaskaran Nair* v. *Security Officer, Southern Range, R.P.F.*, 1982 (2) SLJ 161]

8.26 Gist of the leading judgments of Courts relating to reversion/termination of services of probationers

(i) "A probationer can be reverted during the probationary period itself and even thereafter to the original post, since he is having no legal right to the higher post. But if he is reverted to his original post by way of punishment, the provisions of Article 311 will apply."

[*State of Bombay* v. *F.A. Abraham*, AIR 1962 SC 794]

(ii) "Respondent was posted as Tahsildar on probation. Inquiry started for the purpose of affording him an opportunity to show cause why his probation should not be terminated forthwith. After considering his explanation, his probation was terminated. It cannot be said that by terminating the probation any penalty was imposed. Reversion is not as punishment. There is no violation of Article 311. "

[*State of Uttar Pradesh* v. *Akbar Ali Khan*, (1966) II SCWR 701]

(iii) "A reversion on the ground of unsuitability is an action in accordance with the terms under which the officiating post is held. It is not a reduction in rank by way of punishment to which Article 311 of the Constitution could be attracted."

[*Union of India* v. *R.S. Dhaba*, (1969) 1 SCWR 922]

(iv) "It is well settled that a person appointed on probation does not ordinarily get automatic confirmation on the expiry of stipulated probationary period. After expiry of probationary period he remains a probationer unless the appointment order contains provisions for his automatic confirmation. His services can be terminated if he is found unsuitable. "

[*State of Uttar Pradesh* v. *Tilak Singh*, 1975 LIC 1021]

(v) "The services of a probationer can be terminated before the expiry of probationary period if his work is unsatisfactory or he is not found fit for permanent employment. "

[*Purshottam Lal Dhingra* v. *Union of India*, AIR 1958 SC 36]

(vi) A person who is on probation, and who is deputed to another deputation should be treated as on probation in the parent Department even while he is on deputation. The provision of probation is only to assess whether he is suitable for the post to which he is appointed. Such assessment can be made even by the department to which he is deputed.

[*R.L. Gupta* v. *Union of India*, (1988) 2 SLR 133 (SC)]

(vii) Petitioner was appointed on probation for a particular period which was extended from time to time. Soon after expiry of maximum permissible period of probation (2 years), he was reverted. Petitioner contended that he should be automatically deemed to have been confirmed on expiry of probation. His contention was not accepted.

[*J.C. Kapoor* v. *International Airport Authority*, (1988) 3 SLR 774 (Mad)]

In the above case, the Madras High Court observed as under:

> "In the absence of any rule which contemplates that on the completion of the initial period of probation or in the absence of extension of probation before the lapse of the initial period of probation, the employee must be deemed to have been confirmed or become a permanent member, it is not possible to spell out a theory that such will be the resultant position...The general law is that a Government servant appointed on probation does not automatically become a full member of the service on the expiry of the period of probation, unless and until he is confirmed expressly or by implication."

(viii) Appointment to the post of Director, Physical Education (Female) in Maharishi Dayanand University was at issue. Probation was for one year. Termination of services was ordered after one year. Termination was held invalid as the petitioner would be deemed to have been confirmed on the expiry of the period of one year, as the period of probation was not extended.

[*Rameshwari Devi* v. *Maharishi Dayanand University*, (1992) 5 SLR 421 (P&H)]

(ix) Petitioner was appointed as a Section Officer in a university and worked for four years. The appointment was on the recommendation of the *ad hoc* Selection Committee. After four years, (during which his work was satisfactory) his services were terminated. The termination was held to be illegal petitioner having rendered four years of service, which goes beyond the maximum period of probation provided in the status, could not be eased out in this way.

[*Joginder Paul Jawa* v. *Haryana Agricultural University*, (1989) 3 SLR 524 (P&H)]

(x) Under Supplementary Rules SR 2(viii), probation period of 2 years was provided in the terms of appointment. There is express provision that no employee is to be kept on probation for more than double the normal term. Applicant was kept on probation for 5 years without any express order of confirmation. It was held that confirmation should be implied.

[*A.B. Srivastava* v. *Union of India*, (1989) 6 SLR 334 CAT (Cal)]

(xi) Under Rule 11(2), Haryana Civil Medical Services (Class II) Rules, 1978, if a probation period expires, the officer is deemed to have satisfactorily completed his period of probation. His services cannot thereafter be dispensed with.

[*Dr. Amar Singh Ahlawat* v. *State of Haryana*, (1988) 3 SLR 446 (P&H)]

(xii) Rule 8, Punjab Police Service Rules, 1959 provided for probation for 2 years with the proviso, probation could be extended for not more than one year. It was held that (1) where the rule provides for a fixed period and (ii) Government has power to extend it upto a specified period (and not an unlimited period), than, at the end of the specified period, which is not extendable the probationer is deemed to be confirmed.

[*Paramjit Singh* v. *Ram Rakha*, (1979) 2 SLR 88 SC]

(xiii) Under Rule 12(b), IAS (Probation) Rules, 1984 an I.A.S. Probationer is deemed to have been confirmed on the expiry of the probation period of one year. Hence an order of reversion, passed after the expiry of the period of probation is illegal.

[*S.D. Chaugule* v. *Union of India*, (1989) 3 SLR 315 CAT (N Bom)]

(xiv) Where the rules clearly require an express order of confirmation a probationer cannot contend that there is implied confirmation if he is continued beyond the period of probation.

[*Municipal Corporation, Raipur* v. *A.K. Misra*, (1991) 2 SLR 615 (SC)]

(xv) Appointment was made on contract. Employee was required to serve for five years from the date of completion of training, but employer could terminate the services at any time, if the work or conduct was found to be unsatisfactory. Services were terminated on account of misconduct. Termination was held justified. The employee was to be deemed to be on probation during the relevant time and his services could be terminated as per the agreement.

[*Haryana Hotels Limited* v. *The Presiding Officer*, (1994) 4 SLR 65 (P&H)]

(xvi) An order of discharge of an IPC probationer (during his probation period) must fall to the ground if the circumstances show that it was an alleged act of misconduct (coming late to the gymnasium etc.) which was the cause of the discharge even though the order was non committal.

[*Anoop Jaiswal* v. *Government of India*, (1984) 1 SLR 426 (SC): (1984) 1 SCJ 85]

(xvii) Under the Karnataka Civil Services (Probation) Rules, 1977, period of probation (as specified) cannot be extended. But that does not mean that on expiry of the period, confirmation is automatic. Rule 5 requires specific declaration of satisfactory completion of probation.

[*K. Rajendra Prasad* v. *State of Karnataka*, (1984) 2 SLR 119]

8.27 Case law on legal fiction of "Deemed Confirmation" after the probationary period is over

(I) One Bhikam Singh was appointed as Dy. Engineer in Maharashtra State Road Transport Corporation on 10-12-1976 on probation for a period of one year. It was stipulated in the order of his appointment that he will be governed by B.S.T. Regulations from time to time. His services were terminated on 6-2-1979. He challenged his order of termination before Bombay High Court. The respondents pleaded that maximum period of Probation was neither fixed in the appointment order nor in the Regulations applicable to the petitioner and that so long as express order of confirmation was not passed, the petitioner is deemed to be a Probationer. Further, confirmation does not depend upon passage of time. It depends upon the employee being found fit for confirmation. The following case law was cited by them on the subject:

(i) *S. Sukhbans Singh* v. *State of Punjab*, 1963 (1) LLJ 671

"A Probationer cannot acquire the status of a permanent member of a service unless the rules under which he is appointed expressly provide for such a result."

(ii) *G.S. Ramaswamy* v. *I.G. Police*, 1963 (1) LLJ 118

"Even though a probationer may have continued to act in the post to which he is appointed on probation for more than the initial period of probation, he cannot become a permanent servant merely because of efflux of time, unless the rules of service which govern him specifically lay down that the probationer will be automatically confirmed after the initial period of probation is over."

(iii) *State of Uttar Pradesh* v. *Akbar Ali*, 1967 (1) LLJ 708

"In case an employee is allowed to continue in the post ever after the period of probation without passing an order of confirmation, the only possible view to take is that by implication the period of probation was extended."

(iv) *Kedar Nath* v. *State of Punjab*, AIR 1972 SC 873

"Where a person is appointed as a probationer in any post and a period of probation is specified it does not follow that at the end of this specified period of probation he obtains confirmation automatically even if no order is passed in that behalf. Unless the terms of appointment clearly indicate the confirmation would automatically follow at the end of specified period or there is a specific service rule to that effect, the expiration of the probationary period does not necessary lead to confirmation. At the end of the period of probation an order confirming the officer is required to be passed and if no such order is passed and he is not reverted to his substantive post the result merely is that he continues in his post as a probationer."

(v) *State of Maharashtra* v. *Veerappa R. Saboji*, 1979 SLJ 621

"The plain meaning of the rules is that there is no automatic confirmation on the expiry of the probationary period fixed in the first instance. On expiry of the said period and on the fulfilment of the requirements of rules a Government servant becomes eligible for being confirmed. But it is a matter of a common knowledge that in many branches of Government service including the judiciary that for administrative reasons or otherwise the confirmation is delayed and is made at the subsequent time. It may also be delayed for watching the work of the Government servant for a further period. In my opinion the rule in question, therefore, comes under the ordinary and normal rule that without an express order of confirmation the Government servant will not be taken to have been confirmed in the post to which he was appointed temporarily and/or on probation".

On the other hand, the petitioner cited the following case law to contend that in the absence of any order extending his period of probation, he is deemed to have been confirmed:

(i) *State of Punjab* v. *Dharam Singh,* AIR 1968 SC 1210

(ii) *Supdt. of Police Ludhiana* v. *Dwarka Dss*, 1979 SLJ 230

In both these cases the facts of the case were entirely different. The relevant rules prohibited extension of period of probation beyond three years. It was in this back ground that a finding was recorded. That the probationary service ripened automatically into confirmation as a result of the expiry of the said period.

Having gone through the relevant case law cited by both the Parties, the Court in its judgment dated 28-4-1982 observed as under:

"It will have to be appreciated that the period of probation of an employee is the period of trial affording opportunity to the employer to observe his performance and to make up his mind regarding his confirmation. The very fact that an employee has been put on probation for a certain period implies that the employer has a right to watch his performance till the last day and thereafter to take the decision in the matter. Thus, if he is entitled to wait till the expiry of the whole period, it is but inevitable that some delay in passing the actual order will take place. After all the appointing authority may be having its office at a difference place and he has to take the final decision after receiving various reports from those under whom the employee worked. It will be too much to expect that the decision has to be taken without the passage of any time. Thus, it is practically impossible to pass an order of extension of period of probation, the moment the period is over, unless and until the order is passed before expiry of that period. It is for this reason that it has been held that there cannot be any assumption of confirmation as soon as the period is over. Of course, it is but proper that the order one way or the other should be passed within a reasonable period. The extent of this period is a question of facts depending upon many circumstances. The confirmation thus does not depend upon passage of time. It depends upon an employee being found to be fit for confirmation. This is of course subject to the specific service conditions and the rules. If any ceiling limit on the probation period is prescribed, the inevitable result is that there cannot be extension of probation period and an employee will be deemed to have been confirmed,"

[*Bhikam Singh* v. *Maharashtra State Road Transport Corporation,* 1982 (2) SLJ 540]

(II) One Trivedi was appointed as a Guest House attendant in C.S.I.R. Bhavnagar on 21-11-1977 on probation for one year. On 25-9-1978, he was allowed to continue on the said post till further orders. Subsequently, there were certain adverse reports against him and his services were terminated on 16-7-1980 against which he approached CAT (Ahmedabad Bench) and the Tribunal in its judgment dated 25-7-1989 observed as under:

"It is now well established that in the matter of appointment of an employee on probation, the expiry of probation period does not confirm automatic confirmation. For confirmation, there should be specific order of appropriate authority. No presumption of confirmation can be drawn from the fact that the employee is continued in the employment after the expiry of period of probation. It is true the Court can go behind the formal order of discharge and find the real cause of action and in case simple order of discharge of probation is based upon misconduct alleged against the Petitioner, it is required to hold an enquiry and in absence of proper enquiry it can not be sustained. The material placed on record does not warrant any inference of *mala fide* on the part of the respondents in terminating the services of the petitioner. It is not a case of the petitioner that he was accused of any misconduct on his part by the respondents. A probationer or a temporary employee can be discharged if not found suitable. In such a situation there is no need for holding any enquiry unless services were terminated by way of punishment."

[*M.K. Trivedi* v. *The Cen. Salt and Marine Chemical*, (1990) 1 SLJ 239 CAT]

(III) Where the rules provide for a maximum period of probation of two years with no provision for extension, then allowing an employee to continue in the post without any order of termination of reversion amounts to automatic confirmation of the post.

[*Om Parkash Maurya* v. *U.P. Sugar Co-operative Factories Federation*, (1986) 2 SLR 651]

(IV) All that probationer acquires after completion of probationary period is an eligibility for confirmation and not confirmation itself. Unless such eligibility is found to be satisfactory and order in that behalf is made confirming the probationer, he still remains a probationer.

[*Lakshmiah* v. *K.S.R.T.C.*, 1982 (2) SLJ 49]

(V) One Dr. Savita Mathur was appointed as Medical Officer and was put on probation for the period of two years. The maximum period of probation prescribed under the Rules was three years which was over on 18-1-1996. Certain adverse remarks from her C.R. were conveyed to her. No order of discharge was passed in her case within a reasonable time of the expiry of the date of the completion of three years probationary period but her services were terminated by order simpliciter on

18-11-1997. She challenged this order in Punjab & Haryana High Court which in its judgment dated 4-8-1998 observed as under:

> "By operation of legal fiction, petitioner is entitled to be deemed to have been confirmed. Her confidential Reports for the 1993-94, 1994-95 and 1995-96 reveal that the petitioner has been graded as a "good officer". Her integrity and professional competence etc. have been found to be "good". The only comment which was conveyed to the petitioner was that she did not "maintain her headquarters". The petitioner had explained this position and pointed out that there was no Government accommodation in village Kiorak where she had been posted. The petitioner claims that she had in fact hired a part of a private house and was staying in the village."

Taking the circumstances cumulatively it cannot be said that the petitioner was found wanting so as to be considered unsuitable for continuance in service. Still further, it cannot be forgotten that in the absence of Government accommodation it may not be easy for a lady Medical Officer to get suitable accommodation in a village. Even if the petitioner had been unable to stay in the village for some time, it would not be fair to conclude that she was unfit to continue in service. This is all the more so in view of the fact that she has been continuously graded as a "good officer" in all the reports.

In view of the above, we are unable to sustain the impugned action of the respondents in terminating the petitioner's service. Resultantly, the order dated November 18, 1997 is quashed.

[*Dr. Mrs. Savita Mathur* v. *State of Haryana*, 1998 (4) RSJ 221]

8.28 Two Classic judgments of the Supreme Court relating to the requirements of holding inquiries under Article 311(2) of the Constitution in the cases relating to termination of services of temporary employees on the ground of misconduct

(i) *Nepal Singh* v. *State of Uttar Pradesh*, AIR 1984 SC 84

This was a case of termination of a temporary Sub-Inspector of Police. The Inspector General of Police, Uttar Pradesh had issued a circular letter to the Superintendents of Police throughout the State requiring them to submit a list of Sub Inspectors whose reputation and integrity is very low, who are generally involved in scandals, like drinking, immorality, etc. and where they are a big problem because they encourage gambling, excise offences, brothels, criminals, etc. The applicant Nepal Singh was one of those included in the list of employees whose services were to be terminated. A "note" was appended with his case stating that "he was a corrupt officer; not straight-forward; married two wives against Government servants' Conduct Rules; does not do his duty sincerely, and wherever he goes, he creates problems." The applicant was removed by an innocuous order stating that his services were not required any more and his services were terminated with one month's pay in lieu of notice. The applicant filed a writ petition in the High Court of Delhi against the order of termination of his services. The High Court dismissed the Writ Petition on the ground that the impugned order was *ex facie* innocuous and could not be said to cast any stigma. Supreme Court, however, held that the complaint of the applicant was that his services have been terminated by the Competent Authority treating him unfairly and arbitrarily and that when a Government servant satisfies the Court *prima facie* that an order terminating his services violates Article 14 and 16, the competent authority must discharge the burden of showing that the power to terminate his services was exercised honestly and in good faith. The Supreme Court further held that "where allegations of misconduct are levelled against a Government servant and it is a case where the provisions of Article 311(2) of the Constitution should be applied, it is not open to the competent authority to take a view that holding the enquiry contemplated by that clause would be a bother or a nuisance and that, therefore, it is entitled to avoid the mandate of that provision and resort to the guise of an *ex-facie* innocuous termination order".

(ii) *Jarnail Singh* v. *State of Punjab,* 1986 (3) SCC 277

In this case, the services of certain *ad hoc* employees were terminated by an apparently innocuous order on the ground that posts were no longer required. The fact, however, was that there were certain allegations of embezzlement and also adverse remarks in the C.R. of the petitioners. No inquiry had been held. This case came up before Supreme Court which held as under:—

> "The order of termination was innocuous and the order of termination of the services of a probationer or of an *ad hoc*

appointee is a termination simpliciter in accordance with the terms of the appointment without attaching any stigma to the employee concerned. It is the substance of the order *i.e.* the attending circumstances as well as the basis of the order that have to be taken into consideration. In other words when an allegation is made by the employee assailing the order of termination as one based on misconduct, though couched in innocuous terms, it is incumbent on the Court to lift the veil and to see the real circumstances as well as the basis and foundation of the order complained of. In other words, the Court, in such case, will lift the veil and will see whether the order was made on the ground of misconduct, efficiency or not." In that case there were certain allegations of serious misconduct against the petitioners and also in the service records of the petitioners, which were taken into consideration by the Departmental Selection Committee without giving them any opportunity of hearing and without following the procedure provided in Article 311(2) of the Constitution of India, while considering the fitness and suitability of the appellants for the purpose of regularising their services in accordance with the Government Circular made in October, 1980. Thus the impugned orders terminating the services of the appellants on the ground that "the posts are no longer required were held to be made by way of punishment."

The Supreme Court considered the counter-affidavit filed by the authority and took into consideration the contention of the statement made therein to come to a conclusion that "the impugned order of termination of service of the petitioners had been made on the ground that there were adverse remarks in the service records of the petitioners were really made by way of punishment and they are not termination simpliciter according to the terms of the appointment without any stigma." It was further held that "it is undisputed that the respondents did not follow the mandatory procedure prescribed by Article 311(2) of the Constitution making the purported orders of termination of services of the petitioners on the ground of misconduct and thus there has been a patent violation of the rights of the petitioners as provided in Article 311(2) of the Constitution". The Supreme Court also came to categorical finding on considering the facts found from the entire materials that "there is no room for any doubt that the impugned order of termination of services of the petitioners had been made by way of punishment as the allegations of embezzlement of funds as well as adverse remarks in the service records of these petitioners were the basis and the foundation for not considering the petitioners to be fit for being regularised in their services in accordance with the Government Circular dated October 28, 1980."

[*Jarnail Singh* v. *State of Punjab*, 1986 LIC 1986]

Chapter 9

TERMINATION OF SERVICES OF *AD HOC* EMPLOYEES

"It is now well settled that an ad hoc appointment by its very nature is a stop gap arrangement made for a variety of reasons, particularly when the regular incumbent is not available or a process of regular selection involves time and the exigencies of service are such that the post cannot be allowed to remain unmanned meanwhile."

[*Captain S.M. Kanji Lal* v. *U.O.I.*, 1990 (1) SLJ 264 CAT]

SYNOPSIS

9.1 Law on the subject

9.2 Distinction between "Temporary Employees" and *"Ad hoc* Employees"

9.3 Distinction between Substantive appointment, temporary appointment, Regular appointment and ad hoc appointment

9.4 Difference between ad hoc appointment and temporary appointment

9.5 Difference between the terms "ad hoc", "fortuitous" and "stop-gap" used in service matters jurisprudence

9.6 Vacancies caused due to long-term deputations cannot be called fortuitous

9.7 Rulings of the Supreme Court relating to ad hoc employees enunciated in *State of Haryana* v. *Piara Singh,* AIR 1992 SC 2130

9.8 Circumstances under which administration should resort to making appointments on ad hoc basis

9.9 The practice of making ad hoc appointments in public services should be avoided as far as possible

9.10 An employee can be removed from service even after putting in long years of service on ad hoc basis in accordance with the express language of the appointment order

9.11 There is no need to issue a show cause notice to an *ad hoc* employee for his reversion to his substantive post when the order is not penal in nature

9.12 The services of one ad hoc employee cannot be terminated to appoint another person in his place

9.13 Persons appointed on *ad hoc* basis are required to be replaced when eligible persons become available

9.14 Gist of judgements of the courts relating to termination of services of ad hoc employees

9.15 Observations of the courts on the subject of absorption of *ad hoc* employees into regular cadre

9.1 Law on the subject

An *ad hoc* appointment does not by itself confer any right on the appointee and where, therefore, an appointment is made purely on *ad hoc* basis, the services of such an appointee can be terminated without any notice and the employer can put an end to the employment by exercising the right to terminating the services.

[*Sujata Oberoi* v. *Union of India,* 1987 (1) SLR N Del CAT 625]

9.2 Distinction between "Temporary Employees" and "*Ad hoc* Employees"

Punjab & Haryana High Court in the case of *S.K. Verma* v. *State of Punjab,* (1979) SLJ 477 (P&H) in its judgment dated 19-5-1978 observed as under:

> "*Ad hoc* employee is one who is appointed for a specified period of time as against a temporary employee who may be appointed without specifying the period of his appointment at all. The term "ad hoc employee" is conveniently used for a wholly temporary employee engaged either for a particular period or for a particular purpose and one whose services can be terminated with the maximum of each. The dictionary meaning of *ad hoc* in Webster's New International Dictionary has been given as 'pertaining' to or for the sake of this case alone'. In the Random House Dictionary its meaning has been given as "for this special purpose with respect to this subject or thing". Therefore, having regard to the ordinary meaning of the terms, no distinction can reasonably be drawn between a temporary employee whose services are terminable without notice or otherwise and an employee characterized as *ad hoc* and employed on similar terms. Indeed, it appears to us that in the gamut of services law, an *ad hoc* employee virtually stands at the lowest rung. As against the permanent quasi-

permanent, and temporary employee, the *ad hoc* one appears at the lowest level implying that he had been engaged casually or for a step-gap arrangement for a short duration of fleeting purposes.

The term "*ad hoc*" prefixed with the work "appointment" or "employee" is not a misnomer but represents a "level" in the hierarchy of various holders of post.

9.3 Distinction between Substantive appointment, temporary appointment, Regular appointment and *ad hoc* appointment

The Delhi High Court in *Lashkar Singh* v. *Municipal Corporation of Delhi,* (1978) SLJ 695 (Del) explained the difference between the aforementioned four types of appointments in these words:

(i). A post may be a permanent post or a temporary post. The appointment to a permanent post may be in a substantive capacity sometimes called in a permanent capacity or in a temporary or in an official capacity or in *ad hoc* capacity. Substantive appointment to a permanent post may also be made on probation. When an appointment in a substantive capacity or on probation is made to a permanent post, it would be a regular appointment. If the rules of service permit, temporary appointments to a permanent post may also be made on a regular basis. Officiating appointment or an *ad hoc* appointment can never be a regular appointment.

(ii) The competence to make appointment is to be distinguished from the nature of appointment. In a temporary post, appointment can never be made permanently or substantively. The very nature of the post would make the appointment a temporary appointment. If a post is created for a short tenure or an appointment is made to it, would be a temporary appointment though it may be regular appointment in that capacity depending upon, the rules of recruitment or appointment.

(iii) An officiating or *ad hoc* appointment to a permanent or temporary post is only stop gap arrangement till "regular appointments are made. An officiating appointment falls in a slightly separate category. Sometimes an officiating appointment is made when the incumbent of the post goes on leave and arrangements have to be made for the time being. At other times officiating appointment may be made to test the suitability of a person for a higher post. In the former case, it cannot be called a regular appointment though in a later case it may sometimes be a regular appointment depending upon the rule and would be in the nature of appointment on probation.

9.4 Difference between *ad hoc* appointment and temporary appointment

In *Om Parkash* v. *State of Haryana,* 1984 (1) SLR 314, the Division Bench of the Punjab and Haryana High Court while considering the difference between an '*ad hoc*' appointment and a temporary appointment observed that broadly speaking '*ad hoc*' appointments are generally made outside the rules whereas temporary employments are made within the frame work of rules of a service. In the instant case, it is not the case of the petitioner that the had been appointed under any statutory rules. His appointment and continuation was nothing more than purely *ad hoc* and such he cannot be said to have acquired any vested right or interest in the post. It follows, therefore that since the petitioner had no right to continue to the post either under the rules or under the terms of his appointment, the termination of his services is valid and legally in order."

9.5 Difference between the terms "ad hoc", "fortuitous" and "stop-gap" used in service matters jurisprudence

(i) The dictionary meaning of "fortuitous" is "happening by chance", "luckily". "*Ad hoc*" is something which is formed for a particular purpose. "Stop gap" means a temporary way of dealing with a problem or satisfying a particular need.

(ii) The meaning assigned to the terms while interpreting provisions of service Rules will depend upon the provisions of that Rule and the context and the purpose for which the expressions are used.

[*Rudra Kumar Sain* v. *U.O.I.*, 2000 (4) SLR 787]

9.6 Vacancies caused due to long-term deputations cannot be called fortuitous

It was held by Punjab and Haryana High Court that where the vacancies occur due to persons sent on long term deputations and these are filled on *ad hoc* basis treating them as not available as the deputationists could come back, cannot be said to be fortuitous. In cases where deputation is a long term affair, vacancies will be treated as non-fortuitous. Thus, the promotions made against such vacancies are to be treated as 'regular' from the date of promotion of *ad hoc* promotions of the appellant.

[*Sudarshan Pal* v. *State of Punjab*, 1987(1) SLJ 276]

9.7 Rulings of the Supreme Court relating to *ad hoc* employees enunciated in *State of Haryana* v. *Piara Singh*, AIR 1992 SC 2130

(i) "The normal rule, of course is regular recruitment through the prescribed agency but exigencies of administration may some time call for *ad hoc* appointments to be made. In such a situation, efforts should always be made to replace such *ad hoc* employees by regularly selected employees as early as possible. Such *ad hoc* employee may also compete along with others for such regular action/appointment. If he gets selected, "well and good" but if he does not, he must give way to regularly selected candidate. The appointment of regularly selected candidate cannot be withheld or kept in abeyance for the sake of such *ad hoc* employee.

(ii) Secondly, an *ad hoc* employee should not be replaced by another *ad hoc* employee. He must be replaced only by a regularly selected employee. This is necessary to avoid arbitrary action on the part of the appointing authority.

(iii) Thirdly, even where an *ad hoc* employment is necessitated on account of the exigencies of administration, he should ordinarily be drawn from the Employment Exchange unless it cannot brook delay in which case, the pressing cause must be stated on the file. If no candidate is available or is not sponsored by the Employment Exchange, some appropriate method consistent with the requirement of Article 16 should be followed. In other words, there must be a notice published in the appropriate manner calling for applications and all those who apply in response thereto should be considered fairly.

(iv) Fourthly, unqualified persons ought to be appointed only when qualified persons are not available through the above processes.

(v) Lastly, if for any reason, an *ad hoc* employee is continued for a fairly long spell, the authorities must consider his case for regularization provided he is eligible and qualified according to rules and his service record is satisfactory and his appointment does not run counter to the reservation policy of the State."

9.8 Circumstances under which administration should resort to making appointments on *ad hoc* basis

Ad hoc appointments should be resorted to only when there is "administrative necessity " or "emergency calling" for additional hands for performing administrative task of a given post which is lying vacant. When the administration stands in such dire need of additional hands, the strict meticulous adherence to merit, and at times even in the matter of age and qualifications and also the prescribed procedures for selection are given a go by in the public interest. In the nature of things, it is expected to be a one time act to afford to the administrative authority breathing time to select and appoint candidates in strict compliance with the relevant rules or the executive instructions.

9.9 The practice of making *ad hoc* appointments in public services should be avoided as far as possible

Governments of India have been issuing instructions from time to time to avoid making *ad hoc* appointments as far as possible. It has, however, been noted that despite these instructions, *ad hoc* appointments are continued to be made and consequently proposals for regularisation of such appointments are being made on the ground that the persons concerned have been working against these posts for a long time. This has led to instances where the Courts and Tribunals have directed Government to fix seniority of such employees after taking into consideration the period of service rendered by them on an *ad hoc* basis. This unintended benefits of *ad hoc* service has been bestowed on a number of persons whose appointments were initially made on seniority-cum fitness basis even though the Recruitment Rules for such posts provided for promotion by selection only.

9.10 An employee can be removed from service even after putting in long years of service on *ad hoc* basis in accordance with the express language of the appointment order

One Dr. (Mrs.) Chanchal Goyal was appointed as a lady doctor by Local Self Deptt. Of Rajasthan on 27-11-1974 on purely temporary basis for a period of six months or till the candidate selected by Rajasthan Public Service Commission is available whichever is earlier. She got extension in service from time to time. On 1-10-1988, her services were terminated on the ground that the candidate selected by the Rajasthan Public Service Commission has become available. She moved Rajasthan High Court in the matter and the litigation continued and she continued to work on *ad hoc* basis. Finally, she was removed from service on 11-4-1997 against which she filed a writ petition in the Supreme Court. It was held by the Apex Court that it cannot give any relief to the petitioner against the express language of the appointment order even though, she had put in about 28 years of *ad hoc* service. There is no such term as "deemed regularization". She cannot also claim protection on the doctrine of "Legitimate Expectation" which is still in formative stage in India.

[*Dr. (Mrs.) Chanchal Goyal* v. *State of Rajasthan*, 2003 (3) SLJ 1 (SC)]

9.11 There is no need to issue a show cause notice to an *ad hoc* employee for his reversion to his substantive post when the order is not penal in nature

One Baldev Singh was holding the substantive post of Charge I Mate in Punjab State Electricity Board. He was appointed/ promoted on *ad hoc* basis as Assistant Lineman. He was reverted to his substantive post by an order dated 8-1-1981 without issuing any show cause notice to him. This case came up before Supreme Court which in its judgment dated 6-4-1998 observed as under:

> "We have no hesitation to hold that in the facts and circumstances of the case the question of giving an opportunity of hearing to the plaintiff before passing the order dated 8-1-1981 does not arise. Since the plaintiff's appointment/promotion to the post of Assistant Lineman was purely on *ad hoc* basis and the higher authorities directed to discontinue such *ad hoc* appointment, the competent authority passed the impugned order posting the plaintiff against his substantive post of Charge 1 Mate. The plaintiff had not acquired any right to the post of Assistant Lineman

and further the impugned order dated 8-1-1981 cannot be held to be penal in nature."

[*Punjab State Electricity Board* v. *Baldev Singh*, 1998 (4) RSJ 3]

9.12 The services of one *ad hoc* employee cannot be terminated to appoint another person in his place

This question arose in the case of *S.K. Verma* v. *State of Punjab*, (1979) SLJ 477, before Punjab and Haryana High Court, which in its judgment dated 19-5-1978 observed as under:

> "In the present context of the simple case of termination of services in accordance with the contract of the employment clearly specifying that services may be dispensed with at any time without giving any notice. There is no question of Article 311 being attracted. It is elementary law that Articles 14 and 16 are attracted only when equals are treated unequally or to put it in reversely, unequals are treated equally. An *ad hoc* employee with an existing service record cannot be deemed in the eye of law as identically equivalent to an aspirant for the post which he is likely to vacate. The two do not form the same class, one of them being employed with his service record vice the other who is as yet unemployed and his work and conduct is yet to be assessed in future. The two, therefore, stand on entirely different footing, far from being in an identical class. There is thus a clear differentia existing betwixt them. Consequently, Article 16 can have no application even on this assumption either."

9.13 Persons appointed on *ad hoc* basis are required to be replaced when eligible persons become available

The instructions issued by Government provide that whenever an appointment is made on *ad hoc* basis, the fact that the appointment is *ad hoc* and that such appointment will not bestow on the person a claim for regular appointment is required to be spelt out clearly in the order of his appointment. It should be made clear in the order that the service rendered on *ad hoc* basis will not be counted for seniority and eligibility for promotion to the higher grade.

Government of India have issued instructions on the subject in D.O.P.T. O.M. No. 28036//1/2001 – Estt. (D) dated 23-7-2001, the relevant extracts from which are reproduced below:

"xxxxx

2. Instances have, however, come to the notice that despite the clear provisions, persons appointed on *ad hoc* basis, when replaced, approach the courts of law for regularizing their appointments and in many cases, directions are given by the Courts for regularising the period of *ad hoc* appointment with consequential benefits like seniority, etc.

3. In this regard, it is stated that issue of regularisation of *ad hoc* employees has been considered in several judgements of the Hon'ble Supreme Court. In the case of *R.N. Nanjundappa* v. *Thimmaiah,* AIR 1972 SC 1767 the Supreme Court observed that regularisation is not itself a mode of recruitment and any act in the exercise of executive power of the Government cannot override rules framed under Article 309 of the Constitution. In the case of *State of Orissa* v. *Sukunti Mahapatra,* AIR 1993 SC 1650 the Supreme Court has observed that assuming that their having served for long years is a valid reason for regularization, that without any thing more, will not meet the requirement of the action being in public interest and what has been done under the impugned orders is to regularise the illegal entry into service as if the Rules were not in existence. In another case *K.C. Joshi* v. *Union of India,* AIR 1991 SC 284, the Supreme Court observed that the *ad hoc* appointees cannot be put on a higher pedestal over the candidates who stood the test of merit and became successful in a competitive recruitment and secured ranking according to the merit in the approved list of candidates. In the case of *State of Haryana* v. *Piara Singh,* AIR 1992 SC 2130 the Supreme Court observed that direction to regularise *ad hoc* appointments, work-charged employees would only result in encouraging of unhealthy practice of back door entry – what cannot be done directly cannot be allowed to be done in such indirect manner. In the case of *Dr. M.A. Haque* v. *Union of India,* 1993 (2) SCC 213, the Supreme Court held that the Recruitment Rules made under Article 309 of the Constitution have to be followed strictly and not in breach. If a disregard of the rules and the by passing of the Public Service Commission are permitted, it will open a back door for illegal recruitment without limit. In the case of *Dr. Arundhati A.*

Paragaonkar v. *State of Maharashtra,* AIR 1995 SC 962, the Apex Court has held that a continuous service by itself do not give rise to the claim of regularisation.

4. An *ad hoc* appointee has to be replaced by a regularly selected candidate as per provisions of the Recruitment Rules and in accordance with the prescribed procedure at the earliest possible and in no case such an officer should be regularised. In the cases, where a judicial order is received for regularisation of an *ad hoc* employee, steps may be taken to contest the same in the light of the specific conditions on which the offer of appointment on *ad hoc* basis was made, the policy of the Government in this regard and the various judicial pronouncements of the apex Court. If in a particular case, the Ministry/Department desires to consider acceptance of the judicial order, the matter should be invariably referred to the Department of Legal Affair and the Department of Personnel and Training as per this Department's O.M. No. 28027/9/99-Estt.(A) dated 1-5-2000 which says that whenever there is a court order against the Government of India, pertaining to service matters, no such order shall be implemented by the concerned Ministry/Department without first referring the matter to the Department of Legal Affairs and to the Department of Personnel and Training for advice.

5. It has all along been emphasized in the existing instructions that *ad hoc* appointments should be made only in rare cases and in real exigency of work, where the post cannot be kept vacant until regular candidate becomes available. It has been emphasized, in particular that *ad hoc* appointment by direct recruitment from the open market should be resorted to only as a last resort. This is because once a person is appointed from outside the Government on *ad hoc* basis such arrangement is generally continued for long periods, either because a regularly selected candidate is not available or some other vacancy in the grade/cadre become available against which he is adjusted. Consequently, when efforts are made to replace such an officer, he / she invariably approaches a court of law for regularisation of their appointment. Apart from the fact that regularisation of appointment in such cases is not in public interest as

they have not come through proper selection procedure seniority, promotion, pension, etc. However, notwithstanding these instructions, *ad hoc* appointments by direct recruitment from open market are being made as a matter of routine. In fact, on many occasions, such appointments are being made only to avoid the post getting abolished in terms of the relevant instructions of the Ministry of Finance, providing for automatic abolition of posts if they remain vacant for more than one year. Of late, instances of *ad hoc* appointments from open market have substantially increased resulting in more and more court cases being filed for regularisation of service of such *ad hoc* appointees.

6. In view of the aforesaid undesirable trend, the matter has been reviewed and it has been decided that hereafter no appointment shall be made on *ad hoc* basis by direct recruitment from open market. Where the vacant post cannot be kept vacant for functional considerations, efforts may be made to entrust the additional charge of the post to a serving officer under provisions of FR 49, failing which only appointment by *ad hoc* promotion/ad hoc deputation may be considered. If in an exceptional case (e.g. in the case of an operational organisation), it is inescapable to resort to *ad hoc* appointment by direct recruitment, prior concurrence of the Department of Personnel and Training (Establishment 'D' Section) may be obtained by giving full and complete justification for the same.
7. Continuation of an *ad hoc* appointment beyond one year will, as per the existing instructions, continue to require the prior approval of Department of Personnel and Training as before."

9.14 Gist of judgments of the courts relating to termination of services of *ad hoc* employees

(i) Ad hoc appointees appointed irregularly cannot claim to continue in service as against regular appointees properly selected. Such a claim would in fact violate Article 14 of the Constitution because the very object of service rules (Article 309 of the Constitution) is to afford equal opportunity to all.

[*Bharatiben* v. *State of Gujarat*, (1989) 1 GLR 659 (Guj)]

(ii) A person appointed to a post on an *ad hoc* basis for a specified period cannot claim that until a regular appointment is made, he should be allowed to continue.

[*Bhartendu Sharma* v. *State of Haryana*, (1995) 2 SLR 248 (P&H) (DB)]

(iii) Where a person is initially appointed or promoted in *ad hoc* capacity and continues his service without break and is finally appointed or promoted in the said post on regular basis, the entire period counts for service. He cannot be reverted without adequate reason.

[*C.S. Dubey* v. *Union of India*, (1975) 1 SLR 580 (Del); *N.K. Srivastava* v. *Municipal Corporation, Delhi*, (1991) 1 SLR 727 (Del)]

(iv) Expression *"ad hoc"* appointment connotes an appointment made as stop-gap arrangement. When the period or purpose is not indicated in the order of appointment, it has to be treated as one for short period.

[*Dr. Mohd. Ishaq* v. *Osmnia University*, (1990) 2 SLR 178 (187-190) (AP) (DB)]

(v) Appointment was made on *ad hoc* basis, till such time an approved candidate of Service Selection Board joined service. Termination of services, on the availability of candidate selected by the Board is valid.

[*Balwinder Kaur* v. *State of Haryana*, (1993) 4 SLR 179 (P&H)]

(vi) *Ad hoc* appointees appointed by the Irrigation Department without the State Public Service Commission being consulted have no right to demand their continuance in office. "To permit their continuance in service would not only be the violation of the term contained in the letter of appointment but would also amount to a breach of the requirements of Article 320 of the Constitution and no Court of Law can permit such infraction.

[*Association of Asstt. Engineers* v. *State of Gujarat*, 1988 GLT 395]

(vii) Officiating services in *ad hoc* appointment counts for service if the employee is ultimately regularised.

[*Bhusan Kumar Chaturvedi* v. *Union of India*, (1988) 5 SLR 366 (CAT) (Jabalpur)]

(viii) Where a Principal in the U. P. Education Department appoints a person as Lecturer against a leave vacancy by way of

"Local arrangement", it is not an *ad hoc* appointment and in any case, the appointee cannot claim to continue in the post till P.S.C. appointee is appointed.

[*Dr. Bimal Singh* v. *State of Uttar Pradesh,* (1985) 2 SLR 501 (All) (DB)]

(ix) Where the service of an *ad hoc* employee are terminated on the ground of unsuitability, communication in advance of the deficiency is necessary.

[*Dr. (Mrs.) Sumati P. Shere* v. *Union of India,* AIR 1989 SC 1431]

(x) Petitioner was appointed as LDC. One of the conditions was that the appointment was temporary and *ad hoc* and the candidate was liable to be discharged without notice. Another condition was that the appointment was subject to character verification. On adverse police verification, the petitioner was discharged. It was held that natural justice ought to have been observed before discharging the employee.

[*M. Krishnan* v. *Government of India,* (1988) 5 SLR 60 CAT (Mad)]

(xi) Services of an *ad hoc* employee cannot be arbitrarily terminated while his juniors are retained.

[*I.P. Girija* v. *Union of India,* (1987) 2 SLR 769]

(xii) Termination of services of an *ad hoc* employee for wilful absence without observing the rules of natural justice is illegal.

[*Manjit Singh* v. *State of Punjab,* (1988) 5 SLR 161 (P&H)]

(xiii) An *ad hoc* employee's services cannot be terminated on grounds of conduct without following the procedure prescribed by Article 311 of the Constitution. If an order stigmatizes the petitioner by referring to her absence from duty, Article 311 must be observed.

[*Geeta* v. *State of M.P.,* (1988) 2 SLR 389 (MP) (DB)]

(xiv) *Ad hoc* appointees who have held an appointment for a sufficiently long period, constitute a class by themselves and relaxation of the rules in their favour is valid.

[*Shanti Devi* v. *State of Haryana,* (1988) 1 SLR 483 (P&H)]

(xv) Where the appointment of a person is on *ad hoc* basis, on a regular appointment being made, he must make way for the regular appointee.

[*Dr. Kishore* v. *State of Maharashtra,* (1997) 1 SLR 107 (SC)]

(xvi) *Ad hoc* appointment as temporary Assistant Engineers was made for a specific period and not in accordance with the rules. Initial *ad hoc* appointment extended periodically till their regularization on 26-2-1980. Period spent on *ad hoc* appointment cannot be counted towards seniority. Seniority is to be reckoned from the date of regularisation of service.

[*State of West Bengal* v. *Aghore Nath Dey*, (1993) 2 SLR 528 (SC)]

(xvii) A person was appointed as Sub-Inspector, Food and Supplies on purely *ad hoc* basis (against ex-servicemen quota) for a period not exceeding six months. It was also mentioned in the letter that his services could be terminated even during this period without notice and without assigning any reason. He was subsequently suspended, as criminal proceedings were instituted against him, for cheating. Hence, his services were terminated. It was held that the termination was legal.

[*State of Haryana* v. *Babu Lal*, (1985) 3 SLR 395 (P&H)]

(xviii) The Gujarat High Court has deprecated the practice of making *ad hoc* appointment for 28 or 29 days and then forcing an artificial break. Such a practice is illegal, unfair, unjust and oppressive. It violates Articles 14 and 16 of the Constitution.

[*Dinesh Kumar* v. *State of Gujarat*, (1988) 1 SLR (Guj)]

(xix) Where the principle to be followed for *ad hoc* employees is that of "first come last go" (Punjab Government circular dated 13th December, 1983) it is not permissible to make a distinction between those recruited directly and those taken through employment exchange.

[*Joginder Singh* v. *State of Punjab*, (1986) 2 SLR 442 (P&H)]

(xx) Where a person is appointed temporarily against leave vacancy, the appointment comes to an end when the period of appointment expires. Relieving orders in such a case cannot be treated as termination order.

[*State of Punjab* v. *Avtar Kaur*, (1991) 2 SLR 329 (P&H) (DB)]

(xxi) Candidates, after having undergone training, were available for appointment as Patwaris. In the presence of such candidates, the Collector's action in making an *ad hoc* appointment to bypass the rules is illegal.

[*Gurmail Singh* v. *State of Punjab*, (1986) 3 SLR 684 (P&H)]

(xxii) Where an *ad hoc* appointment is made, then the appointment term cannot be arbitrarily limited to six months. Services cannot be terminated, except where the performance is unsatisfactory or regular candidates are available or the post itself is abolished.

[*Balwan Singh* v. *State of Haryana*, (1997) 1 SLR 624 (P&H) (DB)]

(xxiii) Applicants were promoted as law assistants on an *ad hoc* basis till regular persons were recruited. By mistake, the fact regarding *ad hoc* appointment was not clearly indicated. Mistake was sought to be rectified after about two years. 'Applicants' representation against the action was considered and rejected. Held, there was no violation of Articles 14 and 16 of the Constitution.

[*G.P. Rao* v. *Union of India*, (1995) 8 SLR 515 (CAT) (Guwahati)]

(xxiv) Petitioner was appointed as an *ad hoc* teacher in the Government Middle School, Kairu, but her services were terminated for reasons which were found to be illegal. The reason given by the Government was that she did not have English as a subject in graduation, and that this was a qualification prescribed by the Director of Public Instruction in his letter. It was later found that the letter was prospective only and did not affect the petitioner already appointed. Termination was held to be void.

[*Ram Rati Devi* v. *State of Haryana*, (1985) 2 SLR 770 (P&H)]

(xxv) Where the post is permanent one, the State cannot go on making casual or *ad hoc* appointments, treating the post as a temporary one.

[*Sayare Devi* v. *State of Rajasthan*, (1995) 7 SLR 403 (Raj)]

(xxvi) Where *ad hoc* appointment is continued for long, the court presumes that there is need and warrant for a regular post. Court accordingly directs regularization.

[*State of Haryana* v. *Piara Singh*, AIR 1992 SC 2130]

(xxvii) Denial of salary to *ad hoc* teachers for period of summer vacation deprecated.

[*Rattan Lal* v. *State of Haryana*, AIR 1987 SC 479]

(xxviii) An *ad hoc* employee was convicted under section 294, IPC (doing obscene acts/reciting songs to the annoyance of others) and his services were terminated. It was held that conviction on its own would not involve moral turpitude depriving the opportunity to serve the State.

[*Pawan Kumar* v. *State of Haryana,* 1996 (2) LLJ 703]

(xxix) Mere prolonged continuous *ad hoc* service does not ripen into regular service to claim permanent or substantive status.

[*State of Orissa* v. *Dr. Pyari Mohan Misra,* 1995 (3) SCC 123]

9.15 Observations of the courts on the subject of absorption of *ad hoc* employees into regular cadre

"If the casual labour with six months or 240 days of continuous service have been entitled by judicial pronouncements and Government policy to be absorbed in regular service and given priority for absorption in vacant posts, there is no reason why the superior class of *ad hoc* appointees who have been continued for nine to ten years should not be entitled to absorption in the regular cadre" observed the Hon'ble Supreme Court in *Rattan Lal* v. *State of Haryana,* 1988 (4) SCC 43. That case related to the policy of State of Haryana which it was adopting to appoint teachers on *ad hoc* basis at the commencement of an academic year and then to terminate their services before the commencement of next summer vacation or earlier and to appoint them again on an *ad hoc* basis at the commencement of the next academic year and to terminate the services before the commencement of the succeeding summer vacation or earlier and they are continuously doing so year after year. The Supreme Court deprecated this unhealthy practice of arbitrary "hiring and firing" policy and directed the State of Haryana to take immediate steps to fill up the posts in accordance with the relevant rules the vacancies in which the teachers appointed on *ad hoc* basis were then working and to allow all those teachers who were then holding this post on an *ad hoc* basis to remain till the vacancies were duly filled up. They further directed that the teachers who are now working on such *ad hoc* basis and if they have the prescribed qualification may also apply for being appointed regularly in those posts. The State Government was also directed to consider sympathetically the question of relaxing the qualifications of maximum age prescribed for appointment to those posts in the case of those who have been victims of this of *ad hoc* appointments. If any of the petitioners in these petitions has under any existing rule acquired the right to be appointed as a regularly appointed teacher, his case should be considered by the State Government and an appropriate order passed in his case.

(ii) In *Guru Prasad* v. *Union of India,* 1986 (6) ATC 47, the Jabalpur Bench of the Tribunal held that *ad hoc* appointees continued beyond a period of one year have to be treated as temporary appointee under CCS (Temporary Service) Rules, 1965 and entitled to quasi permanenteys under rule 3 of those rules even though described as *ad hoc.* They have further indicated that the form of appointment order is not conclusive proof of its nature and the court has the power to lift the veil and see its real nature from attendant circumstances like the opening of service books and the reports of medical examinations.

(iii) It is not in dispute that respondents are at liberty to discharge the employees even after seven or eight years of service merely because in the terms of appointment such powers have been agreed to be vested with the employer. In *Ramachandra Hari Karmakar* v. *Union of India,* 1988 (4) SCC 43, the Principal Bench of the Tribunal set aside the order of termination passed under Central Civil Services Temporary Service Rules when juniors were retained on the ground that notwithstanding compliance of contract of service and the service rules such an act would be in violation of Articles 14 and 16 of the Constitution.

Chapter 10

TERMINATION OF SERVICES OF EMPLOYEES APPOINTED ON CONTRACT

"When an employee is appointed to his post on contract, he acquires a status and his rights and obligations are no longer determined by consent of both parties but by statute or statutory rules which may be framed and altered unilaterally by the Government."

(Supreme Court)

SYNOPSIS

10.1 Law on the subject

The law on the subject has been laid down by the Supreme Court in the leading case of *Roshan Lal Tandon* v. *U.O.I.*, AIR 1967 SC 1889 in these words:

"...... It is true that the origin of Government service is contractual. There is an offer, for acceptance in every case. But once appointed to his post or office, the Government servant acquires a status and his rights and obligations are no longer determined by consent of both parties, but by statute or statutory rules which may be framed and altered unilaterally by the Government. In other words, the legal position of a Government servant is more one of status than of contract. The hall mark of status is the attachment to a legal relationship of rights and duties imposed by the public law and not by mere agreement of parties...."

".......But it is obvious that the relationship between the Government and its servant is not like an ordinary contract of service between a master and servant. The legal relationship is something entirely different, something in the nature of status. It is in much more than a purely contractual relationship voluntarily entered into between the parties. The duties of status are fixed by the law and in the enforcement of the duties, society has an interest. In the language of jurisprudence, status is a condition of membership of a group of which powers and duties are exclusively determined by law and not by agreement between the parties concerned."

The implications of this judgment is that once an employee is appointed to a post under Government on contract, he is governed by the rules governing his service conditions and it will not be permissible thereafter for him to rely upon the terms of contract which are not in consonance with the rules governing the service and that the powers of the Government under Article 309 to make rules, to regulate the service conditions of its employees are wide and cannot in any manner, be fettered by any agreement and these powers can be exercised unilaterally without consent of the employees concerned.

10.2 Employees employed on *ad hoc* basis under contract acquire status on the appointment and their service conditions deemed to be governed by Statutory Rules thereafter

One Sukumaran was offered the post of a peon on 19-1-1983 in the office of Project Evaluation office Cochin on a temporary basis on the condition that it will be a short-term appointment and would be terminable on the return of the regular incumbent of that post or at any time even earlier before that and that it will not confer on him any title to his permanent employment. The services of the petitioner were terminated on 20-5-1985 without any notice. The petitioner challenged the order of his termination in *T.I. Sukumaran* v. *U.O.I.,* 1989 (4) SLJ 75 before CAT

Ernakulam Bench which in its judgment dated 8-6-1989 observed as under:

> "..... It has been held by the Apex Court in *Roshan Lal Tandon* v. *U.O.I.*, AIR 1967 SC 1889 (quoted above) that the employees after having been appointed on contract acquire a status and their service conditions are then governed by the statutory laws and not by contract.
>
> Xxxx
>
> In our opinion, the appointment offered by the Respondent to the petitioner was temporary and on his accepting the offer, his services have to be governed by the provisions of Central Civil Services (Temporary Service) Rules, 1965 and under Rule 5 of the said Rules, it was necessary for the contesting Respondents to serve him with a notice of one month for terminating his services. Admittedly, no notice was given to the petitioner as is also evident from the order of his termination. The termination of the services of the Petitioner, thus, being contrary to law is void and of no consequence and he should be deemed to be in service with all consequential benefits permissible under the law."
>
> [*T.I. Sukumaran* v. *U.O.I.*, 1989 (4) SLJ 75]

(ii) One Ashok Kumar was offered the post of a Security Guard in All india Radio Bhagalpur on a purely temporary basis liable to be terminated at any time without any reason. The petitioner accepted the terms and conditions of appointment and joined in the post on 14-7-1978. He was subsequently charged for assaulting his appointing authority in an incident on 26-6-1979 and criminal proceedings were also initiated against him. He was placed under suspension on 26-7-1979 and his services were terminated under Rule 5(1) of CCS (TS) Rules on 31-8-1981 and it was ordered that he will not be entitled to claim any dues from 1-9-1981. He was, thus, not given any notice nor any salary in lieu of any notice period. He challenged this order before CAT Patna Bench, which in its judgment dated 28-10-1986 observed as under:

> ".......In the case of *U.O.I.* v. *Arun Kumar Roy*, 1986 (1) SCC 675, it was laid down that a Government servant whose appointment originates in a contract, acquires a status and terms and conditions of such an employee are then governed

by rules of his service and it will not be permissible thereafter for him to rely on the terms of the contract which are not in accordance with the rules governing his service........... Accordingly, the services of the petitioner can be terminated under Rule 5(1) of CCS (TS) Rules and as provided in proviso to Rule 5(1)(b), he will be entitled to one month's pay. Since his services were terminated on 31-8-1981 forthwith, he can claim relief from the department in the shape of one month's salary for the month of September, 1981."

[*Ashok Kumar* v. *U.O.I.*, 1987 (1) SLJ 187 CAT]

10.3 Distinction between 'Contract for Service' and 'Contract of Service'

In the former, the master or employer may order or require the employee to suggest the manner under which a work is to be done but in the later case, the employer can order and require the employee to do the service under his supervision and direct control. Where an agreement is for personal labour, it is contract of employment.

[*Harish Chandra* v. *Trilok Singh*, AIR 1957 SC 444]

10.4 Appointments of teachers on "contractual basis" on a consolidated salary for fixed terms when vacancies are available is arbitrary, oppressive, unreasonable and violative of Articles 14 and 16 and 39(d) of the Constitution

One Shamsher Singh and others were appointed to the posts of lecturers in Technical Education Deptt., Haryana in various disciplines after being selected by a duly constituted committee and were given appointments on *ad hoc* basis in the scale of Rs. 2200-4000. Their services were later on terminated when regular teachers selected by the Haryana Public Service Commission became available. The effected lecturers claimed that the regular Lecturers had joined against vacant posts only and there was no justification whatsoever for terminating their service. Strangely enough, the Government later informed those Lecturers whose services had been terminated that they should come and join against vacant posts available in the Deptt. as there was sufficient work load and their services were needed. They were now offered a consolidated salary of Rs. 5500 per month on "contract basis" instead of regular Pay Scales. They challenged the offer of the contract made by the State Government to them before Punjab & Haryana High Court which in its judgment dated 20-7-1998 observed as under:-

> "...... The action of the Respondents to appoint the Petitioners on 'contractual basis' at a consolidated salary in spite of the available of vacant posts carrying regular scales is arbitrary, oppressive, unreasonable and violative of Article 14 and 16 of the Constitution. Consequently, the writ petition filed by them are accepted. The condition regarding contractual appointments is declared illegal, unconstitutional and is accordingly struck down. The respondents will allow the petitioners to continue in service till the availability of regularly selected candidate or till the vacant/sanctioned posts are available. The petitioners will be given salary in the regular pay scales after their reappointment on contractual basis as was given to them earlier upon their initial appointments on *ad hoc* basis with all consequential reliefs."

10.5 Gist of the judgments on the subject of termination of services of employees appointed on contract

(i) One Prem Singh was given employment for one day at a time with the issuance of successive letters. It was held that contractual relationship stood terminated at the end of each day. The status of the respondent was at best as that of daily wager.

[*Allahabad Bank* v. *Prem Singh,* 1996 (10) SCC 597]

(ii) The contractual field must be fair, just, reasonable in consonance with constitutional conscience and socio-justice.

[*L.I.C.* v. *Consumer Education & Research Centre,* 1995 AIR SC 1811]

(iii) Ministers appointing persons of their choice in contractual employment which is co-terminus with tenure of ministries. No order of termination is necessary as the appointment dos not attract the rules.

[*State of Gujarat* v. *P.J. Kampavat,* 1992 AIR SC 1685]

(iv) One Dr. Ajay Kumar Jain was appointed as a scientific fellow for one year extendable by three years on year to year basis under "Quick Hire Scheme" in CSIR. After expiry of one year contract of employment, the employment was extended by six months and his request for further extension was rejected. No reason was given in the counter affidavit for such extension of six months period. The action of the appellant was held arbitrary.

[*CSIR* v. *Dr. Ajay Kumar Jain,* AIR 2000 SC 2710]

(v) The petitioner was selected for a post after passing an examination. An offer of appointment was made which was subject to his being declared fit in medical examination. The petitioner resigned his earlier post and presented himself for medical test but was not examined for no fault of his own. It was held that contract of employment had come into existence which the petitioner is entitled to enforce.

[*R.A. Kushwaha* v. *U.O.I.,* 1985 (2) SLR 779 (All) (DB)]

(vi) Appointment of compilers/checkers in census office is contractual. There is no right to regularisation.

[*Seema Pathak* v. *U.O.I.,* 1995 (3) SLR 296 CAT (Chandigarh)]

(vii) When the appointment is contractual and the contract is not renewed because of unsatisfactory performance, there is no cause of auction.

[*Dr. Thenmozhi* v. *Director of Health & Family Welfare,* 1995 (3) SLR 396 CAT (Mad)]

Chapter 11

TERMINATION/REGULARISATION OF SERVICES OF CASUAL WORKERS

"We would be guilty of turning a blind eye to a situation apart from being highly unethical, wholly contrary to constitutional philosophy of socio-economic justice if we fail to point out that Rule 2501 of Railway Establishment Manual which permits a man serving for 10, 20, 30 years at a stretch without break being treated as daily rated servant, is thoroughly opposed to the notions of socio-economic justice and it is high time that the Railway administration brings this part of the provision of the Manual, antiquarian and antediluvian, in conformity with the Directive Principles of State Policy as enunciated in Part IV of the Constitution."

(Supreme Court)

SYNOPSIS

11.10 State as model employer has an onerous duty to timely expedite regularization of services of casual workers and non-availability of a post is not a valid ground to deny the relief

11.11 Orders issued by Government of India relating to regularisation of services of Casual employees

11.12 Gist of Court decision relating to termination of services of casual employees

11.1 Who is a casual worker?

The word "casual" has been defined in Oxford Dictionary as "not regular or firmly established, occasional or temporary casual jobs, happening by chance". A casual worker is, therefore, one who is not employed in regular job and by implication; it means a person whose employment is dependent upon occurrence of any job opportunity by chance. The security of job of such a person is of precarious nature.

11.2 Plight of casual workers employed in the Railways

The Apex Court had occasion to comment adversely on the poor lot of casual workers employed in the Railways in their classic judgment in the case of *D'Souza L. Robert D'Souza* v. *Executive Engineer*, 1982 (1) SLR 864. It found to its horror that casual employees remained employed for over 20 years but even then, they were not treated even as regular temporary employees and that their services could be terminated at the whims and fancies of local straps. The Court had a dig at the Railways in employing large number of work charged staff who remained daily wagers throughout their long service. One could understand such a situation when Planning and Projects were foreign to Indian economy but today, Railways have perspective plans spreading over decades. If one Project is completed, another has to be taken over. Railway administration has miles to go and promises to keep and this became crystal clear from the case of *D'Souza*. It is high time that such utterly unfair provisions wholly denying social economic justice are properly modified and brought in conformity with the modern concept of justice and fair play to the lowest and the lowermost in Railway administration."

11.3 Exhortations of the Judicial Courts to Government for preparing schemes for regularization and absorption of the casual workers as far as possible

There have been a number of judicial pronouncements in which the existing practice of employing casual workers in

Government Deptts. and Public Sector Undertakings have been deprecated by the Courts of the land and it has been exhorted by them that Government should prepare schemes on rational basis for absorbing as far as possible all casual workers who have been continuously working for years together. In the case of *Surindera Singh* v. *Chief Engineer C.P.W.D.*, WP (C) No. 59 60 & 563-70/83 [AIR 1986 SC 584], Supreme Court in its judgment dated 17-1-1986 observed as under:

> "We record our regret that many employees are kept in service on a temporary daily wage basis without their services being regularised. We hope that the Government will take appropriate action to regularise the services of all those who have been in continuous employment for more than six months."

(ii) In another case decided by the Hon'ble Supreme Court on 27-10-1987 in respect of Daily Rated Casual Labour employed under P& T Department *Bhartiya Dak Tar Mazdoor Manch* v. *Union of India,* WP No. 373 & 302/1986, it directed the respondents to prepare a scheme on a rational basis for absorbing as far as possible the casual labourers who have been continuously working for more than one year in the Posts & Telegraphs Department.

(iii) Still in another case *U.P. Income Tax Department, contingent Paid Staff Welfare Association* v. *Union of India,* WP No. 1670 of 1986 decided on December 4-12-1987, the Hon'ble Supreme Court observed as follows:

> "We allow this Writ Petition and direct the respondents to pay wages to the workmen who are employed as the contingent paid staff of the Income Tax Department throughout India doing the work of Class IV employees at the rates equivalent to the minimum pay in the pay scale of the regularly employed workers in the corresponding cadres. Such workmen are also entitled to corresponding Dearness Allowances and Additional Dearness allowance payable thereon. Whatever other benefits which are not being enjoyed by the said workmen shall continue to be extended to them. We further direct the respondents to prepare a scheme on a rational basis for absorbing as far as possible the contingent paid staff of the Income Tax Department who have been

continuously working for more than one year as Class IV employees in the Income Tax Department."

11.4 Observations of the Hon'ble Supreme Court in *L. Robert D'Souza* v. *Executive Engineer, Southern Railway*, 1982 (1) SLR 864 on the grant of temporary status to Casual Labour

D'Souza had been working as a casual labour continuously from 1954 to 1976 and was transferred from one construction unit to another during the said period. He was, however, never treated as a temporary employee. His services were terminated on the ground that he is a mere Project labour and is not entitled to be treated as a temporary employee. In the classic judgment *delivered* by the Apex Court on 16-2-1982 his termination was held illegal. The extracts from the said judgment *are* reproduced below:

(i) "Construction unit is a regular unit all over the Indian Railways. It is a permanent unit and cannot be equated to project. Therefore, the averment of the Railway administration that the appellant was working on project cannot be accepted. He belongs to the construction unit. He was transferred fairly often and he worked continuously for 20 years and when he questioned the *bona fides* of his transfer he had to be re-transferred and paid wages for the period he did not report for duty at the place where he was transferred. Cumulative effect of these facts completely belies the suggestion that the appellant worked on project. Having rendered continuous uninterrupted service for over six months, he had acquired the status of a temporary railway servant under Rule 2501 of R.E.M. (Railway Establishment Manual) and therefore, his service could not have been terminated under Rule 2505 of R.E.M."

(ii) "The test provided for the purpose of determining the eligibility of casual labour to be treated as temporary should be the period of continuous work put in by each individual labour on the same type of work and not the period put in collectively by any particular gang or group of labourers. It is thus abundantly clear that if a person belongs to the category of casual labour employed in construction work other than work-charged projects renders six month's continuous service without a break, by the operation of statutory rule, the person would be treated as temporary railway servant after the expiry of six months of continuous employment. It is equally true of even seasonal labour. Once the person has acquired the status of temporary railway servant by operation of law, the conditions of his service would be governed as set out in Chapter XXIII."

(iii) "The Executive Engineer informed the advocate appearing for Railway administration that appellants other than the present appellant were absorbed as regular railway employees and hence the appeal has become infructuous. Unfortunately for the appellant he was denied this benefit as his service had already been terminated. If the service was not terminated, his case was not distinguishable from the case of his co-appellants and he would have been entitled both in law and facts to the same treatment. The approach of the Railway administration to say the least is amazing. For years they did not act according to law and confer status of temporary railway servant on the appellant and on his colleagues. When appellant espoused this cause he was thrown out but his colleagues were given the benefit richly deserved in law. This discriminatory treatment cannot help the respondent because appellant's case cannot be distinguished. If the status of temporary railway employee was already acquired before the termination of service in the manner brought about, the same would be *ipso facto* invalid. If by operation of law, to wit Rule 2501 the appellant had acquired the status of temporary railway servant by rendering continuous uninterrupted service for more than six months, his service could not have been terminated under rule 2505.".

(iv) There is no dispute that the appellant would be a workman within the meaning of the expression in section 2(s) of the Industrial Disputes Act, 1947. Further, it is incontrovertible that he has rendered continuous service for a period over twenty years. Therefore, the first condition of section 25F of the Act that appellant is a workman who has rendered service for not less than one year under the Railway administration, and that his service is terminated for the reasons which would constitute "retrenchment". It is immaterial that he is a daily rated worker. Accordingly, the termination of service in this case would constitute "retrenchment" and because of not complying with pre-conditions to valid retrenchment, the order of termination would be illegal and invalid.

11.5 Distinction between Project Casual Labour and Open Line Casual Labour in the matter of grant of temporary status to them

In the case of *K.G. Radha Krishna Panicker* v. *U.O.I.*, ATR 1991(1) CAT 578, the Madras Bench was considering the question of discrimination between Project casual labour and open line casual labour employed in the Railways in the matter of grant of temporary status to them and observed as under:

"We are averse to treating differently grouping or classifying the applicants on the basis of grant of temporary status to them for a number of reasons; firstly, it is a well known established fact that temporary status is a merely a concept and it has no formal existence like promotion or confirmation. Temporary status is merely acquired and is not granted or conferred to individuals even according to the Railway rules. It is evident that a casual labourer in the Railways acquires temporary status after putting in continuous service for the prescribed period. There can be no doubt that by mere efflux to time, a casual labourer in continuous service in the Railways automatically acquires temporary status. There is no formality of accord or selection or approval required for acquiring the status. Admittedly, nothing is done by the respondents or required to be done by the casual labourers in order to gain that status which rather comes to them if they but merely continue in service without a break for the prescribed period. In this case, the Madras Bench was considering the case of 49 employees of the Southern Railways for grant of terminal pensionary benefits. They had originally joined as casual labourers in the construction wing in different projects and were absorbed in various capacities in regular service on different dates prior to 1-1-1981. They had claimed that their casual service after completion of six months of their initial appointment should be considered for purpose of retiring benefits like Pension, DCRG, etc. In accordance with Railway Board Circular dated 14-10-1980, it was provided that half the period of casual service after attaining temporary status followed by regular absorption will count for pension. However, this benefit was not admissible to Project Labour who were regularized before 1-1-1981 since there was no scheme of grant of temporary status to casual labour from any date prior to 1-1-1981. It was under the directions of the Supreme Court in *Inder Pal Yadav's* case, 1985 (2) SLR 248 that the concept of temporary status was extended to project casual labour but such temporary status could not be acquired by such project casual labour before 1-1-1981. The question whether there can be any discrimination between a project casual labour and other casual labour for the grant of temporary status prior to 1-1-1981 was adjudicated upon by the Madras Bench. The Tribunal felt that if Project casual labourers who had not been regularized before 1-1-1981 could be given temporary status with effect from 1-1-1981 or a later date and count their service after attaining temporary status till their date of regularization to the extent of 50% for pension, there is no reason why those project casual labourers who had been absorbed before 1-1-1981 should not be given temporary status to count part of their casual service before 1-1-1981 for pension."

11.6 Casual labour with requisite service in whichever capacity it is rendered should be considered for regularisation

In a case services of 44 persons who were engaged as casual labour as Hot Weather Workers in Railways and had worked for more than 120 days and had also acquired the status of Monthly Rated Casual Labour (MRCL) were terminated in the year 1992 on the ground that there is no sanction for their continuation in service. They pleaded that they should be taken back in service and regularised since their juniors are continuing in service. In this connection, they cited the judgment of CAT (Chandigarh Bench) in *Ashok Kumar* v. *U.O.I.*, 1996 (1) SLJ (CAT) 279 in which it was held that various kinds of duties performed by them such as casual labour/Water Man etc. will have to be counted as one fold without any distinction. They also cited the judgment of

CAT (Allahabad Bench) in *Bhagirathi* v. *U.O.I.*, O.A. No. 963/1992 decided on 3-9-1995 in which it was held as under:

"(i) All the applicants shall be considered for regularisation in their own turn and in case any of the juniors has been so regularised the applicants who are seniors will be considered for being regularised from the date of regularisation of such juniors.

(ii) Meanwhile they shall be considered for re-engagement as casual labour in preference to their juniors.

In support of their claim, they further referred to Rule 2001 – [Note 8; sub-para (2) of Indian Railways Establishment Manual Vol. II (I.R.E.M.) which reads as under:

> "Should it become necessary to engage additional casual labourers, then discharged casual labourers who have not been re-employed, will be reengaged against the future requirements in order of priority on the basis of total period of service prior to their discharge...."

This case came up for consideration before CAT (Allahabad Bench) In *All India Hot Weather Watermen Association* v. *U.O.I.*, 2003 (3) SLJ 29 CAT and the Tribunal in its judgment dated 1-1-2003 directed that the decision taken by the Tribunal in the above mentioned *Bhagirithi* case will apply in that case also.

11.7 The services of casual labourers cannot be terminated on the adverse recommendations of a committee made at their back

In the case of *N.F. Rly. Employees Union* v. *U.O.I.*, 1990 (1) SLJ 112 CAT the services of some casual labourers were terminated on the basis of certain adverse recommendations made by a committee in which the concerned casual labourers were not given any opportunity to be heard. The action of the respondents was held illegal and the Calcutta Tribunal in its judgment dated 14-4-1989 observed as under:

> "The main ground urged by the applicants is that they were not given an opportunity to show cause against the finding given by the committee. The enquiry was held without notice to them and the committee did not give any opportunity to the applicants to make their submissions. It is evident from the facts given above that a seniority list had

been published including the names of the applicants. According to the procedure prescribed, the applicants have a right for engagement according to the seniority list. If the seniority is to be changed and their names are to be deleted on the basis of the Committee's report, then the applicants are entitled to represent against the proposed deletion and the names could not have been deleted without an opportunity being given to them to show cause in regard to the deletion of their names."

11.8 Observations of the Courts on the point as to whether the Casual workers can be said to hold civil posts under Government

(i) CAT (Principal Bench) in the case *D.M.S. Employees Union*, [ATR 1988 (1) CAT 183]

"We are not prepared to accept this contention that since the casual workers are not holding any post in D.M.S., no relief can be granted by the Tribunal, since the jurisdiction of the Tribunal extends only to those who are holding any "civil post under the Union" Such workers though not holding any civil post but are yet appointed to *Civil Services* of the Union."

(ii) The view expressed by CAT in *D.M.S. Case* is at variance with the ruling of the Supreme Court, given in *Kanak Chand* case, AIR 1967 SC 884 which is reproduced below:

"Every Civil Post holder has employment but every employment under Government does not amount to holding a civil post......... The contingency paid workers and daily rated employees or Muster Roll Employees are not civil post holders."

(iii) *Vijay Singh* v. *U.O.I.*, 1990 (1) SLJ (CAT) (Jabalpur Bench) 614

"On the question of jurisdiction of this Tribunal we are in respectful disagreement with the view taken by the Principal Bench in the case of *DMS Employees Union*. As held in the case of *Kanak Chand* decided by the Supreme Court every civil post holder has employment but every employment under Government does not amount to holding a civil post and the Supreme Court had also specifically held that contingency paid workers and daily rated employees or Muster Roll employees are not civil post holders.

Xxx

Such employees are not even borne on regular establishment of the department. Being an employee of the Government on contingency basis serving the Government is not the same thing as being appointed in any civil service of the Union. In most cases there is in fact no regular appointment order to any post. If they are not appointed to any post they are also necessarily not appointed to any civil service of the Union, and vice versa, he will necessarily hold a civil post, if he is appointed to a civil service of the union but there cannot be any appointment to a civil service in isolation."

11.9 Brief gist of judgments of the courts relating to regularisation of services of casual workers

In the hierarchy of public employment, permanent service is at the top followed by temporary service, *ad hoc* service, full time casual employment with temporary status, full time casual employment without temporary status, part time casual employment and finally seasonal employment on daily rated or piece rate basis. In addition to above, we have staff employed on contingencies, contract labour, Apprentices, Probationers, etc. etc. The tenure of all these categories of staff is precarious since their services can be terminated with or without notice depending upon their terms of contract or the relevant service rules applicable to them. There have been innumerable cases where services of such employees have been terminated and they have been thrown on the road after they had put long years of service. Judiciary has come to the rescue of such unfortunate victims of official apathy by making classic pronouncements exhorting the Government to grant temporary status to casual labour and to make efforts to regularise them and absorb them in future vacancies wherever possible.

(ii) With reference to the casual workers employed in the Railways, the Supreme Court in *Inderpal Yadav* v. *Union of India,* 1985 (2) SCC 648 while deprecating the rule of "hire and fire" and referring to Articles 41 and 42 of the Constitution prevailed upon the Railway Ministry to formulate a scheme for giving temporary status to them after they have completed 360 days of service. In *Surinder Singh* v. *Engineer-in-Chief C.P.W.D,* ATR 1986 SC 76, the Supreme Court directed that all daily rated employees were to be paid the same salary and allowances as are paid to regular and permanent employees from the date of their employment and "expressed the hope that the Government would take appropriate action to regularise the services of all those who have been in continuous service for more than six months". In *Daily Rated Casual Labour, P & T Department* v. *U.O.I.*, AIR 1987 SC 2342, the Supreme Court held that Clause 2 of Article 38 of the Constitution of India contains one of the Directive Principles of State Policy providing that the State shall in particular strive to minimise the inequality in the income and endeavour to eliminate inequalities in the status, facilities and opportunities, not only amongst the individuals, but also amongst the groups of people residing in different areas and engaged in different vocations. It held that the classification of the employees into regularly recruited employees and casual employees rendering the same kind of service which is being rendered by the regular employees is violative of Articles 14 and 16 of the Constitution. The Supreme Court directed the Posts and Telegraphs Department not only to pay to the casual labourers the same pay equivalent to the minimum pay in the pay scales of the regularly employed workers but also to prepare a scheme on a regional basis for absorbing as far as possible the casual labourers who have been continuously working for more than one year in the Posts and Telegraphs Department. A similar view was taken by them in *U.P. Income Tax Department* v. *Union of India,* 1988 (2) SLJ 38.

(iii) Casual labour appointed irregularly have been allowed temporary status by efflux of time. In *Panama Tanti* v. *Union of India,* ATR 1987 (1) CAT 466, the Calcutta Bench of the Tribunal held that even if there was some mistake or irregularity in the recruitment of casual labour even then they attain temporary status on completion of more than 120 days of work. In that case the applicants were seasonal hot weather water men engaged by the Railways.

(iv) Even volunteers appointed as casual worker seasonally have been given temporary status and protection of certain provisions of the Constitution. In *Samir Kumar Mukherjee* v. *General Manager, Eastern Railway,* ATR 1986 (2) CAT 7 the Calcutta Bench of the Tribunal ruled that if persons engaged as volunteers to assist the Railway Ticket Checking staff for short periods and given extension from time to time are continued for more than a year in Railway employment have to be treated as temporary employees after 180 days of continuous service. It was held that to disengage or dismiss them arbitrarily and without notice or without giving any reason is clearly violative of the principles of natural justice and Articles 14, 16 and 21 of the Constitution. This was also against the Directive Principles of State Policy (Articles 39 and 41) enjoining the right of citizen to adequate means of livelihood.

(v) Even a substitute Extra Departmental Agent in the Postal Department who is nominated by another Extra Departmental Agent during his/her absence on leave has been given priority of being absorbed in the vacant posts. In. *Durga Bhomick* v. *Union of India,* (1989) 11 ATC 255, the Calcutta Bench of the Tribunal held that even a substitute P & T Extra Departmental Agent working for not less than 240 days per year is entitled to permanent absorption in future vacancies. The Department of Posts by its communication dated 14-12-1987 decided that the Extra Departmental Stamp Vendors and eight other categories of Extra Departmental Agents should be employed in the regular cadre of the Department of Posts. The P.M.G. West Bengal Circle clarified in his letter dated 29-3-1988 that only those who had worked as E.D. Substitute or partly as E.D. Substitute and partly as Daily Rated Mazdoor for not less than 240 days in a year from a date prior to 7-5-1985 and continued to work till 13-11-1987 only come under the purview of the consideration for appointment in the vacant post of E.D. Agents.

(vi) Pursuant to the judgment of the Supreme Court in *Surinder Singh* v. *Engineer-in-Chief, CPWD,* the Department of Personnel and Training issued a circular dated 7-6-1988 (printed below) giving guidelines for absorption of Casual workers who have rendered service for more than 240 days in regular cadre. Relying on the circular the Madras Bench of the Tribunal in *National General Employees Union* v. *Union of India,* ATR 1989 (2) CAT 175 noted that the respondents had initiated action for regularisation of the eligible casual workers and directed that until they are regularised, the casual workers should be paid daily wages at the rate of 1/30th of the pay at the minimum of the relevant pay scale plus Dearness Allowances and paid weekly off day after six days of continuous work.

11.10 State as model employer has an onerous duty to timely expedite regularization of services of casual workers and non-availability of a post is not a valid ground to deny the relief

The widow of a causal baildar was appointed on 1-2-1987 on work change basis against a sanctioned post of 13 years but was not regularized since no regular post was available. He expired in the meanwhile and Smt. Guddi, his wife filed an OA in CAT (PB New Delhi) and the Tribunal in its judgment dated 5-5-2005 observed as under:

It is a trite law that this court cannot direct Government to create post but in deserving cases on equitable consideration there are ways and means with the Government to posthumously regularize the services of the late husband of the Applicant which would not divest away her claim for retiral benefits, leaving her to wait on a contingency of creation of post and the said act would not be only inhuman but would be arbitrary.

For the foregoing reasons, the ground of non-availability of post is not a valid ground to deny the relief to the Applicant.

In the result, OA is allowed. Respondents are directed to expeditiously regularize the services of late husband of Applicant posthumously and in that event the Applicant shall be entitled to all retiral benefits due to her.

[*Guddi* v. *National Captial Territory of Delhi*, O.A. No. 1055 of 2004]

11.11 Orders issued by Government of India relating to regularisation of services of Casual employees

(i) Deptt. of P&T O.M. No. 49014/2/96-Estts (C) dated 7-6-1988

"General terms and conditions for employment of casual labour"

1. The Policy regarding engagement of casual workers in Central Government Offices has been reviewed by Government keeping in view the judgment of the Supreme Court delivered on the 17th January, 1986 in the Writ Petition filed by *Surinder Singh* v. *Union of India*, and it has been decided to lay down the following guidelines in the matter of recruitment of casual workers on daily wage basis:

(i) Persons on daily wages should not be recruited for work of regular nature.

(ii) Recruitment of daily wagers may be made only for work which is of casual or seasonal or intermittent nature or for work which is not of full time nature, for which regular posts cannot be created.

(iii) The work presently being done by regular staff should be re-assessed by the Administrative Departments concerned for output and productivity so that the work being done by the casual workers could be entrusted to the regular employees. The Departments may also review the norms of staff for regular work and take steps to get them revised, if considered necessary.

(iv) Where the nature of work entrusted to the casual workers and regular employees is the same, the casual workers may be paid at the rate of 1/30th of the pay at the minimum of the relevant pay scale plus dearness allowance for work of 8 hours a day.

(v) In cases where the work done by a casual worker is different from the work done by a regular employee, the casual worker may be paid only the minimum wages notified by the State Government/Union Territory Administration, as per the Minimum Wages Act, 1948. However, if a Department is already paying daily wages at a higher rate, the practice could be continued with the approval of its Financial Adviser.

(vi) The casual workers may be given one paid weekly off after six days continuous work.

(vii) The payment to the casual workers may be restricted only to the days on which they actually perform duty under the Government with a paid weekly off as mentioned at (vi) above. They will, however, in addition, be paid for a National Holiday, if it falls on a working day for the casual workers.

(viii) In cases where it is not possible to entrust all the items of work now being handled by the casual workers to the existing regular staff, additional regular posts may be created to the barest minimum necessary, with the concurrence of the Ministry of Finance.

(ix) Where work of more than one type is to be performed through out the year but each type of work does not justify a separate regular employee, a multi-financial post may be created for handling those items of work with the concurrence of the Ministry of Finance.

(x) The regularisation of the services of the casual workers will continue to be governed by the instructions issued by this Department in this regard. While considering such regularization, a casual worker may be given relaxation in the upper age limit only if at the time of initial recruitment as a casual worker, he had not crossed the upper age limit for the relevant post.

(xi) If a Department wants to make any departure from the above guidelines, it should obtain the prior concurrence of the Ministry of Finance and the Department of Personnel and Training.

2. All the administrative Ministries/Departments should undertake a review of appointment of casual workers in the offices under their control on a time bound basis so that at the end of the prescribed period, the following targets are achieved:

(a) All eligible casual workers are adjusted against regular posts to the extent such regular posts are justified.

(b) The rest of the casual workers not covered by (a) above and whose retention is considered absolutely necessary and is in accordance with the guidelines, are paid emoluments strictly in accordance with the guidelines.

(c) The remaining casual workers not covered by (a) and (b) above are discharged from service.

3. By strict meticulous observance of the guidelines by all Ministries/Departments, it should be ensured that there is no more engagement of casual workers for attending to work of a regular nature, particularly after the review envisaged above is duly completed. Each Head of Office should also nominate an officer who would scrutinize the engagement of each and every casual worker and the job for which he is being employed to determine whether the work is of casual nature or not.

4. Ministry of Finance, etc., are requested to bring the contents of this OM to the notice of all the appointing authorities under their respective administrative control for strict observance. Cases of negligence in the matter of implementing these guidelines should be viewed very seriously and brought to the

notice of the appropriate authorities for taking prompt and suitable action against the defaulters.

(ii) Deptt. of P& T O.M. No. 51016/2/90-Ests (c) dated 10-9-1993

Scheme for Grant of Temporary Status and Regularisation of Casual Workers

The guidelines in the matter of recruitment of persons on daily wage basis in Central Government offices were issued vide this Department's O.M. No. 49014/2/96-Estt. (C) dated 7-6-1988. The policy has further been reviewed in the light of the judgment of the CAT. Principal Bench, New Delhi, delivered on 16-2-1990, in the Writ Petition filed by *Raj Kamal* v. *Union of India*, and it has been decided that while the existing guidelines contained O.M., dated 7-6-1988, may continue to be followed, the grant of temporary status to the casual employees, who are presently employed and have rendered one year of continuous service in Central Government Offices other than Department of Telecom, Posts and Railways may be regulated by the Scheme printed below:

2. Ministry of Finance, etc., are requested to bring the scheme to the notice of all the appointing authorities under their respective administrative control and ensure that recruitment of casual employees is done in accordance with the guidelines contained in O.M. dated 7-6-1988. Cases of negligence should be viewed seriously and brought to the notice of the appropriate authorities for taking prompt and suitable action.

APPENDIX

DEPARTMENT OF PERSONNEL AND TRAINING, CASUAL LABOURERS

(Grant of Temporary Status and Regularization) Scheme

1. This scheme shall be called "Casual Labourers (Grant of Temporary Status and Regularisation) Scheme of Government of India, 1993."

2. This scheme will come into force with effect from 1-9-1993

3. This scheme is applicable to casual labourers in employment of the Ministries/Departments of Government of India and their attached and subordinate offices, on the date of issue of these orders. But it shall not be applicable to casual workers in Railways, Department of Telecommunication and Department of Posts who already have heir own schemes.

4. *Temporary Status.*—(i) Temporary status would be conferred on all casual labourers who are in employment on the date of issue of this OM and who have rendered a continuous service of at least one year, which means that they must have been engaged for a period of at least 240 days (206 days in the case of offices observing 5 days week).

(i) Such conferment of temporary status would be without reference to the creation/availability of regular Group 'D' posts.

(ii) Conferment of temporary status on a casual labourer would not involve and change in his duties and responsibilities. The engagement will be on daily rates of pay on need basis. He may be deployed any where within the recruitment unit/territorial circle on the basis of availability of work.

(iii) Such casual labourers who acquire temporary status will not, however, be brought on to the permanent establishment unless they are selected through regular selection process for Group 'D' posts.

5. Temporary status would entitle the casual labourers to the following benefits:

(i) Wages at daily rates with reference to the minimum of the pay scale for a corresponding regular Group 'D' official including DA, HRA and CCA [Special Compensatory Allowance or Compensatory (City) Allowance or Composite Hill Compensatory Allowance, etc., *i.e.* only one of the compensatory allowance, more beneficial to them, can be taken into account for the purpose of calculating their wages. O.M. No. 3(2) /95 – E.II (B), dated the 15th January, 1996].

(ii) Benefits of increments at the same rate as applicable to a Group 'D' employee would be taken into account for calculating *pro rata* wages for every one year of service subject to performance of duty for at least 240 days (206 days in administrative offices observing 5 days week) in the year from the date of conferment of temporary status.

(iii) Leave entitlement will be on a *pro rata* basis at the rate of one day for every 10 days of work. Casual or any other kind of leave, except maternity leave, will not be admissible. They will also be allowed to carry forward the leave at their credit on the regularisation. They will not be entitled to the benefits of encashment of leave on termination of service for any reason or on their quitting service.

(iv) Maternity leave to lady casual labourers as admissible to regular Group 'D' employees will be allowed.

(v) 50% of the service rendered under temporary status would be counted for the purpose of retirement benefits after their regularisation.

(vi) After rendering three years' continuous service after conferment of temporary status, the casual labourers would be treated on par with temporary Group 'D' employees for the purpose of contribution to the General Provident Fund, and would also further be eligible for the grant of Festival Advance, Flood Advance on the same conditions as are applicable to temporary Group 'D' employees, provided they furnish two sureties from permanent Government servants of their Department.

(vii) Until they are regularized, they would be entitled to Productivity-Linked Bonus/*Ad hoc* Bonus only at the rates applicable to casual labourers.

6. No benefits other than those specified above will be admissible to casual labourers with temporary status. However, if any additional benefits are admissible to casual workers working in industrial establishments in view of provisions of Industrial Disputes Act, they shall continue to be admissible to such casual labourers.

7. Despite conferment of temporary status, the services of a casual labourer may be dispensed with by giving a notice of one month in writing. A casual labourer with temporary status can also quit service by giving a written notice of one month. The wages for the notice will be payable only for the days on which such casual worker is engaged on work.

8. *Procedure for filling up of Group 'D' posts..*—(i) Two out of every three vacancies in Group 'D' cadres in respective offices where the casual labourers have been working would be filled up as per extent Recruitment Rules and in accordance with the instructions issued by Department of Personnel and Training from amongst casual workers with temporary status. However, regular Group 'D' staff rendered surplus for any reason will have prior claim for absorption against existing/future vacancies. In case of illiterate casual labourers or those who fail to fulfil the minimum qualification prescribed for the post, regularisation will be considered only against those posts in respect of which literacy or lack of minimum qualification will not be a requisite qualification. They would be allowed age relaxation equivalent to the period for which they have worked continuously as casual labourer.

9. On regularisation of casual worker with temporary status, no substitute in his place will be appointed as he was not holding any post. Violation of this should be viewed very seriously and attention of the appropriate authorities should be drawn to such cases for suitable disciplinary action against the officers violating these instructions.

10. In future, the guidelines as contained in this Department's OM dated 7-6-1988, should be followed strictly in the matter of engagement of casual employees in Central Government offices."

(A) CLARIFICATIONS TO OM, DATED 10-9-1993, REGARDING GRANT OF TEMPORARY STATUS AND REGULARISATION OF CASUAL WORKERS

"References are being received from various field formations seeking clarifications regarding orders issued by the D.P. & Trg. In connection with grant of temporary status to the daily rated workers. The clarifications sought for and their reply have been indicated against each clarified as under:

S. No.	*Clarification sought*	*Reply*
1.	Whether the attendance of the casual workers shall continue to be marked on Muster Roll Forms No. COWA-21 (i) Revised or the same is to be marked in the attendance register and paid through Form No. CPWA-29 as is done in the case of Group 'D' employees on Workcharged Estt.?	There will be no change in this regard. The existing practice of marking attendance will continue. The casual workers even after conferment of temporary status continue to be casual workers.
2.	Whether the casual workers who are eligible for temporary status with effect from 1-9-1993 are entitled for any arrears of increment with effect from 7-6-1989?	In Para 2 of D.P. & Trg. O.M. dated 10-9-1993, it has been clearly indicated that these orders are applicable with effect from 1-1-1993. There is, therefore, no question of grant of any arrears to any worker in respect of period prior to 1-9-1993.
3.	Whether the casual workers shall be entitled for payment of gazetted holidays also?	No
4.	Whether service Books in respect of casual workers to whom temporary status is granted are to be opened and if not, how the benefit of grant of annual increments, leave on *pro rata* basis at the rate of 1 day for every 10 days as per the orders, is to be regulated?	This is a matter of convenience. If the field offices feel that it is not essential to open Service Books and they can regulate the benefits extended without opening of Service Books, they may do so. If they find that opening of Service Books is more convenient to maintain the records properly, they can follow this practice. However, for the sake of uniformity, it is advised that

S. No.	*Clarification sought*	*Reply*
		Service Books in respect of such workers are opened.
5.	Whether will be any change in operation of orders regarding payment of OTA to the casual workers, consequent upon implementation of the orders of grant of temporary status?	No
6.	Whether these orders are also applicable to the casual workers who have recently died and what benefits of gratuity/pensions, etc. will be available them?	Kindly refer Para 5, sub-para (v) and (vi) in D.P. & Trg. O.M. dated 10-9-1993.
7.	Whether the deceased casual worker with temporary status will be paid for the accumulated leave?	No
8.	Whether wages of daily rated workers covered under temporary status are to be prepared on Hand Receipt (at present these are being prepared on Hand Receipt) or on Form CPWA-58?	The existing procedure may be followed. As already made clear, even after conferment of temporary status, these workers continue to be casual workers.
9.	Whether the leave accumulated in the account of the workers with temporary status in the 1st year shall be carried forward to the next year. If so, what will be its limit?	The matter is under consideration in consultation with D.P. & Trg. Necessary clarifications will be furnished in due course of time.

(B) CLARIFICATIONS ON GRANT OF TEMPORARY STATUS AND REGULARISATION OF CASUAL WORKERS

With reference to O.M. No. 51016/2/90-Estt. (C) dated 10-9-1993 (printed above) many reference have been received from various Ministries/ Departments, seeking clarifications on certain points relating to grant of temporary status to casual labourers.

2. Clarifications in respect of the points raised in the references are given below:

S. No.	Point	Clarification
1.	Whether the casual employees who were not initially engaged through Employment Exchange are entitled to the benefit of temporary status?	Since it is mandatory to engage casual employees through Employment Exchange, the appointment of casual employees without Employment Exchange is irregular. Hence, such casual employees cannot be bestowed with temporary status.
2.	Whether temporary status could be granted to the part time casual employees?	No
3.	Will the casual labourers initially engaged after crossing the upper age limit prescribed for recruitment to Group 'D' posts be eligible for grant of temporary status?	No age-limit has been prescribed for grant of temporary status. However, for the purpose of subsequent regularisation the conditions regarding age and educational qualifications prescribed in the relevant Recruitment Rules will apply.
4.	Will the wages of casual employees would be debited to the salaries sub-head of the establishment or to the contingent sub-head?	Since the casual employees on grant of temporary status would be entitled for wages on actual basis, their wages will have to be debited to the sub-head 'wages'.
5.	Whether the casual employees working in administrative offices observing 5 days week would be entitled to the benefit of paid weekly off?	Since the facility of paid weekly off is admissible after 6 days of continuous work, this would not be admissible to casual employees working for 5 days in a week.
6.	For the purpose of assessing leave entitlement, how how should qualifying period be reckoned?	Qualifying period should be reckoned with reference to actual number of days duty performed ignoring days of weekly off, leave and absence, etc.

S. No.	Point	Clarification
		All days of duty will be counted irrespective of intervening spells of absence which do not constitute break in service.
7.	Frequency at which leave will be credited.	Twice a year. On the Ist of January and Ist of July, credit will be afforded for the preceding half-year or fraction thereof, on a *pro rata* basis at the rate of one day for every 10 days of work.

(iii) Government instructions regarding regularisation of staff working in Deptt. of Posts

"**1. Part time and full time casual labourers.**—It is hereby clarified that all daily wagers working in Post Offices or in R.M.S. Offices or in Administrative Offices or PSDs/MMS under different designations (mazdoor, casual labourer, contingent paid staff, daily wager, daily rated mazdoor, outside) are to be treated as casual labourers. Those casual labourers who are engaged for a period of not less than 8 hours a day should be described as full time casual labourers. Those casual labourers who are engaged for a period of less than 8 hours a day should be described as part time casual labourers. All other designations should be discontinued.

Substitutes engaged against absentees should not be designed casual labourer. For purposes of recruitment to Group 'D' posts, substitutes should be considered only when casual labourers are not available. That I, substitutes will rank last in priority, but will be above outsiders. In other words, the following priority should be observed:

(i) NTC Group 'D' officials;

(ii) EDAs of the same Divisions;

(iii) Casual labourers (full time or part-time. For purpose of computation of eligible service, half of the service rendered as a part-time casual labourer should be taken into account.

That is, if a part-time casual labouer has served for 480 days in a period of 2 years she will be treated, for purposes of recruitment, to have completed one year of service as full time casual labourer).

(iv) EDAs of other divisions in the same Region;

(v) Substitutes (not working in Metropolitancities);

(vi) Direct recruits through Employment Exchanges.

Note.—Substitutes working in Metropolitan Cities will, however, rank above No. (iv) in the list.

[G.I. of Posts. Lr. No. 65-24/88-SPB.1, dated the 17th May, 1989]

2. Casual labourers (Grant of Temporary Status and Regularisation) Scheme.—In continuance with the directions of the Hon'ble Supreme Court a scheme was drawing up by this Department in consultation with the Ministries of Law, Finance and Personnel and the President as been pleased to approve the said scheme. The scheme is as follows:

1. 'Temporary Status' would be conferred on the casual labourers in employment as on 29-11-1989 and who continue to be currently employed and have rendered continuous service of at least one year, during the year they must have been engaged for a period of 240 days [206 days in the case of offices observing five days week).
2. Such casual workers engaged for full working hours, *viz.* 8 hours including ½ hour's lunch time will be paid at daily rates on the basis of the minimum of the pay scale for a regular Casual labourer official including DA, HRA and CCA.
3. Benefit of increment at the same rate as applicable to a Group 'D' employee would be taken into account for calculating per month rate wages after completion of one year of service from the date of conferment of Temporary Status. Such increment will be taken into account after every one year of service subject to performance of duty for at least 240 days (206 days in establishments observing five days week) in the year.
4. Leave entitlement will be one day for every 10 days' of work. Casual leave or any other kind of leave, except maternity leave, will not be admissible. No encashment of

leave is permissible on termination of services for any reason or on the casual labourers quitting service.

5. Maternity leave to lady full time casual labourers will be allowed as admissible to regular employees.
6. 50% of the service rendered under Temporary Status would be counted for the purpose of retirement benefits after regularisation as a regular Group 'D' official.
7. Conferment of Temporary Status does not automatically imply that the casual labourers would be appointed as a regular Group 'D' employees within any fixed time frame. Appointment to Group 'D' vacancies will continue to be done as per the existing Recruitment Rules, which stipulate preference to eligible ED employees.
8. After rendering three years' continuous service after conferment of temporary status, the casual labourers would be treated at par with temporary Group 'D' employees for the purpose of contribution to General Provident Fund. They would also further be eligible for the grant of Festival Advance/Flood Advance on the same conditions as are applicable to temporary Group 'D' employees, provided they furnish two sureties from permanent Government servants of this Department.
9. Their entitlement to Productivity-Linked Bonus will continue to be at the rate applicable to casual labourers.
10. Temporary status does not debar dispensing with the service of a casual labourer after following the due procedure.
11. If a labourer with temporary status commits a misconduct and the same is proved in an enquiry after giving him reasonable opportunity, his services will be dispensed with.
12. Casual labourers may be regularized in units other than recruiting units also, subject to availability of vacancies.
13. For purpose of appointment as a regular Group 'D' official, the casual labourers will be allowed age relaxation to the extent of service rendered by them as casual labourers.
14. The casual labourers can be deployed anywhere within the recruitment unit/territorial circle on the basis of availability of work.

15. The engagement of the casual labourers will continue to be on daily rates of pay on need basis.
16. The conferment of temporary status has no relation to availability of sanctioned regular Group 'D' Posts.
17. No recruitment from open market for Group 'D' posts except compassionate appointments will be done till casual labourers with the requisite qualification are available to fill up the posts in question.

Further action may be taken in regard to the casual labourers by each unit as per the abovesaid scheme. This issues with the approval of Ministry of Finance and concurrence of Integrated Finance, *vide* their Dy. No. 1282-FA/91 dated 10-4-1991.

[G.I. Deptt. of Posts. Lt. No. 45-95/87-SPB 1, dated the 12th April, 1991]

Clarification (1)—Further to letter No. 45-95/87-SPB 1 dated 12-4-1991 (printed above), it is hereby clarified that the scheme is effective from 29-11-1989 and hence the eligible casual labourers may be conferred temporary status and the benefits indicated in the above said circular with effect from 29-11-1989.

2. Eligibility for weekly off to casual labourers continue to remain the same as before, *viz.* after 6 days of continuous work, they will be entitled to one weekly off. They will also be entitled for 3 paid National Holidays.

3. Leave salary to the casual labourers with temporary status will be paid at the rate of daily wages being paid to the casual labourers concerned.

4. Casual labourers who work in offices observing 5 days a week are not entitled to Paid Off on Saturday or Sunday. In other words, the weekly paid off after 6 continuous working days is permissible only to those Casual workers who work at the rate of 8 hours per day in establishments having 6 days a week.

5. The Scheme is also applicable to casual workers in the civil wing of this Department. It is not, however, applicable to any person working on casual basis in Group 'C' posts.

6. Vacancies of Casual labourers caused by their absorption in Group 'D' posts are not to be filled by recruiting fresh casual

labourers. In other words, engagement of fresh casual labourers is not permissible as already reiterated time and again.

[G.I. Deptt. of Posts. Lr. No. 45-37/91-SPB.1 dated the 5th June, 1991]

Clarification (2).—Attention is invited to the Department of Per. & Trg. O.M. dated 7-6-1988, as per which engagement of fresh full time casual labourers is not permissible. In the said O.M., it has also been made clear that where the work of more than one type is to be performed throughout the year but each type of work does not justify a separate regular employee, a multi-functional post could be created for handling these items with the concurrence of Ministry of Finance. The possibility of creation of multi-functional posts in offices for discharging the items of work each of which does not justify a full time post may be explored in the first instance. In case this is not found possible to entrust, part-time casual hands may be engaged as per the outlines contained on O.M. dated 7-6-1988.

It is once again reiterated that the decision regarding engagement of fresh part-time casual hands should be taken with care and at a fair high level so that the provisions of O.M. dated 7-6-1988 are not diluted.

[G.I. Deptt. of Posts. Lt. No. 45-111/90-SPB 1 dated the 13th January, 1992.

Clarification (3).—1. Casual labourers conferred with temporary status can accumulate leave upto a maximum limit of 240 days.

2. Such casual labourers may be allowed paid leave as and when they require, provided leave is available at their credit.

3. No substitute arrangements should be made on such occasions, since engagement of fresh casual labourers is not permissible.

4. Casual labourers conferred with temporary status are to be paid OTA at the existing OTA rates for casual labourers, if they are engaged for extra hours.

[G.I. Deptt. of Posts. Lt. No. 45-26/92-SPB 1 dated the 28th October, 1992]

Clarification (4).—1. The service book of the casual labourers conferred with the temporary status is required to be maintained as in the case of temporary Government employees.

2. Temporary status casual labourers are entitled to increment on par with the departmental officials on completion of one year of engagement of 240 days, *i.e.* the increment would be taken into account for calculation of wages with effect from 1-11-1990 for the casual labourers conferred with temporary status on 29-11-1989, if they have completed one year of service at least 240 days.

3. The services of temporary status casual labourers can be dispensed with in case of misconduct after giving due opportunity on the lines of those available to regular employees.

4. A ban on employment of casual laboures had been put to by the Government prior to 29-11-1989. Therefore there should not be any casual labourer employed after 29-11-1989. If there are any, their full particulars may be furnished along with the circumstances under which they were taken and under whose orders.

5. Employment of substitutes against the leave vacancy or paid weekly off days of temporary status casual labourer is not permissible.

6. Casual labourers engaged in P&T dispensaries where the full working hours are less than 8 hours daily are not eligible for temporary status.

[G.I. Deptt. of Posts. Lt. No. 45-56/92 dated the 1st March, 1993]

9. Casual labourers recruited after 29-11-1989 and upto 10-9-1993 are also to be conferred 'Temporary Status'.— According to the orders on the scheme issued vide letters No. 45-95/87-SPB.1 dated 12-4-1991 and 66-9/91-SPB.1 dated 30-11-1992, full time casual labourers who were in employment as on 29-11-1989 were eligible to be conferred 'Temporary Status' on satisfying other eligibility conditions.

The question of extending the benefits of the scheme to those full time casual labourers who were engaged/recruited after 29-11-1989 has been considered in this office in the light of the judgment of the CAT, Ernakulam Bench, Ernakulam delivered on 13-3-1995 in O.A. No. 750 of 1994.

It has been decided that full time casual labourers recruited after 29-11-1989 and upto 1-9-1993 may also be considered for the grant of benefits under the scheme.

[G.I. Deptt. of Post, Letter No. 66-52/92-SPB.1 dated the 1st November, 1995 as amended by Letter dated the 8th November, 1995]

11.12 Gist of Court decision relating to termination of services of casual employees

(i) As per general scheme of 1993, the casual labourers who acquired temporary status cannot be removed merely on the whims and fancies of the employer if there is sufficient work and other casual labourers are still to be employed by the employer for carrying out the work. They shall not be removed from service as per clause 7 of the scheme except in case of serious misconduct or violation of service rules.

[*U.O.I.* v. *Mohan Lal*, 2002 (3) RSJ SC 627]

(ii) Clause 4 of the schemes of 1993 is very clear and conferment of 'temporary' status is to be given to casual labourer who were in employment on the date of the commencement of the scheme. It does not appear to be a general guide line to be applied for the purpose of giving "temporary" status to all the casual workers as and when they complete one year's continuous service.

[*U.O.I.* v. *Mohan Lal*, 2002(3) RSJ SC 627]

Chapter 12

TERMINATION OF SERVICES OF EMPLOYEES OF STATUTORY CORPORATIONS/CO-OPERATIVE SOCIETIES, ETC.

"Rules and regulations framed by statutory bodies have statutory force and the authorities functioning thereunder are statutory authorities and the employees of such bodies enjoy statutory status. They are entitled to protection of Articles 14 and 16 of the Constitution but not to the protection of Article 311 of the Constitution".

(Supreme Court)

SYNOPSIS

12.10 Short notes on the subject of jurisdiction of the High Courts under Article 226 of the Constitution to issue writs against statutory corporations/co-operative societies etc.

12.11 The provisions of Article 311 of the Constitution are not applicable to employees of Insurance company Ltd.

12.12 The protection of Article 14 of the Constitution is available to the employees of the Statutory Corporation in the matter of termination of their services

12.13 The services of even a permanent employee of the Corporation can be terminated by order simpliciter on the ground of their unsuitability for the post

12.14 Principles of law applicable to termination of services of employees of Statutory Corporations

12.1 Law on the subject

The Rules and Regulations of the Corporations, State Enterprises, Government Companies, Co-operative Societies, etc. govern the service condition of its employees. The Supreme Court held that the Rules and Regulations framed by such statutory bodies have the force of law and their employees have statutory status and are entitled to a declaration of being in employment when their dismissal or removal is in contravention of the statutory provisions. It is however now well established that Article 311 of the Constitution does not apply to such employees.

[*Sukhdev Singh* v. *Bhagat Ram*, AIR 1975 SC 1331]

12.2 Text of Article 12 of the Constitution of India and its relevance to the employees of Statutory Corporations/ Co-operative Societies, etc. in the matters of security of their service

Article 12 of the Constitution of India defines "State" and stipulates that this term includes the Government and Parliament of India and the Government and legislature of each of the States and all local or "other authorities" within the territory of India or under the control of Government of India. The term "other authorities" has come in for interpretation by courts in a number of cases in the wake of the emergence of numerous corporations, co-operative societies, Government companies, etc. which employ large number of workers and where their services were terminated. It has been held that statutory corporations carrying on business of public importance are "authorities" within the meaning of Article 12 despite the fact that they have no power to issue binding directions entailing penal consequences. There is widening concept of the term 'State'. The employees of Statutory Corporations can claim protection of Articles 16 and 14 against the Corporations. The status of regulations framed under Oil and Natural Gas Commission, 1959, LIC Act, 1956 and the Industrial Finance Corporation Act, 1948 etc. have force of law. Orders of removal from service of employees of these Corporations in contravention of the regulations framed under the respective Acts would enable an employee to a declaration against the Corporations for continuance in service and not relegate him to a claim of damages alone. However, protection of Article 311 is not available to them.

It has also been held that the term "other authorities" does not include institutions such as Council of Scientific and Industrial Research which are sponsored and controlled by Central Government and registered under the Societies Registration Act within the meaning of the Article 12 of the Constitution. Employees of such institutions have no standing to impeach circulars of such institutions relating to service matters on the ground of infraction of their rights under Articles 16 and 14 of the Constitution. This point has however been dealt with in depth in the light of some later judgment of the courts in the succeeding sub-paras.

12.3 Interpretation of the term "Other authorities" as used in Article 12 of the Constitution of India

The term "State" as defined in Article 12 of the Constitution includes Government and Parliament of India and the Government and Legislature of each of the States and all local and "other authorities" within the territory of India or under the control of Government of India.

A large number of Corporations are coming into existence from time to time which are carrying on business of public importance. Further, there are also institutions which are sponsored and controlled by the Central Government and registered under Societies Registration Act. Whether such Corporation, etc. can be held to be "other authorities" within the meaning of Article 12 of the Constitution depend on the question as to whether such bodies are "agencies" or "instrumentality" of the State. The tests for determining whether a Corporation can be said to be an instrumentality or agency of the Government have been laid down by the Supreme Court in *Ramana Dayaram Shetty* v. *International Airport Authority of India*, AIR 1979 SC 1628 in these words:

"(1) If the entire share capital of the corporation is held by Government it would go a long way towards indicating that the corporation is an instrumentality or agency of Government.

(2) Where the financial assistance of the State is so much as to meet almost entire expenditure of the Corporation, it would afford some indication of the corporation being impregnated with governmental character.

(3) It may also be a relevant factor whether the corporation enjoys monopoly status which is the State conferred or State protected.

(4) Existence or 'deep and pervasive State Control' may afford an indication that the Corporation is a State agency or instrumentality.

(5) If the functions of the corporation are of public importance and closely related to governmental functions, it would be a relevant factor in classifying the Corporation as an instrumentality or agency of Government.

(6) Specifically, if a department of Government is transferred to a Corporation, it would be a strong factor supportive of this inference of the Corporation being an instrumentality or agency of Government"

If on consideration of aforesaid factors, it is found that a particular Corporation is an 'instrumentality' or 'agency' of Government, it would come within the meaning of "other authorities" in terms of Article 12 of the Constitution. It is immaterial whether such a Corporation is created 'by' a statute or 'under' a statute. The test is whether it is an instrumentality or agency of the government and not as to how it was created. The Hon'ble Apex Court went on further to point out as under in the above mentioned case:

"We are inclined to think that no particular test has a predominant role to play. The cumulative effect has to be looked into. Where the functions are closely related to Governmental functions and where a department of Government is transferred to a Corporation or where rule-making or regulation- making power has been given which when made would regulate the conduct of the people at large are clear features in support of treating the institution as an instrumentality or agency of Government. Where, however, Government while embarking upon a commercial activity putting the entire money, exercise direct or indirect control and receive the profits - these by themselves may not be adequate to hold the institution to be an agency or instrumentality of Government….."

12.4 Judgments of the Supreme Court on the subject of Statutory character of Corporations/Cooperative societies

(a) "The Society (Council of Scientific and Industrial Research) does not have a statutory character like the Oil and Natural Gas Commission, or the Life Insurance Corporation or Industrial Finance Corporation. It is a society incorporated in accordance with the provisions of the Society Registration Act. The fact that the Prime Minister is the President or that the Government appoints nominees to the Governing Body or that the Government may terminate the membership will not establish anything more than the fact that the Government takes special care that the promotion, guidance and co-operation of scientific and industrial research, the institution and financing of specific researches, establishment or development and assistance to special institutions or departments of the existing institutions for scientific study of problems affecting particular industry in a trade, the utilization of the result of the researches conducted under the auspices of the Council towards the development of industries in the country are carried out in a responsible manner."

[*Sabajit Tewari* v. *U.O.I.*, 1975 SLJ 410]

(b) A three judge Bench was considering a claim to protection of service in the College which was a society registered under the relevant Co-operative Societies Act. The question arose as to whether the Executive Committee of the College which later got affiliated to a University became a statutory body and, therefore, work under such College amounted to public employment and the majority decision was in the negative. In paragraph 9, the majority opinion was expressed thus:

> "It is, therefore, clear that there is a well marked distinction between a body which is created by the statute and a body which after having come into existence is governed in accordance with the provisions of the statute. In other words, the position seems to be that the institution concerned must owe its very existence to a statute which would be the fountain head of its powers. The question in such cases to be asked is, if there is no statute would the institution have any legal existence. If the answer is in the negative, then undoubtedly it is a statutory body, but if the institution has a separate existence of its own without any reference to the statute concerned but is merely governed by the statutory provisions it cannot be said to be a statutory body....."

[*Executive Committee of Vaish Degree College, Shamli* v. *Lakshmi Narain*, AIR 1976 SC 888]

(c) "....Corporation established by or under an Act of Legislature can only mean a body corporate which owes its existence, and not merely its corporate status, to the Act. For example, a municipality, a Zilla Parishad or a Gram Panchayat owes its existence and status to an Act of Legislature. On the other hand, an association of persons constituting themselves into a company under the Companies Act or a society under the Societies Registration Act owes its existence not to the Act of legislature but to acts of parties though, it may owe its status as a body corporate to an Act of legislature."

[*S.S. Dhanoa* v. *Municipal Corporation, Delhi*, 1981 (3) SCC 431]

12.5 Implications of termination of services of employees of Societies etc. which are held as ' Not State' within the meaning of Article 12 of the Constitution

The rulings of the Courts on this question have far reaching consequences on termination of services of the persons employed in such societies etc. In such cases, the jurisdiction of High Court under Article 226 of the Constitution cannot be invoked and restoration of the services cannot be ordered. The employment of persons in such Societies which are held to be 'Not State' is nothing more than a mere contract between a Master and servant. The Hon'ble Supreme Court has dealt with three different types of cases of termination of services of the employees in *Sirsi Municipality* v. *Ceceila Francis Tellis,* 1973 SC 855: (1973) SCWR 55. The Apex Court observed:

> "The cases of termination of a servant fall under three broad heads. The first head relates to relationship of master and servant governed purely by contract of employment. Any breach of contract in such a case is enforced by a suit for wrongful dismissal and damages. Just as a contract of employment is not capable of specific performance similarly breach of contract of employment is not capable of finding a declaratory judgment of subsistence of employment. A declaration of unlawful termination and restoration to service in such a case of contract of employment would be indirectly an instance of specific performance of contract for personal services. Such a declaration is not permissible under the law of Specific Relief Act.
>
> The second type of cases of master and servant arises under Industrial Law. Under that branch of law, a servant who is wrongfully dismissed may be reinstated. This is a special provision under Industrial Law. This relief is departure from the relief's available under the Indian Contract Act and the Specific Relief Act which do not provide for reinstatement of a servant.
>
> The third category of cases of master and servant arises in regard to the servant in the employment of the State or of other public or local authorities or bodies created under statute.
>
> Termination or dismissal of what is described as a pure contract of master and servant is not declared to be a nullity however wrongful or illegal it may be. The reason is that dismissal in breach of contract is remedied by damages. In the case of servant of the State or of local authorities or statutory bodies, courts have declared in appropriate cases the dismissal to be invalid if the dismissal is contrary to rules

of natural justice or if the dismissal is in violation of the provisions of the statutes. Apart from the intervention of statute there would be a declaration of nullity in the case of termination or dismissal of a servant of the State or of other local authorities or statutory bodies.

The courts keep the State and the public authorities within the limits of their statutory powers. Where a State or a public authority dismisses an employee in violation of the mandatory procedural requirements or on grounds which are not sanctioned or supported by statute the courts may exercise jurisdiction to declare the act of dismissal to be nullity. Such implication of public employment is thus distinguished from private employment in pure cases of master and servant."

12.6 Corporations/Societies/Undertakings/Institutions etc. held as "Not State" within the meaning of Article 12 of the Constitution

(i) Government aided schools are not an instrumentality of the State. Writ of *mandamus* cannot be issued directing them to reinstate an employee. They remain private organizations even if they receive aid from Government and are subject to regulations by various statues.

[*K.P. Mohammad* v. *State of Kerala*, 1983 (2) SLR 540]

(ii) Sikkim Co-operative Milk Producers' Union created for development of milk industry is not 'State'. Hence rules of natural justice do not bind the termination by it of services of employees.

[*Dalal Chandra Karmakar* v. *Sikkim Co-operative Milk Producers' Co-operative Union*, 1985(1) SLJ 706]

(iii) Red Cross Society constituted under Red Cross Society Act, 1921 is not a "State" and is not subject to Fundamental Rights but it must observe natural justice.

[*Pant Raj Sachdev* v. *Indian Red Cross Society*, 1986 (1) SLJ 675 (P&H)]

(iv) A writ is not maintainable against a non-statutory educational institution, private owned and maintained.

[*Gurpreet Singh* v. *Punjab University*, 1983 (1) SLR 220 (P&H)]

(v) Writ cannot be issued against Air Force Central School, Air Force Station, Race Course, New Delhi which is not an aided school and not a statutory body.

[*Wing Commander S.K. Singh* v. *Lt. Governor Union Territory of Delhi*, 1987 (1) SLR 98 Del]

(vi) Gujarat State Co-operative Cotton Federation is not a "State".

[*B.J. Soni* v. *Gujarat State Co-operative Cotton Federation*, (1985) 2 SLR 788 (Guj)]

(vii) Co-operative society is not a statutory body. A writ cannot lie against an order of the society calling upon the employee to make good the loss caused by the employee's negligence.

[*M.N. Siddeswraiah* v. *Managing Director, Bangalore District Co-operative Bank*, (1981) 2 SLR 647 (Karn)]

(viii) The Bihar State Co-operative Marketing Union Ltd., Patna is not "State". It is not created under statute but is registered under the Co-operative Societies. State Control is not deep and pervasive. The fact that entire share capital is held by the State is not conclusive.

[*H.N. Banker* v. *State of Bihar*, (1986) 2 SLR 256 (Pat) (DB)].

(ix) The Institute of Constitutional and Parliamentary Studies, New Delhi, a society registered under the Societies Registration Act, is not an "authority" within Article 12 of the Constitution. Though it receives grant from Government. It is autonomous. It is not subject to "deep and pervasive" control of the Government. It is not an organ of the Government and does not speak the mind of the establishment.

[*Tekraj Vasndi* v. *Union of India*, (1983) 3 SLR 393 (Del)]

(x) "The Delhi High Court, in a Division Bench ruling pronounced on 11th September, 1991, has held that a writ petition cannot be filed against the Maruti Udyog Limited. That company cannot be regarded as falling within the concept of "State" within the meaning of Article 12 of the Constitution. The judgment *was* pronounced by Mr. Justice S.B. Wad and Mr. Justice Mohammed Shamim in a writ petition filed by *P.B. Ghayalod* against *Maruti Udyog Limited*. Even though a part of the share capital in the company is held by the Government of India, there were other factors which militated against holding the company to be within the concept of "State". Government had only a bare majority of the share capital and not the entire capital in the company. A substantial part of the share capital belonged to a foreign company. The fact that some directors were appointed by the Central Government did not become conclusive. Rulings in earlier cases which related to public sector corporations could not be applied indiscriminately without regard to the facts. There was no deep and pervasive control of the Central Government over the Maruti Corporation. It was further pointed out by one of the Judges that case similar to Maruti Udyog stand apart from the normal run of cases of public corporations. "Their mainstay is the technology transfer, importation of foreign capital in terms of equity participation and loans which the foreign collaborator is able to bring. The new economic realities have forced us to substantially liberate the economy from licensing, controls and restrictions on capital inflow from abroad. Foreign companies are now being invited in a big way to invest in India and to transfer technology. Raising foreign equity participation to 51% is one such step. Foreign investors would prefer to collaborate with public corporations because they require Government guarantees to protect their interest. Proper territorial location, means of communication and transport, peaceful atmosphere for running an industry and assurance of repatriation of profits are some such protections. If they pay handsome remunerations and perquisites to their employees, they would also expect stringent work culture and discipline from the employees."

12.7 Corporations/Societies/Undertakings etc. held as "State" within the meaning of Article 12 of the Constitution

(i) The Hindustan Steel Ltd. (a public sector corporation) falls within the category of "State". It is an instrumentality of the State and is subject to constitutional and statutory obligations.

[*Hindustan Steel* v. *Rabindra Nath*, (1985) 1 SLR 147 (Cal) (DB)]

(ii) The Indian Council of Agricultural Research, a registered society is an instrumentality of the State.

[*P.K. Ramachandra Iyer* v. *Union of India*, (1983) 3 SLR 495 (SC)]

(iii) An Industrial Development Corporation is a "State".

[*Manabendranath Jha* v. *Chairman, Industrial Development Corporation, Orissa,* (1986) 1 SLR 340 (Ori) (DB)]

(iv) The Indian Tourism Development Corporation is "State".

[*O.P. Bhandari* v. *I.T.D.C.,* (1986) 3 SLR 710 (SC)]

(v) The National Dairy Development Board falls within the concept of "State", as its day to day function is subject to the control of Government of India. Termination of Services of its employee on the ground of alleged trade union activities without hearing is illegal.

[*S.A. Rahim* v. *National Dairy Development Board,* (1983) 3 SLR 575]

(vi) The National Textile Corporation is an agency of the State.

[*Ganesh Chandra Mukherjee* v. *National Textile Corpn.,* (1983) 2 SLR 664 (Cal)]

The National Textile Corporation falls within the category of "State". Termination of services of an employee arbitrarily and without complying with the rules is void and the Court can direct reinstatement of the employee. Service contract cannot violate a fundamental right.

[*Ganesh Chandra Mukherjee* v. *National Textile Corpn.,* (1983) 1 SLR 187 (Cal)]

(vii) Nationalised Banks are instrumentalities of State. They fall under Article 12 of the Constitution. But their employees are not entitled to the protection of Article 311.

[*G.S. Shambhani* v. *State Bank of India, Ahmedabad,* (1984) 2 SLR 765 (Guj)]

(viii) A nationalised Insurance Company (United India Insurance Co.) which came into being as an instrument of State policy is an instrumentality of the State.

[*A.L. Kalra* v. *Project & Equipment Corporation,* (1984) 3 SCC 316: (1984) 2 SLJ 82 followed; *Rajmohnan* v. *Asstt. General Manager,* (1984) 2 SLR 782 (Ker)]

(ix) The Project and Equipment Corporation of India Ltd. is an instrumentality of the State. It is bound by its own regulations, even though not statutory. Contract of personal service can be enforced against it was an employee is entitled to obtain declaration of continuance of service.

[*A.L. Kalra* v. *Project & Equipment Corporation*; (1984) 2 SLJ 82: (1984) 2 SLR 446 (SC)]

(x) A private college aided by Government and affiliated to the Osmania University is amenable to writ jurisdiction.

[*Harjinder Singh* v. *Kakatiya College*; AIR 1975 AP 351; *S. Savaranul* v. *State of Tamil Nadu*, (1985) 1 SLR 765 (Mad)]

(xi) The Kerala State Road Transport Corporation is "State".

[*A. Aziz* v. *Managing Director K.S.R.T.C.*, (1986) 2 SLR 78 (Ker)]

(xii) *Registered Society.*—The Institute for the Physically Handicapped (a registered society) is an instrumentality of the State. It is completely funded, managed and controlled by Government. The President of the General Council is the Secretary to Central Government. The Chairman of the Standing Committee is a representative of the Department of Social Welfare. Appointments have to be approved by Government. Even for dissolution, prior consent of Government is required.

[*Raghunandan Prasad* v. *Institute for Physically Handicapped*, (1984) 3 SLR 355 (Del)]

(xiii) The Steel Authority of India which is a Government owned company is a "State" within the meaning of the Constitution.

[*Officers' Association, Bhilai Steel Plant* v. *Steel Authority of India*, (1983) 1 SLR 477 (MP)]

The Steel Authority of India is an instrumentality of the State.

[*Bihar State Harijan Kalyan Paishad* v. *Union of India*, (1985) 1 SLR 667 (SC)]

(xiv) The State Bank of India is an instrumentality or agency of the Central Government and falls within "State" in Article 12 of the Constitution.

[*Gurudas* v. *State Bank of India*, (1983) 1 SLR 735 (Cal)]

State Bank of India is "State"

[*K. Indira* v. *State Bank of India*, (1983) 2 SLR 376 (AP)]

(xv) The State Bank of Bharat Co-operative Society is an instrumentality of the State, as it is under the control of

Government and its financial resources are controlled and contributed mostly by Government.

[*Ismail Khan* v. *State of Rajasthan*, (1986) 1 SLR 556 (Raj)]

(xvi) The Trade Fair Authority of India is "State" and amenable to writ jurisdiction, in view of "deep pervasive" control exercised by the State.

[*S.D. Sharma* v. *Trade Fair Authority of India*, (1985) 1 SLR 670 (674): (1985) 1 SLJ 160 (Del) (DB)]

(xvii) The Central Inland Water Transport Corporation Ltd. (a Government company as defined in section 617, Companies Act) is "State". "If there is an instrumentality or agency of the State which has assumed the garb of a Government company as defined in section 617 of the Companies Act, it does not follow that it thereby ceases to be an instrumentality or agency of the State."

[*Central Inland Water Transport Corporation Ltd.* v. *Birjo Nath*, (1986) 2 SLR 345 (SC): (1986) 2 SCJ 201]

(xviii) The Central Co-operative Bank Ltd. Bharatpur is "State" and writ against it is maintainable.

[*Phool Chand* v. *State of Rajasthan*, (1986) 1 SLR 222]

(xix) The Indian Statistical Institute a society registered under the Societies Registration Act and governed by the Statistical Institute Act, is an instrumentality of the State. Writ can be issued against it. As required by its bye-laws, before the Director of the Institute is appointed, the vacancy must be published.

[*B.S. Minhas* v. *Indian Statistical Institute*, (1983) 3 SLR 150 (SC)]

(xx) The Defence Metallurgical Research Laboratory (DMRL, Hyderabad) Hyderabad founded and funded exclusive by the Government of India is "State" and its employees are entitled to the protection of Article 16 of the Constitution.

[*A Manik Rao* v. *Metallurgical Research Laboratory*, (1985) 1 SLR 165 (AP)]

(xxi) Food Corporation of India (FCI) is an instrumentality of the State.

[*Workmen of Food Corporation of India* v. *Food Corporation of India*, (1985) 1 SLR 625]

(xxii) Government Aided School – Government aided schools remain private institutions even if they receive aid from Government and are subject to regulation of institutes. Writ of Mandamus cannot be issued to direct the management of such institutes.

(xxiii) Although normally, co-operative societies are not subjected to writ jurisdiction, yet where the society fails to perform a statutory requirement prejudice of any person, that person can seek *mandamus*.

[*Subhas Chander Jain* v. *State Federation of Consumer Co-operative Wholesale Stores Ltd.*, (1986) 1 SLR 8]

12.8 Co-operative Societies are amendable to writ jurisdiction only in cases relating to performance of legal obligations and duties imposed by a statute

Normally Co-operative Societies are not amendable to the writ jurisdiction of the High Court but whenever the society fails to perform a statutory requirement to the prejudice of some one, the later is entitled to approach the High Court for seeking writ of mandamus to direct the Society not to commit breach of statutory requirement. So long as no case is made out of any breach of statutory provisions which a society is obliged to comply with, no writ can be issued against it. But whenever, it is pointed out that any statutory provision requiring the society to act in a particular manner creates a right or interest in favour of a person, it will be permissible for such a person to seek remedy of writ against the Society. It may well be understood that the Cooperative Society will be amendable to writ jurisdiction only in cases relating to performance of legal obligation and duties imposed by a statutes creating a corresponding legal right.

[*S.C. Jain* v. *Haryana State Federation of Consumer Co-operatives*, 1980 (1) SLJ 108]

12.9 The Courts of appropriate jurisdiction have the omnibus powers to issue writs in all cases whenever any person is wronged irrespective of the source of scourge

When any citizen or person is wrong, the High Court will step in protect him. Be that wrong be done by State, an instrumentality of the State, a company or a co-operative society or association or body of individuals whether incorporated or not or even an individual. Right that might have been infringed may be under Part III of the Constitution or any other right which the law validly made might confer upon him.

[*U.P. State Co-operative Land Development Bank Ltd.* v. *Chandra Bhan Dubey*, AIR 1999 SC 753]

12.10 Short notes on the subject of jurisdiction of the High Courts under Article 226 of the Constitution to issue writs against statutory corporations/co-operative societies, etc.

(i) Bank of Rajasthan is neither held to be a State nor an instrumentality of the State. But still, writ of *mandamus* can be issued against it by the High Court, under Article 226 of the Constitution if it has wrongly deprived its employee of his right of livelihood.

[*K.M. Mohnot* v. *Chairman, Bank of Rajasthan*, (1994) 3 SLR 442 (Raj)]

(ii) Writ can be against a private body if the duty imposed upon it is a statutory duty or a public duty which may be imposed by character, common law, custom or even contract.

[*Ganesh Morto Naik* v. *Goa State Co-operative Bank Ltd.*, (1992) 6 SLR 251 (Bom) (DB)]

(iii) Writ jurisdiction is exercisable against Registrar, Cooperative Societies, if it is a statutory authority and the by-laws confer appellate jurisdiction on the Registrar.

[*Jullundhar Central Co-operative Bank* v. *Registrar, Co-operative Societies*, 1983 (1) SLR 64 (P&H)]

(iv) Rules and Regulations framed by statutory bodies have statutory force and the authorities functioning thereunder are statutory authorities and the employees of such bodies enjoy statutory status. There is statutory obligation on the statutory authorities not to deviate from the conditions of service and any deviation can be enforced by legal sanction of judicial declaration which can invalidate actions taken in violation of rules and regulations. The employees of such bodies are entitled to declaration and relief under Act. 226 of the Constitution.

[*Sukhdev Singh* v. *Bhagat Ram*, 1975 (1) SLR 605]

(v) A society merely registered under Punjab Co-operative Societies Act, 1961 is not amenable to the writ jurisdiction under Article 226.

[*Ajmer Singh* v. *Registrar Co-operative Societies, Punjab*, 1980 (3) SLR 347 (FB)]

(vi) A Corporation, Society or Company amenable to writ jurisdiction must be a body being an instrumentality or agency of State within the ambit of Article 12 of the Constitution.

[*R.D. Shetty* v. *International Airport Authority of India*, AIR 1979 SC 1628]

(vii) Writ can be issued against the U.P. State Co-operative Land Development Bank Ltd. Since the affairs of the Bank are controller by the State Government though it functions as a Co-operative Society. It is an extended area of the State – an instrumentality of the State or authority as mentioned under Article 12 of the Constitution.

[*U.P. State Co-operative Land Development Bank Ltd.* v. *Chandra Bhan Dubey*, AIR 1999 SC 753]

12.11 The provisions of Article 311 of the Constitution are not applicable to employees of Insurance company Ltd.

One Arun Tandon was an employee of Insurance Company Ltd. He was reverted to his original post on the ground of unsatisfactory work. His case came up for consideration before Jammu & Kashmir High Court which in its judgment dated 11-6-1982 observed as under:

> ......The provisions of Article 311 are not applicable to him. Assuming, though not granting that the Insurance Company of which the Petitioner is the employee is an "authority" within the meaning of Article 12, still its employees cannot have the status of Government employees to attract the provisions of Article 311. This point is no more *resintegra. Sukhdev* v. *Bhagat Ram,* AIR 1975 SC 1331; *Ajay Hasia* v. *Khalid Majid*, 1981 (2) SLJ 651].

[*Arun Tandon* v. *Insurance Co. Ltd.*, 1982 (2) SLJ 362]

12.12 The protection of Article 14 of the Constitution is available to the employees of the Statutory Corporation in the matter of termination of their services

Rule 26 of Delhi State Industrial Development Corporation (Staff Rules), 1978 provides that management may terminate the services of an employee by giving prescribed notice if management is satisfied that it is expedient to terminate the services of the employee on specified grounds: One of the grounds is "Non availability of the services of the employee arising out of prolonged or irregular absence without permission or any other reason". It was held that this Rule violated Article 14 of the Constitution. "A power which excludes the rule of natural justice in the matter of termination of service in public employment is itself bad even though the exercise of this power is conditional.

[*Ajaib Singh* v. *DSIDC*, 1984 (2) ILR 734]

12.13 The services of even a permanent employee of the Corporation can be terminated by order simpliciter on the ground of their unsuitability for the post

One Bansal joined Indian Air Lines Corporation on 20-10-1955 as Office Assistant. He was a permanent employee. In October, 1973, there was a general strike in the Corporation and a lock out was declared. After the lock out was lifted, the Corporation demanded an undertaking from its employees and those who signed the same were permitted to join. Shri Bansal, too, gave the undertaking in the form demanded but he added the following foot note therein:

> "I save all my previous claim on reciprocal basis in accordance with the law of the land".

The said undertaking was not accepted and he was not taken back in service. He filed a Writ Petition in the Delhi High Court raising several issues and the Corporation was directed to take him back in service subject to his rights in the Writ Petition. He joined his services on 26-6-1974 but his services were terminated on 24-7-1974 under Rule 13 of the Regulations applicable to him.

The background of this case is that on 15th March, 1974 the petitioner had written a letter to the President of India in which he said that the lock-out declared by the Chairman, Air Chief Marshal P.C. Lal, was illegal and that the Air Chief was mismanaging the affairs of the Corporation. On 3rd May, 1974 he wrote another letter to the "President of India, Prime Minister, and her colleagues in the Cabinet Ministers, Brothers and Sisters Member of Parliament of India". Here again he said that the lock-out was illegal. P.C. Lal, it was said, had stopped catering and transport to the passengers and had transferred the bus fleet of the Indian Airlines to his own enterprise by the name of Ex-Servicemen Air Links Transport Service Pvt. Ltd. where according to what the petitioner had heard P.C. Lal was the major shareholder of the firm. The petitioner said several other unsavoury things about P.C. Lal in these two letters which it is unnecessary to repeat here.

In their counter affidavit, the Corporation sought to justify the order of termination on the ground that they "found that the wild personal allegations and aspersions made by the petitioner against the Chairman of the Indian Airlines which were defamatory in character, were wholly false, frivolous and mischievous and undermined and defamed the institution in which he was employed.

Counsel for the petitioner submitted that it is one of those cases where the petitioner's services have been terminated on account of his writing letters. This, he says constitutes a misconduct within the meaning of Regulations 16. A case of misconduct, it was further argued, must be dealt with under the "Rules of Conduct and Disciplinary Procedure" which form part of the Regulations. In other words, the argument was that to a case such as the petitioner's, Regulation 17 was attracted and the petitioner was entitled to a show cause notice, a charge sheet and an enquiry. This having not been done the termination of the petitioner's services simplicitor under Rule 13 is void.

Counsel for the Corporation on the other hand submitted that Rule 13 and Regulations 17 give two separate and independent powers to the Corporation. It is open to the Corporation to exercise one or the other as it thinks fit according to the nature of the case. Whether the petitioner's services can simply be terminated under Rule 13 and the Corporation need not resort to Regulation 17 is the question which fell to be decided in this case.

The Hon'ble Court in its judgment dated 10-8-1976 observed as under:

> "It is well established that to an employee of a statutory corporation Article 311 of the Constitution does not apply.
>
> The Indian Airlines Corporation is statutory Corporation. If it wishes to punish an employee for misconduct, it must take action under Regulation 17. If it does not want to punish the employee for misconduct it can pass an order of discharge simpliciter under Rule 13. It can also do a third thing. It can start proceedings against the employee under Regulation 17. It can level a charge. It can hold an inquiry. And even if at the conclusion of the enquiry the employer finds him guilty of misconduct it may not impose the penalty enumerated in Regulation 17. It can pass an order of discharge simpliciter under Rule 13. This was exactly what had happened in *Jabalpur Electric Supply Co.* v. *Sambhu Prasad*, AIR 1966 SC 1288. In that case, the employer on enquiry was satisfied that an act of misconduct for which the employee was liable to dismissal had been proved but he took a merciful view of his conduct and passed an order of discharge as distinct from the order of dismissal. The court said "this is a case in which the employer has acted, fairly and even generously in terminating the services of the employee". This shows that the two powers can commingle.
>
> The Corporation had two alternatives in this case. If the Corporation preferred to act under Rule 13 it would not be reasonable to say that the Corporation should have charged the petitioner with misconduct and held an enquiry. The fact that it did not do so but exercised its power under Rule 13 cannot render the order *mala fide* or one passed in colourable exercise of its power.
>
> In my opinion the order in this case does not show that the petitioner's services were terminated because of any misconduct. Nor can I hold that the termination of service is *mala fide* or a colourable exercise of power vested in the management. The opinion formed by the management about the suitability of the petitioner in view of his admitted authorship of the letter is, I think, not open to judicial review. On the material I cannot hold the action of the management any thing but *bona fide*."
>
> [*K.S. Bansal* v. *Indian Airlines*, (1977) SLJ 385]

12.14 Principles of law applicable to termination of services of employees of Statutory Corporations

(1) The employer cannot "hire and fire" the employee as he pleases. Otherwise this will completely negative security of service secured to industrial employees through industrial adjudication. There is no unfettered right of the employer under the contract of employment.

(2) If the employer terminates the employment simpliciter, the action must be bona fide. If the termination of service is a colourable exercise of the power or a result of victimization or unfair labour practice the Industrial tribunal would have the jurisdiction to intervene and set aside such termination.

(3) The form of the order is not conclusive. The tribunal can go behind the order to find the reasons which led to the order and then consider whether the termination was a colourable exercise of the power or was a result of unfair labour practice or victimization.

(4) "If the exercise of such power is challenged on the ground of being colourble or *mala fide* or an act of victimisation or unfair labour practice, the employer must disclose to the court the grounds of his impugned action so that the same may be tested judicially."

[*Michel's* case, 1975 SLJ 369]

(5) "The loss of confidence is no new armour for the management, otherwise security of tenure ensured by the industrial jurisprudence and authenticated by a catena of cases of the Supreme Court will be subverted by this neo-formula. (*Michel* case)". It is wrong reading of the Supreme Court decision in *Rebellow's case* that loss of confidence was held to be an independent ground for termination simpliciter. It is "not that the loss of confidence was exalted as a ground but the special circumstances of the case exhibited bad faith in discharge simpliciter". (*Michel* case)

(6) Article 311 does not apply to an employee of the Statutory Corporation.

[*K.S. Bansal* v. *Indian Airlines*, (1977) SLJ 385]

Chapter 13

RETRENCHMENT AND TERMINATION OF EMPLOYEES

"The days of "hire and fire" of workmen in Industry are gone with the introduction of Industrial Disputes Act, 1947 and promulgation of Industrial Employment (Standing Orders) Central Rules, 1946. The Principles of natural and social justice have been imported in industrial jurisprudence which must be kept in mind while dealing with industrial disputes."

[*Ajaib Singh* v. *Sirhind Co-op Mktg,-cum-Processing Service Society*, AIR 1999 SC 1351]

SYNOPSIS

13.1 Gist of Industrial Dispute Act, 1947 relating to the provisions of Retrenchment/termination of services of workers

13.2 Note on up-to-date amendments made in Industrial Disputes Act, 1947 particularly relating to Retrenchment compensation etc. payable to the workers

13.3 Observations of the Hon'ble Supreme Court with regard to the objectives of Industrial Disputes Act, 1947

13.4 Gist of the Industrial Employment (Standing Orders) Act, 1946

13.5 Interpretation of the term "Appropriate Government" used in section 10 of Industrial Dispute Act, 1947 for making reference to the Labour Court in an industrial dispute

13.6 Definition of the term "Retrenchment" as given in section 2(oo) of Industrial Disputes Act, 1947

13.7 "Retrenchment" is another name for termination of services of an employee in an Industrial establishment

13.8 Observations of the Supreme Court as to the interpretation of the term "Retrenchment"

13.9 Does the term "Retrenchment" as defined in section 2(oo) of the Act merely means discharge of "surplusage in a continuing business or that it also includes the discharge of the staff on closure of the business concern itself?

13.10 Short notes on the rulings of the courts on the subject matter of retrenchment/termination of services of workers

13.11 Termination of services of a Probationer in an industrial establishment on the ground of his unsuitability for the job amounts to retrenchment

13.12 Termination of service of an employee on account of his having become surplus due to recession in industry amounts to 'Retrenchment'

13.13 Even where there is no specific mention about the age of superannuation of workers in the Standing Orders, the action of the Management in superannuating the worker at the age of 58 years does not amount to 'Retrenchment'

13.14 The Industrial Tribunal should exercise its powers under section 11A of the Act judiciously

13.15 The Industrial Tribunal is duty bound to adjudicate the dispute once it has been referred to it under section 10 of the Act and cannot surrender its jurisdiction to another authority

13.16 The management has the full right to terminate the services of a worker who has been appointed on a temporary basis for specific period

13.1 Gist of Industrial Dispute Act, 1947 relating to the provisions of Retrenchment/termination of services of workers

The Act came into effect from 11-3-1947. It deals with provisions relating to investigation and settlement of industrial disputes. During the last over 50 years of the operation of the Act, it became expedient to effect certain changes in the provisions from time to time consistent with the social philosophy of the country of shielding the weak against the all-mighty industrial giants etc. keeping in view the necessity of maintaining industrial peace. The more important provisions of the Act are discussed below:

(i) The Act provided for two institutions for the prevention and settlement of industrial disputes namely the "Works Committee" and "Industrial Tribunals". The former consisted of representatives of the employers and the workmen, while the latter consisted of one or more members possessing qualifications ordinarily required for appointment of judges of the High Court. It was envisaged that Works Committees will be constituted in every industrial establishment employing 100 workmen or more and their duties will be to remove causes of friction between the employers and the workmen in the day to day working of the establishment. It was provided that reference to Industrial Tribunal will lie where both parties to any industrial dispute apply for such reference or where the appropriate Government considers it expedient to do so.

(ii) The Act sought to re-orient the administration of the conciliation machinery provided in the Trade Disputes Act. Conciliation was to be compulsory in all disputes in public utility services and optional in the case of other industrial establishments. With a view to expedite conciliation proceedings time limits were prescribed for conclusion thereof – 14 days in the case of conciliation officer and 2 months in the case of Board of Conciliation from the date of notice of strike. A settlement arrived at in the course of conciliation proceedings would be binding for such periods as may be agreed upon by the parties and where no period has been agreed upon, for a period of one year, and will continue to be binding until revoked by a 3 months' notice by either party to the dispute.

(iii) Another important new feature of the Act related to the prohibition of strikes and lockouts during the pendency of conciliation and adjudication proceedings of settlements reached in the course of conciliation proceedings and of awards of Industrial Tribunals declared binding by the appropriate Government. The underlying argument was that where a dispute has been referred to conciliation for adjudication, a strike or lock out in furtherance thereof, is both unnecessary and inexpedient. Where on the date of reference to conciliation or adjudication, a strike or lock out is already in existence; power was given to the appropriate Government to prohibit its continuance lest the chances of settlement or speedy determination of the dispute should be jeopardized.

(iv) The Act also empowered the appropriate Government to declare, if public interest or emergency so requires, by notification in the Official Gazette, any industry to be a public utility service, for such period, if any, as may be specified in the notification.

13.2 Note on up-to-date amendments made in Industrial Disputes Act, 1947 particularly relating to Retrenchment compensation etc. payable to the workers

A number of amendments to the Act have since been carried out from time to time in the light of the experience gained in its actual working, case laws and industrial relation policy of the Government. Brief description about some of the more important changes are given below:

(i) *Amendment Act 41 of 1956.*—Doubts were raised whether retrenchment compensation under the Industrial Disputes Act, 1947, becomes payable by reason merely of the fact that there has been a change of employers, even if the service of the workman is continued without interruption and the terms and conditions of his service remain unaltered. This had created difficulty in the transfer, reconstitution and amalgamation of companies and it was proposed to make the intention clear by amending section 25F of the Act.

(ii) *Amendment Act 36 of 1964.*—There were certain difficulties in getting suitable persons for appointment as Presiding Officers of Tribunals. Section 7A of the Act was modified by relaxing the qualification for appointment of such officers.

(iii) *Amendment Act 35 of 1965.*—(a) In construing the scope of industrial dispute, Courts had taken the view that a dispute between an employer and an individual workman cannot *per se* be an industrial dispute, but it may become one if it is taken up by a Union or a number of workmen making a common cause with the aggrieved individual workman in view of the cases of individual dismissals and discharges could not be taken up for conciliation or arbitration or referred to adjudication under the Industrial Disputes Act, unless they are sponsored by a Union or a number of workmen. It was now proposed to make the machinery under the Act available in such cases.

(b) Changes were made in section 25C of the Act providing for payment of compensation to workmen during lay off periods not earlier provided.

(c) Section 29 of the Act was amended providing for punishment in case of continuing breach of settlement or an award by the employers after conviction for the first breach.

(iv) *Amendment Act 45 of 1971.*—(a) A new section 11A was introduced which was intended to give enhanced powers to the Tribunals. It was provided that the Tribunal's power in an adjudication proceeding relating to discharge or dismissal or a workman should not be limited and that the Tribunal should have the power, in cases wherever necessary, to set aside the order of discharge or dismissal and direct reinstatement of the workman on such terms and conditions, if any, as it thinks fit or give such other relief to the workman including the award of any lesser punishment in lieu of discharge or dismissal as the circumstances of the case may require.

(b) Section 25FFF was amended to provide for payment of full compensation to workmen in the event of closing down of a mining undertaking due to exhaustion of its reserves subject to the condition that no retrenchment compensation would be payable to the workmen concerned when an employer provides them with alternative employment with effect from the date of closure at the same remuneration as they were entitled to receive and on the same terms and conditions of service as were applicable them immediately before the closure.

(v) *Amendment Act 32 of 1972.*—Provision was made in the Act to provide for the service of a notice at least sixty days before the intended closure of an undertaking is to become effective, so that within the period prompt remedial measures could be taken, where the circumstances permit to prevent such closure. No notice will be required to be served in the case of undertakings set up for construction of buildings, roads, canals, dams and other construction works and projects or in the case of small establishments employing less than fifty persons. The Act also provided for penalty for closing down any undertaking without serving the requisite notice.

(vi) *Amendment Act 32 of 1976.*—It was sought to amend the Act to make prior approval of the appropriate Government necessary in the case of lay off, retrenchment and closure in industrial establishments where 300 or more workmen are employed. A new Chapter VB was inserted in the Act in the interest of rehabilitation of workmen and for maintenance of supplies and services essential to the life of the community, there is a provision in the Bill for restarting the undertakings which were already closed down otherwise than on account of unavoidable circumstances beyond the control of the employer.

(vii) *Amendment Act 46 of 1982.*—The terms "appropriate Government". "Industry" and "workman" were redefined in the light of the experience gained in actual working, *case laws* and industrial relations policy of the Government.

It was made obligatory for every industrial establishment employing 100 persons or more to set up time bound grievance redressal procedure.

The provisions relating to closure of industrial establishment were recast in the light of the observation of the Supreme Court in *Excel Wear* case, AIR 1979 SC 25.

The special provision relating to lay off, retrenchment and closure as contained in Chapter V-B of the Act applied to establishment employing 300 workmen or more. With a view to extending this statutory protection to workmen of smaller establishment also, it was provided to reduce the then existing limit from 300 to 100.

(viii) *Amendment Act 49 of 1984.*—The definition of the term 'Retrenchment' given in section 2(oo) was amended and it was provided that termination of service of a workman as a result of non-renewal of the contract of employment on the expiry of its term will not amount to Retrenchment.

(ix) *Amendment Act 24 of 1996.*—Section 2(a) of the Act relating to the definition of the term 'Appropriate Government' in relation to industrial disputes was amended:

13.3 Observations of the Hon'ble Supreme Court with regard to the objectives of Industrial Disputes Act, 1947

(i) "The object of the Industrial Disputes Act, 1947 and settlement of industrial peace by reference to adjudication is to bring about industrial peace; it is to be presumed ordinarily that what has been so referred is a genuine industrial dispute which needs to be resolved. Thus, during judicial review, the Courts should try, as far as possible, to sustain the awards rather than pick holes here and there on trivial and hyper-technical points and thereby frustrate the entire adjudication process.

[*Calcutta Port Shramik Union* v. *Calcutta R.T. Association*, AIR 1988 SC 2168]

(ii) The Industrial Disputes Act was brought on the statute book with the object to ensure social justice to both the employers and employees and advance the progress of industry by bringing about the existence of harmony and cordial relationship between the parties. It is a piece of legislation providing and regulating the service conditions of the workers. The object of the Act is to improve the service conditions of industrial labour so as to provide for them the ordinary amenities of life and by the process, to bring about industrial peace which would in its turn accelerate productive activity of the country resulting in its prosperity.

[*Ajaib Singh* v. *Sirhind Co-op Mktg.-cum-Processing Service Society Ltd.*, AIR 1999 SC 1351: (1999) 6 SCC 82]

13.4 Gist of the Industrial Employment (Standing Orders) Act, 1946

(i) Earlier the economic law of demand and supply in the labour market settled, by mutually beneficial bargain between the employer and the workman. It was taken as granted that such a bargain would secure fair terms and conditions of employment to the workmen. They had an abiding faith in the unity of this law. But the working of this law belied their faith. Later workmen found that they did not possess adequate bargaining strength to secure fair terms and conditions of service, they organized themselves in trade unions and insisted on collective bargaining with the employer. The advent of trade unions and collective bargaining created new problems for maintaining industrial peace and production for the society. Workmen started putting forth their demands. Recognising the rough deal that was being given to the workers by employers who would not define their conditions of service and the inevitability of industrial strife in such a situation, the legislature made an attempt to intervene by introducing the Industrial Employment (Standing Orders) Bill, 1946.

(ii) *Statement of the Act.*—Experience had shown that 'standing orders' defining the conditions of recruitment, discharge, disciplinary action, holidays, leave etc., go a long way towards minimizing friction between the management and workers in industrial undertakings. Discussion on the subject at the tripartite Indian Labour Conference revealed a consensus of opinion in favour of legislature. A Bill was accordingly introduced to provide for the framing of 'standing orders' in all industrial establishments employing one hundred or more workers.

In the first instance it was intended that the Act will apply to the categories of industrial establishments specified in clause (2)(e) thereof which include, besides factories and railways, mines, quarries and oil fields, tramway or motor, omnibus services, docks, wharves and jetties, inland steam vessels, plantations and workshops. Government was empowered to extend the Act to other classes of industrial establishments or to grant exemptions where necessary, by notification.

Within 6 months from the date on which the Act became applicable to an industrial establishment, the employer was required to frame draft 'standing orders' and submit them to the Certifying Officer for certification. The draft should cover all the matters specified in the Schedule to the Act and any other matter that Government may prescribe by rules. The Certifying Officer was empowered to modify or add to the draft standing orders so as to render them certifiable under the Act. It was not his function (nor of the Appellate Authority) to adjudicate upon their fairness or reasonableness. There will be a right of appeal against the decisions of the Certifying Officers.

The Industrial Employment (Standing Orders) Bill, 1946 was passed by the legislature and it received the assent on 23rd April, 1946. It came on the statute book as the Industrial Employment (Standing Orders) Act, 1946 (20 of 1946)."

13.5 Interpretation of the term "Appropriate Government " used in section 10 of Industrial Dispute Act, 1947 for making reference to the Labour Court in an industrial dispute

One Ram Lal was an officer working in State Bank Chandigarh. He was sent on deputation to Primary Bank at Bhatinda. While on deputation, his services were terminated by State Bank Chandigarh. The petitioner raised an industrial dispute. The point at issue was whether it was Chandigarh Administration or the Punjab Government which had the power to make a reference to the Labour Court under section 10 of I.D.A., 1947, about the industrial dispute. Punjab & Haryana High Court in its judgment dated 25-2-1982 observed as under:

> "The petitioner was holding the deputation post with the Primary Bank at Bhatinda by virtue of his being an employee of the State Bank. The relationship between the State Bank and the petitioner came to an end when the latter's services were terminated by the former at Chandigarh. As a result, the deputation of the petitioner with the Primary Bank at Bhatinda automatically came to an end. The order terminating the services of the petitioner at Chandigarh was a complete action in itself. The fact that the order terminating the services of the petitioner was served on him at Bhatinda cannot be taken as a circumstance to infer that the cause of action arose substantially at Bhatinda and not at Chandigarh. I am, therefore, of the opinion that the cause of action in the matter of dispute relating to the termination of the services of the petitioner by the State Bank exclusively arose at Chandigarh and that it did not arise at Bhatinda. In this view of the matter, the appropriate Government in terms of section 10 of the Act is Union Territory, Chandigarh and not the State of Punjab.
>
> [*Ram Lal* v. *Presiding Officer Labour Courts, Patiala,* 1982 (2) SLJ 44]

(ii) In a Union Territory, it is the Central Government which is competent to make a reference of Industrial dispute under Industrial Dispute Act 1947, section 10(1)(d) and as such, such reference cannot be quashed on the ground that it should have been made by the State Government.

In relation to a Union Territory, the concept of 'State Government' as such has no relevance.

[*Goa Sampling Employees' Association* v. *General Superintendence Co. of India*, 1984 (3) SLR 97]

13.6 Definition of the term "Retrenchment" as given in section 2(oo) of Industrial Disputes Act, 1947

"Section 2(oo) "retrenchment" means the termination by the employer of the service of a workman for any reason whatsoever, otherwise than as a punishment inflicted by way of disciplinary action but does not include—

(a) voluntary retirement of the workman; or

(b) retirement of the workman on reaching the age of superannuation if the contract of employment between the employer and the workman concerned contains a stipulation in that behalf; or

(bb) termination of the service of the workman as a result of the non-renewal of the contact of employment between the employer and the workman concerned on its expiry or of such contract being terminated under a stipulation in that behalf contained therein; or

(c) termination of the service of a workman on the ground of continued ill health."

13.7 "Retrenchment" is another name for termination of services of an employee in an Industrial establishment

"Retrenchment" is another name for termination of services of an employee. The management has the power under Industrial Disputes Act, 1947 to put an end to his employment for "any reason whatsoever" subject to the provisions of section 2 (oo) of the Act as reproduced in the preceding sub-head. However, the employer can resort to "Retrenchment" of an employee only after complying with the provisions of sections 25F, 25FF, 25 FFF etc. of the Act although the certified Standing Orders have statutory force and do not expressly exclude the application of principles of natural justice, yet the provisions in the Act relating to Retrenchment make an exception to the application of principles of Natural Justice. The Retrenchment of an employee effected in accordance with the provisions of the Act cannot be termed as "penal" in nature.

There can be situations in industrial establishments when there is a sudden rush of work of a short duration which may necessitate employment of large number of temporary hands to cope with the work. But as soon as the work is over, there is no justification to keep those temporary hands any longer and the need to dispense with their services arises. In that situation, the employees can certainly be retrenched after compliance with the provisions of section 25F of the Act. It has been held by the Supreme Court in *Ralstan John* v. *Central Government Industrial Tribunal-cum-Labour Court*, AIR 1994 SC 131 and also in other numerous court judgment that non compliance with the provisions of section 25 F before resorting to Retrenchment is illegal and the order is liable to be set aside. The employer cannot and should not therefore, be burdened with excess man power and he may award compensation instead of reinstating such workers.

Retrenchment does not amount to penalty calling for compliance with the principles of natural justice or resorting to departmental proceedings. As stated earlier, such Retrenchment only calls for compliance with the various provisions of the Act and nothing more. When compliance with the provisions of the Act is made, Retrenchment is held valid and the employee has no other protection. But if the retrenchment is held illegal and unjustified in the circumstances of any particular case, then the retrenched employee has the right to be reinstated in service or to be compensated having regard to the facts of that particular case.

13.8 Observations of the Supreme Court as to the interpretation of the term "Retrenchment"

Note.—

The judgment referred to hereunder were delivered before 1984 when the definition of the term "Retrenchment" was amended to include clause (bb) as an additional accepted category of cases which is not included in the term "Retrenchment". This clause reads as under:

> "(bb) termination of the service of the workman as a result of non-renewal of the contract of employment between the employer and the workman concerned on its

expiry or of such contract being terminated under stipulation in that behalf contained therein.

(i) "Leaving out the excluding sub-clauses (a), (b) and (c) for the time being – the definition when analysed consists of the following four essential requirements (a) termination of service of workman: (b) by the employer; (c) for any reason whatsoever and (d) otherwise than as a punishment inflicted by way of disciplinary action. It must be conceded that the definition is in very wide terms. When a portion of the staff or labour force is discharged as surplusage in a continuing business, there are (a) termination of the service of a workman; (b) by the employer; (c) for any reason whatsoever and (d) otherwise than as a punishment inflicted by way of disciplinary action. The termination of service which follows may be due to a variety of reasons e.g. for economy, rationalization in industry, installation of a new labour-saving machinery, etc. The legislature in using the expression "for any reason whatsoever" says in effect:

> "It does not matter why you are discharging the surplus; if the other requirements of the definition are fulfilled, then it is retrenchment."

[*Hari Prasad* v. *A.D. Divelkar*, AIR 1957 SC 121]

(ii) "If the definition of 'retrenchment is looked at unaided and unhampered by precedent, one is at once struck by the remarkably wide language employed and particularly by the use of the words "termination....for any reason whatsoever". The definition expressly excludes termination of service as a 'Punishment inflicted by way of disciplinary action'. The definition does not include, so it expressly says, voluntary retrenchment of the workman or retrenchment of the workman on reaching the age of superannuation or termination of the service of the workman of the ground of continuous ill health. Voluntary retrenchment of a workman or retrenchment of the workman on reaching the age of superannuation can hardly be described as termination, by the employer, of the service of a workman. Yet, the Legislature took special care to mention that they were not included within the meaning of 'termination by the employer of the service of a workman for any reason whatsoever. This, in our opinion, emphasizes the broad interpretation to be given to the expression 'retrenchment'.

[*Santosh Gupta* v. *State Bank of Patiala*, (1980) 3 SCR 884]

(iii) "Niceties and semantics apart, termination by the employer of the service of a workman for any reason whatsoever would constitute retrenchment except in cases expected in the section itself. The excepted or excluded cases are where termination is by way of punishment inflicted by way of disciplinary action, voluntary retirement of the workman, retirement of the workman on reaching the age of superannuation if the contract of employment between the employer and the workman concerned contains a stipulation in that behalf, and termination of the service of a workman on the ground of continued ill health. It is not the case of the respondent that termination in the instant case was a punishment inflicted by way of disciplinary action. If such a position were adopted, the termination would be *ab initio* void for violation of principle of natural justice or for not following the procedure prescribed for imposing punishment. It is not even suggested that this was a case of voluntary retirement or retirement on reaching the age of superannuation or absence on account of continued ill-health. The case does not fall under any of the excepted categories. There is thus termination of service for a reason other than the excepted category. It would indisputably be retrenchment within the meaning of the word as defined in the Act."

[*Mohan Lal* v. *Management of M/s Bharat Electronics Ltd.*, (1981) 3 SCR 518]

13.9 Does the term "Retrenchment" as defined in section 2(oo) of the Act merely mean discharge of "surplusage in a continuing business or that it also includes the discharge of the staff on closure of the business concern itself?

This proposition of law was considered at length by Hon'ble Supreme Court in *Karnataka State Road Transport Corporation* v. *M. Boraiah,* 1984 (1) SLJ 142. The Apex Court analysed the definition of the term and also quoted a judgment of the Constitution Bench and observed as under:

"Section 2(oo) of the Industrial Disputes Act, 1947, defines 'retrenchment' to mean.

'Retrenchment' means the termination by the employer of the service of a workman for any reason whatsoever, otherwise, than as a punishment inflicted by way of disciplinary action, but does not include – (a) voluntary retirement of a workman; or (b) retirement of the workman on reaching the age of superannuation if the contract of the employment between the employer and the workmen concerned contains a stipulation in that behalf; or (c) termination of the service of a workman on the ground of continued ill-health."

(ii) A Constitution Bench of the Apex Court in *Hariprasad Shivshankar Shukla* v. *A.D. Divikar*, AIR 1957 SC 121 examined the true meaning of the expression "retrenchment", and posed the following question:

"The question, before us is – does this definition merely give effect to the ordinary, accepted notion of retrenchment in an existing or running industry by embodying the notion in apt and readily intelligible words or does it go so far beyond the accepted notion of retrenchment as to include the termination of service of all workmen in an industry when the industry itself ceases to exist on a *bona fide* closure or discontinuance of his business by the employer."

It went to say:

"There is no doubt that when the Act itself provides a dictionary for the words used, we must look into that dictionary first for an interpretation of the words used in the statute. We are not concerned with any presumed intention of the legislature; our task is to get at the intention as expressed in the statute. Therefore, we propose first to examine the language of the definition and see if the ordinary, accepted notion of retrenchment fits in, squarely and fairly, with the language used. What is the ordinary, accepted notion of retrenchment in an industry......... Let us now see how far that meaning fits in, with the language used. We have referred earlier to the four essential requirements of the definition, and the question is, does the ordinary meaning of retrenchment fulfil those requirements? In our opinion it does. When a portion of the staff or labour force is discharged as surplusage in a continuing business, there are (a) termination of the service of a workman; (b) by the employer; (c) for any reason whatsoever and (d) otherwise than as a punishment inflicted by way of disciplinary action".

The Constitution Bench further said:

"The legislature in using the expression "for any reason whatsoever" says in effect: "it does not matter why you are discharging the surplus: If the other requirements of the definition are fulfilled, then it is retrenchment". In the absence of any compelling words to indicate that the intention was even to include a *bona fide* closure of the whole business, it would, we think, be divorcing the expression altogether from its context to give it a wide meaning. What is being defined is retrenchment, and that is the context of the definition. It is true that an artificial definition may include a meaning different from or in excess of the ordinary acceptation of the word which is the subject of definition; but there must be compelling words to show that such a meaning different or in excess of the ordinary meaning is intended Where, within the frame work of the ordinary acceptation of the word, every single requirement of the definition clause is fulfilled, it would be wrong to take the definition as destroying the essential meaning of the word defined."

13.10 Short notes on the rulings of the courts on the subject matter of retrenchment/termination of services of workers

(i) Termination of service of a workman for a fixed period for non-renewal of contract will amount to retrenchment and section 2(oo)(bb) of the Act will not be attracted when the letter of appointment was a camouflage to circumvent the benefit of permanent.

(ii) Termination of a workman given periodical appointments without compliance of section 25F of the Act will amount to retrenchment and section 2(oo)(bb) of the Act will not be attracted.

[*Manager Jayabrath Printers & Publishers (P) Ltd.* v. *Labour Court Kozhi Kode*, 1993 LLR 413 (Ker HC)]

(iii) Termination of an employee without payment of retrenchment compensation on the ground that his appointment was illegal will be unjustified and will amount to illegal retrenchment.

[*Mithilesh Kumar Singh* v. *State of Bihar*, 1995 LLR 183]

(iv) Termination of a daily wager or a casual employee who has completed 240 days will amount to retrenchment.

[*Chairman-cum-Managing Director, Orissa Road Transport* v. *Ramesh Chandra Gouda*, 1995 LLR 458 (Ori)]

(v) Termination of clerks in a bank even engaged against leave vacancies will amount to retrenchment and will be entitled to re-employment.

[*Oriental Bank of Commerce* v. *U.O.I.*, 1997 LLR 462 (All)]

(vi) Termination of a workman by retaining 55 junior employees will amount to retrenchment.

[*National Cooperative Development Corporation* v. *Manohar Singh Rawal*, 1999 LLT 405 (Del)]

(vii) Termination of trainee under Standing Orders will be retrenchment.

[*T.I. Diamond Chain Ltd. Madras* v. *Presiding Officer, Madras*, 202 LLR 1059 (Mad)]

(viii) When an employer has not paid retrenchment compensation at the time of terminating the services of a workman, reinstatement will be appropriate relief and the High Court will not interfere in its writ jurisdiction.

[*M.C.D.* v. *Sanjay Kumar*, 2004 LLR 162 (Del)]

(ix) Reinstatement of part time employees of the University of Delhi cannot be faulted by the High Court when their services were terminated without compliance of section 25F of Industrial Dispute Act.

[*University of Delhi* v. *R.K. Sharma*, 2003 LLR 893 (Del]

(x) Petitioner was appointed as trainee officer for six months which was extended by three months. He failed in the written test and his services were terminated as his service was unsatisfactory. It was held that his termination is not retrenchment within he meaning of section 25F of the Act.

[*Anthony Olinto Silva* v. *S.V. Nevaji*, 1990 LLR 191 (Bom)]

(xi) Termination of services of a probationer in terms of his appointment does not amount to retrenchment.

[*Divisional Manager LIC* v. *M. Venugopal*, 1993 LLR 317 (AP)]

(xii) Termination of employees engaged during crushing season for less than 240 days will not amount to retrenchment.

[*Morinda Corp. Sugar Mills* v. *Ram Kishan*, 1996 LLR 214 (SC)]

(xiii) Termination of a workman on completion of a Project will not be retrenchment.

[*Telecom District Manager* v. *A.A. Angali*, 2000 LLR 1219 (Kar)]

(xiv) Termination by way of punishment will not be retrenchment.

[*Maria Thomas Gonsalvies (Mrs.)* v. *Concept Pharmaceuticals (P) Ltd.*, 2001 LLR 755 (Bom)]

(xv) When engagement of daily wagers comes to an end, no retrenchment compensation will be payable.

[*Nuclear Fuel Complex* v. *K. Penta Reddy*, 2002 LLR 608 (AP)]

(xvi) Retrenchment compensation will be calculated at 30 days and not 26 days of a month.

[*Parry's (Cal) Employees Union* v. *Third Industrial Tribunal West Bengal*, 2001 LLR 462 (Cal)]

(xvii) Retrenchment of an employee by abolishing his post will be illegal since he had demanded the benefit of figment in terms of award pertaining to working journalists.

[*Management of Daily Pratap* v. *Delhi Administration*, 1991 LLR 552 (Del)]

(xviii) Termination of service on ground of unauthorized absence tantamount to retrenchment.

[*Uttar Pradesh State Spinning Mills Co. Ltd.* v. *N.K. Tripathi* , 2000 LLR 996 (All)]

(xix) Termination of a workman engaged for specific period will not be retrenchment.

[*Haryana State F.C.C.W. Store Ltd.* v. *Ram Niwas*, 2002 LLR 865 (SC)]

(xx) 'Diabetes' will not amount to "continuous ill health" and therefore termination of workman on this ground will be illegal.

[*Harvilas Kushwah* v. *Sports Authority of India*, 1995 LLR 820 (MP)]

(xxi) When the services of an employee are terminated on the ground of security and interest of industrial establishment, it is not retrenchment.

[*Piparaich Sugar Mills Ltd.* v. *Piparaich Mills Mazdoor Union*, AIR 1957 SC 95]

(xxii) Striking of the name of a workman from the Rolls of the Management is termination of his service and retrenchment within the meaning of section 2(oo) of the Act and attracts the provisions of section 25F (a) and (b), violation of which makes retrenchment invalid.

[*Delhi Cloth and General Mills Co. Ltd.* v. *Shambu Nath Mukherjee*, 1977 SLJ 628 SC]

13.11 Termination of services of a Probationer in an industrial establishment on the ground of his unsuitability for the job amounts to retrenchment

One M. Boraiah was a probationer in Karnataka State Road Transport Corporation. His services were terminated on the ground of unsatisfactory service. An industrial dispute was raised and after passing through various judicial channels, the case came up before Supreme Court for determination whether or not the termination of the services of Boraiah amounted to retrenchment within the meaning of section 2(oo) of the Industrial Dispute Act, 1947. The Apex Court observed as under:

"xxx

Once the conclusion is reached that retrenchment as defined in section 2(oo) of the Industrial Dispute Act covers every case of termination of service except those which have been embodied in the definition, discharge from employment or termination of services of a probationer would also amount to retrenchment...."

[*Karnataka State Road Transport Corporation* v. *M. Boraiah*, 1984 (1) SLJ 142]

13.12 Termination of service of an employee on account of his having become surplus due to recession in industry amounts to 'Retrenchment'

One Niranjan Das was employed as a Senior clerk in Gammon India Ltd. on 10-4-1962. He was served with a notice on 14-9-1967 terminating his services which read as under:

"Due to the reduction in the volume of business of the Company as a result of the recession, your services will not be required by the company after the 14th October, 1967 and this may be treated as statutory notice of one month of termination of your service.

We take this opportunity to thank you for your past services and it is very unfortunate that the present circumstances have compelled us to issue this notice.

Should it be possible for us to offer you a job at any of our works sites at a later date, we shall make you a fresh offer at that time."

The question that came up for consideration before the Supreme Court was whether the termination of the employee amounted to retrenchment. The Apex Court in its judgment dated 5-12-1983 observed as under:

"The termination of service for the reasons mentioned in the notice is not covered by any of the clauses (a), (b) and (c) of section 2(oo) which defines retrenchment and it is by now well-settled that where the termination of service does not fall within any of the excluded categories, the termination would be *ipso facto* retrenchment. It is therefore indisputably a case of retrenchment. It is not disputed that the pre-requisite for a valid retrenchment as laid sown in section 25F has not been complied with and, therefore, retrenchment bringing about termination is *ab initio* void."

[*Gammon India Ltd.* v. *Niranjan Dass*, 1984 (1) SLJ 150]

13.13 Even where there is no specific mention about the age of superannuation of workers in the Standing Orders, the action of the Management in superannuating the worker at the age of 58 years does not amount to 'Retrenchment'

One Sahu, an employee of Prajatantra Prachar Society was informed by the Secretary of the Society that he was being superannuated since he has already reached the age of 58 years. There was no specific clause in the Standing Order of the Management about the age of superannuation of workers. It was contended by the petitioner that his superannuation was, in fact, 'Retrenchment' within the meaning of section 2(oo) of Industrial Disputes Act, 1947 and there has been violation of mandatory provisions of section 25F of the Act. The petitioner challenged the order of his retrenchment in Orissa High Court and the Hon'ble Court observed as under:

> "Clause (b) of section 2(oo) excludes retirement on reaching the age of superannuation. True, that retirement has the effect of "termination" of service but all termination of service is not retrenchment. The impugned order, therefore, *prima facie* is not an order of retrenchment unless it is shown that either the Samity was not competent to take the decision to retire its employees at the age of 58 years or that the decision is otherwise unreasonable and unwarranted."
>
> [*Mathuri Sahu* v. *Secretary Prajatantra Prachar Society Cuttack*, 1977 SLJ 428]

13.14 The Industrial Tribunal should exercise its powers under section 11A of the Act judiciously

One Jaswant Singh was a driver in PEPSU Roadways. He consumed liquor. This constituted misconduct under the relevant Standing Order. An enquiry was held and as a disciplinary measure he was dismissed from service. An industrial dispute was raised questioning the correctness of dismissal from service of the appellant and the matter was referred to the Labour Court, Patiala. The Presiding Officer, Labour Court held that the driver was drunk but looking to the circumstances of the case the punishment of dismissal from service was rather on the heavier side and therefore, he directed reinstatement of the appellant in service denying back-wages. The High Court in civil writ petition by respondent employer set aside the decision of the Labour Court holding that the jurisdiction under section 11A was exercised by the Labour Court on extraneous and irrelevant considerations. The High Court confirmed the punishment of dismissal from service. The Petitioner filed an appeal before Supreme Court against the judgment of the High Court and the Apex Court in its judgment observed as under:

> "We are also clearly of the opinion that a driver of a passenger bus or for that matter any mechanically propelled vehicle cannot and should not consume intoxicating liquor while on duty because that endangers the safety not only of those in the vehicle but those using the roads also. However,

looking to the conduct of the appellant it appears to be his first offence and the Labour Court in exercise of its jurisdiction under section 11A of the Industrial Disputes Act was of the opinion that in the facts of the case, punishment of dismissal was rather heavy and was not called for and, therefore, reduced the punishment. But the reduction was to a level of mere refusal of back wages, which would be inadequate punishment in the facts of this case. We are of the opinion that the Labour Court was right and justified in directing reinstatement of the appellant in service. Further appellant is not entitled to back wages for the reasons that appealed to Labour Court. This is not adequate penalty for the misconduct proved. In our opinion to keep the appellant within the bounds of well disciplined conduct a further punishment is also called for and should be imposed so that our humanistic approach may not induce him to repeat his intemperate performance. Accordingly, we direct that the appellant should not be given three increments in the time scale in which he would be reinstated, for the next three yeas. For all other benefits he will be treated as continuing in service."

[*Jaswant Singh* v. *PEPSU Roadways*, 1984 (1) SLJ 244]

13.15 The Industrial Tribunal is duty bound to adjudicate the dispute once it has been referred to it under section 10 of the Act and cannot surrender its jurisdiction to another authority

One Jai Bhagwan, a clerk in Ambala Central Cooperative Bank Ltd. was removed from service on the basis of a complaint for presenting some bogus cheques. No charge sheet was issued to him. An industrial dispute was raised by the workmen for adjudication before Industrial Tribunal Haryana as to whether his termination was justified or not. The Tribunal did not go into the merits of the case but upheld the decision of the management for his removal from service.

The case came up for consideration before the Supreme Court which in its judgment dated 29-9-1983 observed as under:

"Raising an industrial dispute is well recognized and legitimate mode of redress available to a workman and we fail to see why the statute recognized mode of redress should be denied to a workman because of the existence of availability of another remedy. Now, we are able to understand how an additional Tribunal to whom a dispute has been referred to for adjudication can refuse to adjudicate upon it and surrender jurisdiction which it undoubtedly has to some other authority..... Once a reference has been properly made to the Tribunal, the dispute has to be resolved by the Tribunal Resolution of the dispute cannot be avoided by the Tribunal on the ground that the workman ought to have availed the right of appeal to the Board of Management..... The appellant is entitled to be reinstated...."

[*Jai Bhagwan* v. Ambala *Central Co-operative Bank Ltd.*, 1984 (1) SLJ 245 (SC)]

13.16 The management has the full right to terminate the services of a worker who has been appointed on a temporary basis for specific period

One X was appointed as a Fitter on probation on 16-4-1982 upto 30-9-1982. Thereafter, he was a fitter on temporary basis on 1-1-1983 for a period of 2 years and the terms of the appointment read as under:

"This is purely a temporary appointment for a period of two years upto 31-12-1984. During or at the expiry of this period if your work or conduct is not found satisfactory or your services are no longer required by the Company these would be terminated as per clause 8 above."

Before the stipulated period of 2 years was over, the Management sent a communication to him on 14-12-1984 warning him of action for misconduct because of his union activities. X replied to the said letter on 21-12-1984 stating that he had been educating the workers on Hindu-Sikh unity during the lunch break and this did not amount to interference with the working of the factory. On 28-12-1984, the Management wrote to X that he had been appointed on temporary basis for a period of 2 years ending 31-12-1984. The letter stated:

"The above temporary appointments ends on 31-12-1984 by efflux of time automatically and, therefore, you cease to be in service of factory thereafter. Although your ceasing to be in service does not constitute any action on our part, yet as abundant caution, the following dues are remitted to you by

Bank Draft NO. 284426 dated 28-12-1984 in full and final settlement of your account."

This case became the subject matter of adjudication before the Labour Court, High Court and finally the Supreme Court which in its judgment dated 24-4-1998 observed as under:

"The real question is whether 'X' had a claim to employment beyond 31-12-1984. Having regard to the clear terms of his appointment order, which he accepted by signing at the foot thereof, the management was entitled to bring his employment to an end at the conclusion of the period of temporary employment. The letter stating that X' s service would come to an end on 31-12-1984 did not say that the services were being terminated of any misconduct. There was no stigma whatsoever cast by that letter. The High Court was, not in the circumstances, justified in concluding that the services had been terminated because X's misconduct and upholding his reinstatement with fullback wages"

[*Birla VXL Ltd.* v. *State of Punjab*, 1998 (4) RSJ 311]

SUBJECT INDEX

L

M

N